The relevance of the wisdom traditions in contemporary society:
the challenge to psychology

The relevance of the wisdom traditions in contemporary society: *the challenge to psychology*

Edited by
Mark Blows, Saroja Srinivasan, Johanna Blows,
Peter Bankart, Michael DelMonte & Yutaka Haruki

Eburon Publishers
Delft, 2004

Also available in this series of publications:

Comparative and Psychological Study on Meditation. Edited by Y. Haruki, Y. Ishii & M. Suzuki. Eburon, Delft 1996. ISBN 90-5166-483-4.
Western and Buddhist Psychology. Clinical Perspectives. Edited by M.G.T. Kwee & T.L. Holdstock. Eburon, Delft 1996. ISBN 90-5166-477-X.
The Embodiment of Mind: Eastern and Western Perspectives. Edited by M.M. DelMonte & Y. Haruki. Eburon, Delft 1998. ISBN 90-5166-638-1.
Meditation as Health Promotion: A Lifestyle Modification Approach. Edited by K.T. Kaku. Eburon, Delft 2000. ISBN 90-5166-785-X.

ISBN 90 5972 034 2

Eburon Academic Publishers
P.O. Box 2867
2601 CW Delft
The Netherlands
tel.: +31 (0) 15 - 2131484 / fax: +31 (0) 15 - 2146888
info@eburon.nl / www.eburon.nl

Cover design: Jan Kees Schelvis / Travaux Publics, Groningen

This book was funded by Ibuka Foundation at Advanced Research Center for Human Sciences, Waseda University, Tokyo, JAPAN.

Contents

Clinical Papers

Experimental Reports

POETRY

Foreword

The Australian provenance of this collection of papers on the relation between contemporary psychology and global spirituality is significant and stimulating. Perhaps no other western society has so genuinely discovered its relationship with an aboriginal tradition of wisdom. This was brought home to me strongly years ago on my first visit to Australia. I had just delivered a talk on the Christian tradition of meditation, a tradition which, I pointed out, was not invented in the sixties any more than it is a done-over version of eastern traditions. The Christian meditation tradition, I said, goes back to the gospels: the Sermon on the Mount shows that Jesus is as much, and as essentially, a teacher of contemplation as of non-violence. And, I added, without a distinctively Christian historical and theological understanding of meditation, we will be unable to explore the further reaches of inter-religious dialogue that are so important for the peace of the modern world. After the period of meditation a Christian aboriginal offered his comment. He said that I had spoken of a 2000 year old tradition. He belonged to a 40,000 year-old wisdom in which what I spoke of as contemplation is called *dadirri*. This is what Miriam Rose Ungunmer, who has done so much to make friends (which is an aim of all dialogue) between her aboriginal and Christian roots, describes as an 'inner deep listening, a quiet still awareness'. Miriam Rose further illustrates the connection between contemplation and therapy that is the subject of this collection, when she speaks of the effects of *dadirri*. 'When I experience *dadirri*', she says, 'I am made whole again. I sit on the river bank or walk through the trees. Even if someone has passed away I can find peace in this silent awareness. There is no need for words. A big part of *dadirri* is listening.' Many of the therapists writing in the following pages say no more and no less than this but they say it in ways that build a substantial bridge between disciplines and traditions that have too long been isolated or mutually suspicious. If Jesus is a teacher of contemplation, he is no less a healer of human wounds and a reliever of human suffering. The Buddha teaches the congruence of wisdom and compassion.

Once the fundamental connections between psychology and contemplation have been recognized and accepted a shift begins to occur in both fields as techniques begin to be transformed into disciplines. It is this shift that both accompanies and facilitates the more inclusive, less mechanistic understanding of human happiness. St Irenaeus in the second century transforms dualistic understandings of praise and worship when he says that the "glory of God is the human being fully alive", In other words, we glorify God by growing in well-being. But he completes his insight by adding that "the life of man is the vision of God." Happiness requires a sense of growth, of meaning and purpose. To experience one's own growth is to taste transcendence and to feel the beginning of a participation in the divine that the early Christians called *theosis*, or divinisation.

Is the language of therapy consonant with this kind of sequence, this logic of theology? Many of the contributions that follow suggest that to admit and name the spiritual dimension of the psychotherapeutic arts is to expand the vocabulary by which psychology itself may be understood and described. The shift from techniques (among which medication should be included) to discipline (among which meditation ranks high) changes not only the way we think about therapy but also the ways we approach it. Take the crucial practice of attention which itself receives much attention in the following pages. Freud's 'evenly hovering attention' and his attendance to the 'unexpected' in therapy reveal an appreciation, in the most un-religious of the founding fathers of modern psychology, for that quality of spiritual consciousness which Simone Weil understood to be the secret of prayer. To pay attention, to *give* our attention to another, cannot be reduced to the mechanisms of any technique though it can, like anything else, be faked. We can pretend to pay attention but the false will not evoke the desired truth. Nor is attention the same as concentration which consists of techniques of objectification and appropriation. To pay attention is to give oneself in a way that makes one present to another, with all that one may have to give yet without intruding or imposing the gifts one lightly bears. It is itself a gift. Like Simone Weil's prayer, it is about both listening and waiting. Not to scare the therapist concerned with transference, it is also about love.

To listen requires silence. It is hard to talk and listen at the same time. A spiritual approach to therapy is quick to recognize the potential of silence in the encounter between patient and therapist. Interesting brain research shows that the meditative state changes the frequency of mental consciousness and seems to reduce the 'synaptic clatter' the meditator knows as distraction. This does not reduce silence to the mere abstention from speech but shows, as the Bhagavad-Gita puts it, that 'silence is work'. It requires courage and poise in the therapist as well as a high level of discretion. True silence is the highest level of communication (it too can be faked) which explains Meister Eckhart's statement that 'there is nothing so much like God as silence'.

Jung it was, I think, who said that the most influential element in the therapeutic relationship is the self-knowledge of the therapist. The ultimate goal of therapy and the immediate goal of meditation is to grow in self-knowledge. This is greatly facilitated by being in relationship with someone who knows himself better than you know yourself – whether it is the teacher within or the therapist. But again the comparison between the spiritual and the therapeutic raises a distinction. Self-knowledge may include but is not quite the same as self-awareness. To know useful and necessary things *about* oneself is not the same as to know oneself. The Christian contemplative tradition speaks about the contemplation of nature (including one's own) in distinctive relationship to the higher contemplation of God. Self-knowledge is seen as the necessary stepping-stone to the knowledge of God. Knowing certain things about oneself, reducing the level of repression and neurosis helps one to do the deeper work of self-knowledge that is reached more by sustainedly *being* oneself than by endlessly *thinking* (or talking) about oneself. At its best the formation of contemplatives in monastic life was about this. Hence the vexed questions about the relationship between priest and therapist, psychology and religion, therapy and prayer can become less antagonistic. Both have the same ultimate goal though this may be differently expressed. But from the meditator's point of view therapy helps to get one to the point of taking up, in solitude, the discipline of taking the attention off oneself.

Both the therapist and the meditator accept that both arts take time. There is much still to understand about the way the developmental models of therapy and the stages of the contemplative journey can be related to each other. No one better to do this than the therapist who is also a serious practitioner of meditation. This will require rare individuals who possess a substantial knowledge of the theory and practice of both psychotherapy and meditation as well as of the contemplative traditions. It will be very rare to have equal competence in the western and eastern traditions. At present it is eastern wisdom and especially Buddhism, with its high science of mental consciousness, and Hinduism, with its science of the body as an instrument of consciousness, that seem more acceptable to western psychologists. The language of the western mystics often seems too scriptural and symbolic for the scientifically minded, or perhaps merely too familiar, to be useful. But the existentialism of the 'Cloud of Unknowing' or the ascetical theology of John of the Cross are not the only sources in the classical western mystical tradition to illuminate the spiritual dimension of psychotherapy. A deep and broad rediscovery of the roots and branches of Christian mysticism, from the Desert Fathers to today, has yet to be undertaken; and without it the wisdom dimension of therapy as well as the spiritual healing of western culture is hardly possible.

The biblical understanding of the self as 'created in the image and likeness of God' is not an impediment to this collaboration. Diadochus of Photike uses an image of the portrait that is popular among eastern mystical writers to illustrate this. God created the image, the outline of the person whose portrait is being painted. But the person himself or herself participates fully in the development of this outline into a true likeness, adding colour, light and shade and using every available skill. The crowning achievement of the portrait is then the creation of the smile by which the true and whole self of the person is revealed. This smile rising from the depths of a contented and healed soul is the goal of therapy and meditation alike.

Several of the writers who follow refer to the Dalai Lama's authoritative witness to a meaning of happiness that satisfies both psychology and religion. "My religion is kindness," he says in a simple distillation of the various philosophical schools of which he is a master. But, as he would be the first to admit, this is obvious and common sense. Religious observance can only be evaluated by the kind of people it turns out and this is surely no less true of psychotherapy. The fruits of therapy and the fruits of meditation may not be so different but they represent different stages of the ripening process. Ultimately the goal is a smile that does not fade.

Laurence Freeman, OSB
June 2004

Laurence Freeman OSB is a Benedictine monk and director of the World Community for Christian Meditation (www.wccm.org).

Editor's foreword

This book arose from the Seventh International Conference of the Transnational Network for the Study of Physical, Psychological and Spiritual Wellbeing, held at the University of Wollongong, 18th – 21th July 2002. The Transnational Network was based on informal connections between social scientists, mainly psychologists, across the world. One of our main intentions was to cross the barriers between Eastern and Western approaches to the study of the mind. Understanding of each others' culture was essential for this work. Our international meetings were facilitated by the Ibuka Fund, ably administered by Professor Yutaka Haruki and Dr. Rika Kawano at the Advanced Research Centre for Human Studies, Waseda University, Japan. That funding has finished and because of that, and a change in policy, the original Network no longer exists. In its place there is the Transnational Society for Clinical Meditation, administered by Dr. Maurits Kwee. This is part of the International Constructivist approach, led by Professor Michael Mahoney, known internationally for his innovative work in the field of cognitive behavioural therapy. Constructivism aims to unify the three approaches to study of the mind, third person observation as in most Western academic psychology, first person, introspective report as in the Wisdom Traditions and much clinical work and physiological and neurological psychology. This gives continuity to the work that was done by the Transnational Network.

As the Japanese Nandina bush spreads its roots, so that new plants arise, so the original Network has many offspring. Some participants have been inspired to study Wisdom traditions with increased enthusiasm. Others have taken up research projects or have developed deeper understanding of aspects of their interaction with clients in ways not so well articulated in Western science. It would be wrong to claim any exclusive linear causation here for the Network. Many people have an interest in this type of interaction and the Network's effects have combined with other streams of communication. It is not of particular importance that the original Network has dissolved, others are doing this type of work. Over a period of fourteen years or so, it has generated enthusiasm among scholars and had led to enduring friendships.

At the conference, there was an unanswered question, one that has troubled me. The question appeared to be a non sequitur in the context of the discussion, at the time. It was:

> "It is all very fine to discuss the Wisdom Traditions here but what is being done to involve decision makers, the politicians?"

It is fine that scholars discuss what concerns them behind the closed doors of the conference room. If what concerns them happens to be vital questions of ethics and conduct towards those with whom we are interdependent, and thus of general interest to those concerned with the wellbeing of individuals and the communities in which they live, then it may very well be appropriate to open those doors and to extend the communication.

I was recently intrigued by a book by an Australian ex-prime minister, Malcolm Fraser, *Common Ground: Issues That Should Bind and Not Divide Us* (Penguin Books). In a chapter on a proposed Bill of Responsibilities, to complement the United Nations' Bill of Rights, he describes the results of discussion between leaders of the world religions and senior politicians. Commonality of values was sought and the basic one was: *Do not do to the other person what you would not like him/her to do to you*. There is more to commonality than this aphorism but that is the most important ethical principle in a nut shell; one that is common to all the world religions. The discussion in Mr. Fraser's book could have, but obviously did not, flow from this book. Educators and decision makers in business and in politics may be interested in the book and so a reply may be supplied to that unanswered question.

There are chapters in the book that are psychologists' business and so not easily assimilated by the general reader. On the other hand, a number of the more philosophical articles may very well interest people well beyond the profession. These chapters challenge the prevailing direction of the Western academic discipline of psychology. Such a challenge is inevitable after an examination of Eastern approaches and also traditional contemplative Christian traditions (Early Christianity). Particular psychologies are a product of the societies from which they arise. They are then used to reinforce the values of those societies. Today, if we are to achieve peaceful co-ordination between nations, we have to become aware of each others' perspectives, beyond our self reinforced blinkering. I am writing at a time when many of us have been shocked by the debasement of values in a context of war.

Self centred grasping is common to everyone. Transcendence of it is what spiritual growth is all about. Many Westerners have turned to Buddhism to be taught how to make steps towards that transcendence. Various chapters in the book point to some of these steps. It is important to add that one cannot really learn these methods from reading. Reading arouses interest and establishes a direction but oral teaching and practising are important for this sort of learning. Just as we cannot learn to ride a bicycle, play a musical instrument or swim by reading, so we cannot reconstruct our habitual ways of reacting just by reading. In all these efforts we have to be tolerant of our frequent mistakes.

Professor Jean Kristeller gives an overall framework for studying meditation, one of the more common sets of methods for taming our mind. Her sketch covers various levels of meditation, from the very practical, applied ones to the spiritual levels. Later in the book, she describes a set of practical methods for bringing the disturbance of binge eating to rest, in the form of an experimental trial. Professor Yosuke Sakairi deals with the cognitive changes that follow from meditation. From China, with Professor Weidong Wang and his research team, there is a study about the use of a type of walking meditation for lung cancer patients. Professor Fusako Koshikawa and her research colleagues show that there could be an alternative method of achieving non-attachment after trauma apart from learning a form of Zazen meditation, which takes a long time to mature. Rients Ritskes, with his team, shows some important changes in brain functioning with a form of Zazen. He used updated neurological techniques. Much early work of that kind was done in Japan at Komazawa University, Tokyo in the 1970's, under the leadership of Professor Yosiharu Akishige.

We are very pleased to include a chapter by Emeritus Professor Shoji Nakamura, a familiar visitor to Australia and one of the foundation members of the Network, who worked in the original research team at Komazawa. He has followed up the philosophy of Zen originally set out by Yoshiharu Akishige. This article and many of the others provide what to many westerners may seem to be a radical view of the self. Professor Peter Bankart, as he usually does, gives a good draught to help blow away misconceptions about the self. This is taken up in a different way in my article about the Tibetan sage, Shantideva, touching on the issue of rendering a tradition relevant in a contemporary context. Dr Saroja Srinivasan points to a different direction for psychological research based on her experience of Hindu Vedanta. Similarly Dr Usha Ram, from Poona University, draws out implications of the Hindu tradition. Dr Elizabeth Stutchbury, who is an assistant teacher of the Tibetan Dzogchen tradition, provides an over-view of some seminal research into loosening reflexive construing and some alternative ways of reducing misconceptions in the mind. Emeritus Professor Yutaka Haruki describes the traditional Zen Bull pictures, as used to orientate students to the steps in the development of wisdom.

Useful clinical chapters, that could inspire and perhaps even transform clinical practice, are provided by three contributors. Lynne Bousfield, using Early Buddhist techniques, discusses the management of chronic pain. Michael Anderson reminds us that *suspended attention*, which is akin to meditation, is necessary for creative listening and presence in clinical consultation, something that is omitted from conventional clinical training. Professor Bill Mikulas's chapter, *Working with the Clinging Mind*, rounds out this clinical section, showing how to teach people to reduce attachment, the blinkers that we carry as part of our personality. His websites and books are available for in-depth study.

The American Indian *multi-modal* approach, if psychological jargon may be used with tongue in check, is an eye opener for Western clinicians who generally think in a unidimensional fashion. Professor Chris Rybak has provided a chapter on that.

Why have we a chapter on animals? Surely this is rather odd. In the Buddhist tradition, we are to act responsibly towards *all sentient beings.* Buddhist prayers attest that. At the conference, Dr Val Plumwood and Dr Barbara Noske conducted a seminar on our relationship to animals. Clearly if the *four noble truths* are to be followed, animals should be included in responsible action. So we are glad to publish an article on attitudes to animals, by the Dutch scholar, Barbara Noske.

Dr Michelo DelMonte, experienced in many cultural traditions, is not only a foundation member of the Network but helped in the very early days of its conception in Australia. His opening chapter offers some surprising leads into the European Wisdom traditions.

As is consistent with the constructivist approach, we have several poems. A long one by Professor Michael Mahoney and two short ones by Dr Otto Reichard. Dr Reichard also gives a diagrammatic summary of the differences between Eastern and Western understanding of the self and of therapeutic intervention.

Although the chapters break into four sections, theoretical, clinical, experimental and poetry, they overlap. For instance, what may be sketched out in a theoretical chapter may be illustrated in a more concrete fashion in an experimental study or a clinical one.

At the conference we went further than provide poetry. We ended it with a musical production, including songs from various cultures as well as humorous songs telling the story of the Network. The latter included an *Amsterdam Waltz* to celebrate the contributions of Dr Maurits Kwee. The use of art as well as verbal discussion broadened the avenues of communication and led to a strong feeling of wellbeing and cohesion at the conference.

As a father (and grandfather) I remember an intriguing children's book, using figure ground puzzles, called "Where is the Green Parrot?" Now where is the chapter in this book by Maurits Kwee, a master of humour and story telling? At the conference, Dr Kwee chose to give a PowerPoint display. This was spectacular and innovative, a totally different method of communication than reading as in a book. We were unable to do justice to his contribution in written media, so in the body of the book, we give directions for following up his work.

There is one major shortcoming in this book: That is there is no article written from a Muslim perspective. This is a serious omission in view of the recent events in the Middle East. Having seen the so called "whirling Dervishes" practising a type of moving meditation, and in one of our Network newsletters, having read about conventional Muslim (Sufi) meditation, it is plain that Muslim spirituality should be included in any complete account of the interface of psychology and the wisdom traditions. I hope others will take up this point. A very good paper on Sufi practice was read at an early Network conference in the Belgian city of Bruges. The inclusion of Islam was advocated by Professor Akira Onda, one of the foundation members of the Network, in Japan. It was he who suggested the title for our group.

Despite shortcomings, it is hoped that this book will arouse interest in both professional groups and in the general public.

Let the doors be flung open.

ACKNOWLEDGEMENTS

I particularly thank my Japanese friends, Professor Yutaka Haruki for many years of support both financial and professional, Dr Rika Kawano and Professor Yasutomo Ishii who were always there to help and to many other Japanese friends.

The editorial team provided enjoyable company during the long hours of preparation. Saroja Srinivasan, co-convenor of the conference, co-editor and constant adviser, Peter Bankart, whose comments were very much to the point, Michelo DelMonte whose thoroughness was greatly appreciated and Johanna Blows, whose mastery of the English language prevented many a mishap, all helped in the production of the book.

I thank the contributors, those whose articles are published and also those who contributed to the conference but not to the book with workshops, videos, PowerPoint presentations and so on. Jan Pether spoke informally about her work in Indian villages and Professor Sompoch Iamsupasit spoke about his academic aims in Thailand.

Thanks also to A/Professor Patrick Heaven, Head of the Department of Psychology, University of Wollongong, for opening the conference and to the musicians, Eleftherios Kostoglou, Brenda Drake and team who realised the musical programme which cannot be reproduced in the silent written language of a book.

As an extension of the conference, it was a great pleasure to be the guests of Sr. Hildegard at the beautiful Benedictine Abbey, at Jamberoo Mountain, where we were introduced to the spiritual teaching of the Benedictine tradition, and where we enjoyed the generous hospitality for which the order is famous. Also, as an extension of the conference, Johanna Blows arranged a visit to the Central Australian Aboriginal sacred site, Uluru, where the Arrernte people spoke about some of their tradition.

Mark Blows
(mjblows@tig.com.au)

Ways of understanding: meditation, mysticism and science – bridging the gap between east and west

M.M. DelMonte
Fellow of the Psychological Society of Ireland
Principal Psychologist, St. Patrick's Hospital, Dublin

Abstract

There are varying approaches to, and levels of, understanding. The (Western) scientific approach is the most objective. It tends towards the concrete and is concerned, in the main, with the material world, e.g. as in physical medicine. At a more abstract level we have the rather more subjective understandings underpinned by psychological theory as exemplified by the various schools of psychotherapy. Finally, at the most abstract level, we have the traditional spiritual insights associated with relatively ineffable religious experiences linked to trans-symbolic practices such as meditation. This paper explores some of these relationships in the context of Eastern and Western approaches to well-being.

1. Introduction

"In the beginning God created the heaven and the earth. And the earth was without form, and void; and darkness was upon the face of the deep..... And God said, let there be light: and there was light" (Genesis, p.1). This scenario was described nearly three millennia ago and conjures up a recognisable image within the Judeo-Christian tradition. It implies a sudden beginning to the universe, a spiritual equivalent of the postulation of theoretical physics and of astronomy that our universe began precipitously with a "big-bang" (Capra, 1975). This hypothetical "big-bang" led to the creation of time and space out of a void. But what is a void: Does it really contain nothing? Could it be full of potential? "Form and emptiness cannot be conceived as a state of mutually exclusive opposites, only as two aspects of the same reality, which co-exist and are in continual co-operation" (Govinda, 1973). Putting this in Capra's language of physics – "The distinction between matter and empty space finally had to be abandoned when it became evident that virtual particles can come into being spontaneously out of the void, and vanish again into the void... According to field theory, events of that kind happen all the time. The vacuum is far from empty. On the contrary, it contains an unlimited number of particles which come into being and vanish without end" (Capra, 1975, p.234).

In other words, everything, including our universe can be created, can vanish and be re-created endlessly. This idea was already postulated about 500 years before Christ in The Bhagavad Gita, a Hindu text:-

> "At the end of the night of time all things return to my nature; and when the new day of time begins I bring them again into light" (Bhagavad Gita, Mascaró 1962).

What is implied here is a dynamic transitory creation with death and re-creation – continuing endlessly. Hence there is a cycle of impermanence in the context of beginninglessness – i.e. there is no true beginning or end! Impermanence, however, has its source in the infinite, which is itself unchanging but contains all potential. This observation has relevance to many Eastern beliefs and practices such as meditation.

In meditation one strives to create a mental void or silence. This laying fallow of the mind prepares it for a new beginning, i.e. for the unfolding of unexpressed potential. We typically associate meditation practice with the Eastern wisdom traditions such as Hinduism and Buddhism, yet meditation may be one of the early links between East and West, in that meditation was no stranger to the emerging Christian church in the Mediterranean area (DelMonte, 1995).

The practice of meditation, like other approaches to esoteric experience, usually involves a quest for knowledge, largely subjective, and it can be contrasted with the more objective methods of inquiry which characterise Western science.

2. Methods of inquiry

There are many ways of thinking, understanding and knowing based on different methods of inquiry. On the one hand, we have the relatively recent scientific tradition of the West. Since René Descartes and others, this approach has emphasised knowing about the world by using reason, logic, measurement, controlled experimentation and, indeed, the intellect. This rational approach of scientists was very much needed as an "anti-dote" to some of the "wild" superstitious speculations rampant in the past. Their methodology has become firmly established in the scientific community including, amongst others, cognitive-behavioural psychologists. Their scientific theories tend to be readily verbalisable, tightly constructed and easily put to the test. Psychologists who work in this tight way typically confine their understandings to conscious rational observations made by (personal) mind on the functioning of an objective universe. This can also be described as the logical positivist position. It draws its findings and confidence from empirical research. The concept "positivism" was developed by Auguste Compte (1855) who saw intellectual development as passing through three evolutionary phases – i.e. the religious (or superstitious), then the metaphysical (or confused) and finally the scientific (or rational). The superiority of the rational approach is implied herewith.

3. Ancient wisdom traditions

Is the knowledge gleaned by this positivist approach really adequately comprehensive when one tries to understand the human condition? Does the much older tradition based on introspection, meditation and even mysticism have anything to offer at all? This older approach can be traced back to the ancient wisdom traditions of the Orient, i.e. back about 4,000 years to early Hinduism, back at least 3,000 years ago to Judaism, about 2,700 years ago to Japanese Shintoism, about 2,500 years ago to Chinese Taoism, and can also be found in a further developed form in Buddhism (which emerged 2,600 years ago from Hinduism), and even in early Christianity (see DelMonte, 1995). Islam, the "youngest" religion, is less than 1,500 years in existence. Thus, all the world's major religious traditions have their origins in the East. In the first millennium the Christian Church had a greater geographical diffusion in the East than in the West, extending to Persia, Afghanistan, India, Tibet and China (Freeman, 2002).

The early Christian tradition, with its roots in Judaism and with the influence from the Orient, especially Persia, had much more in common with the ancient wisdom traditions of the East than does contemporary Christian Protestantism. The ancient Greeks, and the Hellenistic culture in general, were also in contact with Eastern cultures. This was especially so after the conquests of Alexander the Great (356-323 B.C.) whose control spread from Greece to Egypt, Persia, Mesopotamia, Afghanistan and Northern India. A reading of the third century Greek philosopher, Plotinus, reveals how similar Greek mysticism was to ancient Eastern mysticism. (See later and O'Brien, 1964). There are other east-west links and similarities. Zoroastrianism, the official religion of ancient Persia, had teachings which were similar to, and most probably influenced, early Jewish sects such as the Essenes, and thus, later on also left its mark on early Christianity (see DelMonte, 1995).

Zarathustra was an ancient mythical figure born in Persia around 660 BC, who preached on the end of the world, heaven and hell, the resurrection of the dead, life after death, the last judgement of the soul, a future saviour born of a virgin who ascends into heaven and angels who are guardians over man and nature in our struggle between good and evil. The parallels with Judaism and Christianity are self-evident.

The Christian Orthodox and Roman Catholic Churches with their (former) emphasis on devotion, ritualistic and repetitive prayer, the Holy Ghost, silence, meditation, contemplation, candles, sacred music, and the use of ancient Greek and Latin may have fostered dissociative experiences and thereby rendered a mysterious aspect to worship. Hereby, they also nurtured a sense of security and satisfied the needs of the heart. However, viewed through the lenses of logical positivism these practices would now be deemed as "irrational" – especially in the face of concomitant superstitious practices such as exorcism, the Inquisition, and the buying of indulgences to ward off the works of the devil. The Judaic Christian God was not all love and forgiveness. He was also capable of creating the devil and sending souls to eternal damnation in hell!

With the Enlightenment in Europe and with the development of rational thought and scientific enquiry, traditional religious values were challenged by Luther, Calvin and many others. These led to a demand to reform the Christian church, with numerous splits as witnessed by the birth of several Protestant churches. These "new" churches tended to emphasise the individual and his or her direct relationship with the scriptures and with God. Intermediaries such as angels, the Virgin Mary, saints, statues and even priests were no longer valued as heretofore. The communal struggle for good and God increasingly became transformed into one's individual burden.

Gradually, countries which still were nominally Roman Catholic became more Protestant (i.e. Reformed) in attitude. The "Protestant work ethic" spread throughout the West. For example, in the Republic of Ireland, despite the large decline in the proportion of Protestants in the population since independence in 1922, the country has never been as "Protestant" (i.e. reformed) in mind-set as now. The move away from ritual, devotion, the Latin Mass, collective obedience, etc., towards a more rational, individualistic, materialistic and monetary view of ethics (e.g. the compensation culture) is quite remarkable. Fewer people appear to publicly acclaim the value of confession, forgiveness, divine revelation or grace as heretofore. Contemplative introspection in general and mysticism in particular have given way to the rationality of humanism and of the scientific method of enquiry. But are these ancient wisdom traditions really so irrational, or are they more aptly described as non-rational?

4. RELIGIOUS EXPERIENCE: THE EVIDENCE

Religious experience is remarkable for its prevalence in historical time and geographical space. The oldest written texts were often religious, and every society has had its devotees and practitioners. There is continuity to such spiritual quests across time. "Heaven does not change nor does Toa". (See

Mingyi, 1998). The Western equivalent could be, "plus ça change, plus c'est la meme chose". In other words, some predispositions rarely change.

But is religious experience really a valid "learning" experience linked to these ancient wisdom traditions, or is it more akin to dissociative hysteria, schizotypic projective hallucination or borderline psychosis? Or, put differently, do people prone to such experiences ever have insight (albeit perhaps unwelcomed and premature at times) which can inform us – as propounded by Carl Jung, or is religious experience (e.g. mysticism) no more than superstitious projection? After all, Freud suggested that there is a link between engagement in religious rituals and obsessional neurosis. However, research in this area fails to find any positive correlation between religiosity on the one hand and various psychiatric disorders such as neurosis, psychosis, schizotypy and borderline personality on the other (Cowie, 1997; Joseph & Diduca, 1997). On the contrary, a few studies have shown that religiosity is negatively correlated with psychosis (Joseph & Diduca, 1997). Freud was not entirely wrong, however, because religiosity (in terms of beliefs and practices) is correlated with obsessional personality, but not with psychiatric obsessional symptoms (Lewis, 1997). Moreover, those who have an extrinsic orientation to religion, i.e. those instrumentally motivated by secondary gain – rather than those pursuing it for its intrinsic value per se – are more likely to show psychiatric obsessional symptoms (Lewis, 1997). Here I am more concerned with the intrinsic value of religion, i.e. its pursuit per se as a spiritual quest for meaning. This quest may be enhanced by practices which foster adaptive dissociative experiences.

5. The quest for meaning

Spiritual and mystical understanding (in its broadest sense) is, arguably, the opposite of the rational, logical, linear and tight construing which so characterises the positivist scientific approach. Religious experience is more likely to be seen as an "irrational", dissociated, intuitive, holistic and loose form of sense-making. Its "findings" are not readily communicated with words, which gives it an ineffable quality. Instead of dealing with the measurable objective world, religious experience appears to be more concerned with the "subjective" domain, and is more likely to be communicated via music and art, for example as found in icons. However, some word forms, especially as expressed in poetry and in chanting, convey a mystical flavour, e.g. that of the 16th century St. John of the Cross (Barnstone, 1972) and of the 14th century Julian of Norwich (Doyle, 1983).

However, verbality and mystical experience are not easy partners as the latter is more likely to be fostered by deep silence as in meditation (see later and also see DelMonte, 1995). Moreover, religious experiences do not confine themselves to the personal subjective domain. They include ethical and transcendental aspects of mind. In other words, they go beyond the manifest "mentalism" of personal mind ("the psyche") to embrace the spiritual domain.

Spirituality can stretch beyond the here and now of personal mind, i.e. it is not limited by time and space. Jung's (1958) postulation of the "collective unconscious" would come to mind here. So do Jung's four ways of knowing, namely, thinking, sensation, intuition and feeling. Whereas thinking is central to scientific endeavour, intuition, feeling and sensation are strongly implicated in religious experience, especially in mysticism, but also in Vipassana meditation, for example. With respect to sensation, both sound and sight can evoke strong mystical feelings as with some types of music, e.g. sacred music, classical music and jazz, as can awesome skylines, landscapes, seascapes and the like. Such experiences can be conceptualised as forms of adaptive dissociation. Religious, spiritual and mystical experiences are commonly reported world-wide, yet Western psychologists tend to remain sceptical of religion (Cowie, 1997). At its highest level, spiritual experience transcends the written word. The latter cannot attempt to convey the full complexity of such experiences without showing up the potential limitations and contradictions inherent in much thinking.

6. Ways of knowing: the spectrum?

It can of course be argued that no attempted understanding of life is complete without the complementary inputs of science, the humanities, religion and mysticism. Western science deals, above all, with an objective experience of the material world. However, the scientific approach may "dip" into the subjective (i.e. psychological) domain, as long as it is confined to personal intra-psychic experience. However, science does not typically address the trans-personal domain. In other words, "hard" scientists usually are most comfortable when studying the material world (including our bodies), somewhat less confident when inquiring into mental phenomena (at the level of personal mind), and uncomfortable when dealing with the social aspects of the "collective" mind (for example as described in systems theory in relation to systemic family and group therapy), and many are outright uncomfortable when asked to consider "universal mind", the collective unconscious or other aspects of the trans-symbolic domain.

The trans-symbolic lies beyond both the sensing body and the thinking mind, i.e. beyond the physical domain and beyond language. It may correspond to what Lacan denotes as the "Real" (Lacan, 1966) and is largely unconscious. For some, it can also be referred to as the spiritual domain. In contrast, the pre-symbolic domain is found in early pre-verbal childhood where language acquisition is only beginning. Moreover, much emotional and sensory experience remains sub-symbolic in adulthood, i.e. unverbalised

– as we cannot readily put the "right" words on all our feelings, sensations and intuitions.

The scientific method, when used to build up our knowledge base, is biased in favour of objective observation, thinking and languaging. Scientists characteristically set out to discover and communicate "the truth" and make nature reveal her secrets to us. Those drawn to spiritual and meditative experience on the other hand, are engaged with the less readily verbalisable domain at or beyond the borders of normal consciousness, as revealed subjectively.

In between the "tight" scientists and the "loose mystics" we have a wide spectrum of individuals, e.g. those who identify themselves as humanistic psychotherapists, psychoanalysts, existentialists, and so forth. Many of them are less sure of discovering universal truths at all, but instead concern themselves with hermeneutics, i.e. with interpretations of our descriptions of our experiences. This phenomenological approach unavoidably requires a degree of experiential "immersion" out of which new understandings may arise. Apropos the word "understand", it hails from the old Anglo-Saxon "under standan", literally meaning to "stand under". Intuition, feeling and sensation appear to be implicated herewith just as much as "thinking" is. Deeper understanding is multi-faceted – as practitioners of mindfulness meditation, such as Vipassana, know only too well.

According to the constructivist George Kelly, creativity is borne out of the cyclical dance between loose and tight construing (Kelly, 1955). If we consider loose sense-making as "yin", then tight construing is "yang". Tight sense-making is more logical, scientific and mathematical – and characterises the Western scientific method. Loose construing, on the other hand, is associated with the insights gleaned from meditative, spiritual and aesthetic experiences. Loose yin and tight yang are the complementary sides of the same coin of discovery.

7. East versus west

In the West humanistic values have to a great extent replaced religious ones. Herewith there has been a notable shift towards a more materialistic and reductionistic reasoning. It has been argued (Bankart, *et al.*, 1992) that the Eastern world-view "values contemplation over dissection, understanding over analysis and concern for the whole over the reductionistic isolation of the individual". (p.142).

Western psychotherapy is a child of the rational, humanistic and irreligious values of the Enlightenment. (See McDonagh, 1982 and Black, 2002, for a fuller discussion). The current Western focus on individual identity, personal analysis, individuation and personal success can be contrasted with the traditional Oriental approach which tends to emphasise interpersonal relationships. According to Bankart *et al.* (1992), "In the Eastern tradition, identity is defined much more directly by one's ties to ancestral, kinship, neighbourhood, and occupational/educational groups" (p.144). In this context analysing one's personal mind as in psychoanalysis may make less sense. Hence the Zen admonition to "loose your mind and come to your senses" (Bankart, *et al.*, 1992).

Viewed from the East, the West (especially North America) appears to be in the grasp of social-Darwinianism, where tough, competitive, careerist, goal-orientated striving "lone-rangers" are idealistically portrayed. This behaviour appears to many Eastern observers "as self-limiting egoism and psychologically counter-productive selfishness" (Bankart, *et a.l*, 1992). O'Donoghue (1997) cautioned – "when you extend yourself frenetically outwards, seeking refuge in your external image or role, you are going into exile" (p.154). In the East, spirituality, family, community unison and co-operation appear to have suffered less from the cult of competitive individualism, but for how long? For O'Donoghue (1998) "Individualism is the enemy of real individuality (p.371), and is described by him as "lost islands of desiccated individualism" (p.372).

Bankart (1998) reviewed the Westerner's pre-occupation with self-enhancement through psychotherapy and meditation. This attitude has been depicted as a "culture of narcissism" (Lasch, 1979) and "solipsistic self-indulgence" (Benjamin, 1988). For many Westerners, meditation should be stripped of its spiritual attributes so as to render it an acceptable clinical technique for personal development. What is missing here is the social and ethical frame so important to Eastern wisdom traditions in which a sense of family, community, continuity and spirituality are essential (De Vos, 1986; Russell, 1986; Mingyi, 1998). For O'Donoghue (1998) "much of the modern fascination with mysticism is more self-indulgent than ascetic" (p.112).

Whilst it is interesting, and undoubtedly somewhat simplistic, to contrast Oriental and Occidental approaches, it must be borne in mind that all living systems (including humans) seek balance. The desire for individuality is probably attenuated by a fear of isolation; just as a desire for fusion with idealised others can be tempered by a fear of bondage (see Epstein, 1990). The heroic solitude depicted metamorphically by a fortified lighthouse in the throes of an Atlantic storm may be temporarily appealing and even, for some, enlightening, but is difficult to sustain, even for Westerners, as a stance in life.

It may well be that in the past the early Christian Western world view was not too dissimilar in many respects from what we now tend to regard as "Eastern values". (Likewise, it is unlikely that the East has escaped modernisation without some Westernisation). A reading of John O'Donoghue's (1997) book, "Anam Chara" (Soul Friend), on Celtic spirituality reveals beautiful parallels in attitudes between the early Christian church in Ireland and Eastern thought. Both valued inner development, e.g. "If we become addicted to the external, our interiority will haunt us" (O'Donoghue, 1977, p.14), and both encouraged some detachment from the external world, e.g. "The mystical life has always recognised that to come deeper into the divine presence within you need to practice detachment" (p.246). Such parallels were probably found throughout Europe in the past. "East" and "West" are probably more than geographical locations – they reflect attitudes and mentalities found beyond their respective shores. Maybe "East is East and West is West" and forever the twain shall meet! Let us not become bogged down in East/West dualism (see Fleischman, 1995). The growing interest in the West to Eastern approaches to physical and mental well-being, as exemplified by the increased practice of Chinese medicine, acupuncture, yoga, Tai Chi, Buddhism and so forth, may be an awakening of an older spirituality. It may also be a reaction to the increasing emphasis on rationality and externality in the contemporary Christian world.

Much psychological theory and most psychotherapy practice have evolved, and is conducted, in the context of the Western scientific tradition. This includes the work of the "grandfather" of psychotherapy, Sigmund Freud, who saw himself as first and foremost a scientist. So let us take a closer look at his thinking.

8. RELEVANCE TO CLINICAL PRACTICE

Freud (1912, 1930) the "grandfather" of psychotherapy was, philosophically speaking, a "naturalist" who perceived mind as part of nature. For example, he saw personality formation as being linked to bio-developmental stages of life – the so-called oral, anal and genital phases with their associated defences and emergent personality structures. However, Freud was also concerned with meaning. But meaning, as Freud discovered, cannot solely be extracted from the biological domain, as meaning must be holistic. Nor can meaning (the "text") be reduced simply to internal mental factors as propounded by some psychoanalysts. It has thus been argued (see Langs & Badalament, 1996) that meaning is not simply located in our heads (or even in our whole bodies), as meaning is always holistic and thus contextual (e.g. social). Thus systems theory (von Bertalanffy, 1968), in acknowledging this, is a form of "externalism". Comprehensive systems theory could, therefore, usefully include the spiritual domain in its sense making – as well as the more obvious biological and psycho-social domains (see DelMonte, 1989, 1996). But does the work of psychotherapists typically suggest that they are even aware of this spiritual or mystical dimension, and more to the point, do they care to incorporate aspects of it into their practice? I hope to show, with some examples, that this is being attempted by some practitioners.

Allow me to continue with some pertinent quotations. Freud stated that a psycho-analyst should maintain an "evenly hovering attention" between patient and self in the selection of material during analysis, but "if one's expectations are followed in this selection, there is the danger of never finding anything but what is already known" (Freud, 1912, pp.111-112). To my knowledge Freud did not go on to describe how this interesting advice could be cultivated. Did Bion (1970) take him up when he advised psychoanalysts to forsake "memory, desire and understanding" during practice? By suggesting that analysts eschew these three functions was Bion reformulating Freud's original advice not to follow one's expectations in therapy? In a similar vein Bion quoted from a letter by the poet John Keats, written in 1817, in which Keats referred to "negative capability" as "when a man is capable of being in uncertainties, mysteries, doubts, without any irritable reaching after fact and reason" (Bion, 1970, p.125). It is my hope that a deeper understanding of meditative silence shall allow us to address, later on, the issues just raised by my quotations from Freud and Bion. Some of Bion's conceptualizations were among the most mystical in orientation of all the psychoanalysts, and it is thus to mysticism that we now return.

9. MYSTICISM: THE LINK BETWEEN EAST AND WEST

Those familiar with the writings of Jan van Ruisbroek and Meister Eckhart (both born in the 13th century) will know about the very long tradition of mysticism in the West. Let us look again at Plotinus, the third century Greek philosopher, whose writings, The Enneads, (O'Brien, 1964) reflect views which lie comfortably with both the Eastern wisdom traditions and Western mysticism. Contemplation was of central importance to Plotinus. Let me quote him: "I am myself born of contemplation; mine is a contemplative nature. The contemplation in me produces the object contemplated" (P.165). "Contemplation rises from Nature to Soul, from Soul to Intelligence". (P.169). For Plotinus everything derives from "The One". The One is totality, unity, infinity and, as such, unknowable in the intellectual sense. The One precedes all, is the source of all things. It begets "The Good", "Being" and "The Intelligence" from which, in turn, Beauty, Eros, Ideas and The (Divine) Soul are begotten. Individual souls and Nature flow from The Soul, i.e. the Soul contains the body and not vice versa.

For Plotinus The One is the primal begetter. It is "perfect – seeking nothing, having nothing, needing nothing – The One "overflows" and its excess begets an other than itself, begotten turns back towards begetter and is filled and becomes its contemplator, "The Intelligence" (P.107). What begets is thus always simpler than what is begotten. The One is unity – its derivatives are multiples and complex, hence the drift towards evolutionary complexity.

Being is the object of thought. Knowledge (thought) implies duality. Nevertheless, we aspire to the One, to dance around it. "In this dance the soul looks upon the source of life, the source of The Intelligence", the origin of

Being, the cause of The Good, the root of the Soul. All these entities emanate from The One..." (P.84). The One being everything is also nothing. Meditation, East and West, has been seen as a means to access this "nothingness", this pregnant void, the All. Many contemporary writers have taken an interest in contemplation, meditation and mysticism.

10. Mysticism: some contemporary views

According to O'Donoghue (1997) "The eternal comes to us mainly in terms of nothingness and emptiness" (p.266). Let me continue with a paradox. Ria Weyens stated, "We are afraid of the void" (Weyens, 1992). Yet she also said that "emptiness is the source of fullness", and that to develop fullness "We must find the no-self or selfless-self". To help resolve the above paradoxes it is useful to look more closely at the tradition of mysticism. The words mysticism and mystery have a similar origin. Both come from the Greek "mustikos" suggesting closed lips and eyes. Mysticism, like psychoanalysis, is a quest into the unknown, i.e. into the realm of the mysterious motivated by a desire for knowledge beyond the level of appearances. The mystic appears to be exploring the depths of the unconscious while remaining wholly conscious (Bomford, 2002). For Louth (1992) this journey is more likely to be characterised by the workings of Eros than by Logos. Hence according to Louth the unknowable reality of the Divine cannot be logically apprehended, but is experienced by "transformation of the soul" via Eros. Eros, meaning love, is characterised by feeling and intuition, whereas Logos (or logic) connotes the thinking rational mind. For O'Donoghue (1998) "Mystery cannot be unravelled by thought" (p.137).

Mysticism is thus concerned with moving beyond, i.e. transcending our habitual thinking or dualistic construing of the world. According to Stace (1960) mysticism has to do with the essential unity of experience, e.g. "the seer and the seen are one". Techniques used to gain access to the experience of this unity include yoga, Qi-gong and meditation among others. With such techniques practitioners regularly report that the usual dimensions of time and space become perceptually distorted (dissociated) – often accompanied by an upsurge of cathartic emotion (DelMonte, 1990). However, mystical experiences do not depend on such special techniques. They can be evoked in a variety of natural situations like remote seascapes and majestic landscapes, and may involve awareness of timelessness and of the sheer imponderability by humans of infinite space or time. For O'Donoghue (1998) "A life that has closed off mystery has deadened itself" (p.137).

When it comes to gaining knowledge and understanding there are two main approaches – the "via positiva" and the "via negativa". The former, based more on logic and objectivity tends to focus on what the objective world has to offer, and, as already mentioned, is exemplified by the logical positivist tradition of scientific enquiry. The mystical path, the via negativa, is, on the contrary, concerned with emptiness, void and nothingness and tolerance thereof. Bion's views on the importance of "negative capability" come to mind here. Through "unknowing" one opens up the possibility of mystical understanding. To understand creatively one must first suspend previous notions and thinking patterns so as to produce a temporary "tabula rasa" or fallow state, i.e. to produce "something from nothing" (see Barnstone, 1972, on St. John). "Nothing is the sister of possibility" (O'Donoghue, 1997, p.267).

In meditation, by focusing exclusively and continuously on one meaningless and monotonous stimulus (e.g. a mantra), all contrasts fall away. As contrasts are necessary for ordinary rational sense-making one is left with nothing to construe, i.e. with no news of a difference or "no-thought" (see DelMonte, 1987). No thought can thus be envisaged as deliberately fostered adaptive dissociation or dis-identification involving the suspension of habitual cognitive construing. This void is the still and silent nothingness of the via negativa. In a way the mind is taking a vacation by being vacant. Fresh ideas can flow into such empty places. "Until you really listen to the call of this void, you will remain an inner fugitive, driven from refuge to refuge, always on the run with no place to call home" (O'Donoghue, 1997). This inner void can also be described as the unknowable in that it cannot really be understood intellectually, despite being a source of inspiration. In this sense it can be ascribed as being part of the (Jungian) collective unconscious.

11. Meditation's ethical base

Historically meditation had an ethical base. Feelings of love emergent from the experience of unity with the Divine are to be translated into acts of love and kindness. According to Laurence Freeman (1992) – "The human good is not found only within people, but also between them". On first impression one often thinks of mysticism as being concerned with finding goodness (or Godness) within. The relational aspect of love (and spirituality), as expressed behaviourally, is not always adequately highlighted. Ria Weyens (1992) made the point that "as long as all our energy is absorbed in self-occupation (self-fascination) we remain restless, diseased." Yet, paradoxically, John Main would contend that we need to regularly and systematically turn inwards to deal effectively with this self-fascination.

Sustained silence produces a fertile state of mind open to experiences beyond language. It may lead to an ineffable transcendental state of non-attachment, non-clinging and equanimity, in which one experiences undifferentiated unity, i.e. the Infinite or the Absolute (see Main, 1982, 1984, 1989; DelMonte, 1995). This is just one example of how the ancient practice of meditation is embedded in mysticism and spirituality. I shall now try to make some links between this simple example and the practice of psychotherapy.

12. THE ROLE OF SILENCE: BEYOND LANGUAGE AND SYMBOLISATION

Psychotherapy, compared with meditation, is a neophyte on the world stage. Most forms of psychotherapy use verbalisation as their modus operandi. A common view held by psycho-analysts is that those who do not learn to "think" (i.e. to symbolise verbally) are bound to go on suffering – as with the hysterically inclined who tend to "feel" too much. While one would not dispute that there is great merit in the "talking cure" approach there is, nevertheless, a growing corpus of opinion on the value of fecund silence in therapy. For example, people who are overly obsessional, in thinking and often talking too much, demonstrate that we cannot always "think" our way out of problems. In therapy they typically have difficulty in being "in touch" with feelings – their own and those of others – and are usually very uncomfortable with silence. Hence the endless chatter, which is often split off from feeling. This is sometimes pejoratively referred to as "free dissociation" (Perls, *et al.*, 1973) or split-off intellect. These people may need to learn that speech, like music, is given deeper meaning by being punctuated by fertile silence so that something else besides words may emerge. According to O'Donoghue (1997) "If you are outside of your self, always reaching beyond your self, you avoid the call of your own mystery. When you acknowledge the integrity of your solitude, and settle into its mystery, your relationships with others take on a new warmth, adventure and wonder".

However, silence on the part of the patient was seen as resistance by Freud (1912). But, Balint (1958) argued that "if we can change our own approach – from considering silence as a symptom of resistance to studying it as a possible source of information – then we may learn something about this area of mind". Later authors saw silence as indicative of shyness, shame, sorrow, anger, hostility, psychic absence and fear (Shafii, 1973; Coltart, 1992). Silence has also been construed, at times, as adaptive regression to pre-verbal sense-making (as opposed to malign or psychotic regression – Shafii, 1973). In keeping with this theme Shafii (1973) sees words as creating communication, and silence as fostering communion. The psychoanalyst Coltart (1992) goes as far as saying that "my own preference", above all others, is for a silent patient". This may be because the relatively silent patient allows the analyst ample time to work with the visceral felt-sense of the counter-transference. It should come as no surprise that Coltart also described herself as a practitioner of meditation and Buddhism. This is a long way from Freud who did not work with the counter-transference at all, and who saw religious experience, meditation and mysticism as regressive, irrational and mal-adaptive phenomena, i.e. forms of "oceanic" fusion and oneness with mother, or the wish to re-experience intra-uterine life (Freud, 1930). To facilitate the patient in adaptive regression the therapist must also be capable of silence, e.g. by avoiding premature, aggressive and excessive interpretations, instructions or comments. In this way pre-verbal traumata can be "re-experienced and mastered again in silence" (Shafii, 1973). There are probably several ways in which therapists can learn to be comfortable with silence. One pathway is via the practice of meditation (see DelMonte, 1995).

13. MEDITATION FOR THE PSYCHOTHERAPIST

Many authors have written on how the practice of meditation by psychotherapists can enhance their receptivity, empathy, insight, staying in the "hic et nunc" (here and now), and their use of counter-transference (Lesh, 1970; Carrington & Ephron, 1975; Keefe, 1975; Fromm, 1977; Speeth, 1982; Rubin, 1985; DelMonte, 1987, 1990; Coltart, 1992; Fleischman, 1995). For example, Speeth argued cogently that meditation can be a form of attention training. She sees that concentrative meditation is a training in narrowly focused or specifically invested attention, whereas mindfulness meditation trains one to adopt a non-attached, panoramic or wide-focus attention, which is evenly invested in everything that comes to mind – namely a kind of "choiceless awareness". Allied to these two approaches Speeth also describes a third (and higher) level of integrated attention which she calls "witness consciousness". This involves an awareness of the type of attention being given (narrow or panoramic), as well as the object of attention. Is this "witness consciousness" similar to Freud's "evenly hovering attention"? Bion's advice to forsake "memory, desire and understanding" when listening to patients also comes to mind here.

In a similar vein, Rubin (1985) argued that training in both concentrative and mindfulness meditation enhances "psychoanalytic listening". He postulated that meditation produces a "laying fallow" state of mind. Such an open state would be more receptive to any pregnant silence emergent from the analytic dyad. Fromm (1977), in an excellent article, descriptively contends that the practice of meditation helps to make the unconscious conscious by enhancing ego receptivity, primary process mentation, fantasy, imagery, free-floating attention and adaptive regression. Finally, on this theme, Coltart (1992) argues that may be dealt with at the level of language. Instead she uses her training in meditation to enhance neutral or "bare attention", both "sharply focused and scanning" to tune into the patient's transferences, and especially, into her own counter-transference. It is worth quoting her conclusion on this subject. "The discipline of meditation practice enhances the discipline of one's contribution to an analytic session which sometimes is, in fact, itself almost indistinguishable from a form of meditation" (p.147). I would call this mindfulness meditation. Such mindfulness aids attunement with both the patient and one's own counter-transference.

An aim of mindfulness meditation is also to enhance reflexivity, i.e. the ability to perceive events and oneself in wider context. Reflexivity is thus much broader than "ordinary thinking". It includes an awareness of personal, social, historical and spiritual factors, so that we can place our narratives (texts) in an evolving contextual awareness.

All of this is not to argue that during therapy, patient and therapist must sit out session after session in blissful silence! Rather, the ability to suspend, at critical moments, the complex cognitive processes involved in "memory, desire and understanding" (Bion) is a stance in therapy which meditation training enhances. However, I think that it is not so much a question of forsaking or eschewing memory and desire like Bion advised, but rather temporarily holding them in abeyance. This is precisely what mindfulness meditation is all about. This process has also been referred to as the "de-automatization" of cognitive construing (Fromm, 1977; DelMonte & Kenny, 1985; DelMonte, 1987, 1990), and is akin to Bion's use of the expression "negative capability", which, as already mentioned, refers to the therapist's capacity to suspend logic and dwell in uncertainties, mysteries and doubts while "containing" the patient emotionally. Hence we can conceptually link Bion's "negative capability" and Freud's "evenly hovering attention" to the mindfulness fostered by meditation. In contemplative prayer God is felt to be one's witness, and therewith one's capacity for reflexivity is enhanced, in that one watches God observing one's innermost thoughts. The free-association in psychoanalysis to an attentive "other" likewise fosters reflexivity, in that one reflects on the analyst's reflection of us. This self-observation process is then internalised and becomes habitual.

14. Critique and conclusions

Traditional schools of meditation usually have little to say about finding, owning and coming to terms with our inner so called "badness" or destructiveness (e.g. anger, hatred, greed, envy and the like). Zen Buddhists refer to "Makyo" as morbid, unwanted (often unconscious) material which interferes with meditation by arising spontaneously during its practice (Russell, 1986). Eastern meditation instructors usually do not seek to analyse these emergent makyo. In this respect the practice of traditional meditation differs from Western psychotherapy. With the latter, there is an attempt to integrate split off "goodness" (ego-ideals and idealised objects) with "badness" (our "shadows") rather than "side-stepping" our unwanted parts (see Main, 1982, 1984, 1989; DelMonte, 1995). Psychoanalysts see splitting as weakening the ego. The approach in meditation is to move beyond the dictate of the ego. A difficulty with this approach, especially in the West, could be that individuals who have rather fragmented selves tend to be drawn to meditation, yet may experience considerable difficulty, especially with inadequate supervision, in transcending their unintegrated ego functioning. Paradoxically, we need reasonably good "ego-strength" to help us move beyond those unintegrated ego yearnings that temporarily yield some satisfaction but ultimately little happiness. Hence such transcendence depends for its success on a healthy ego being able to temporarily suspend its habitual functioning (DelMonte, 1987, 1990, 1995).

Another worry is that schizoid individuals may use meditation as a defence to escape even further from the world, and rather than feeling "connected" they may become even more pathologically dissociated and cut off from others. They may meditate in order to distance themselves even further from their unwanted feelings of aggression, sexuality, envy and competitiveness. It may be wiser to acknowledge and integrate this shadowy aspect of self.

A problem with those who exclusively advocate the "via negativa" is that they tend to deify all "no-self" or "nothingness" experiences. Although such experience can have considerable spiritual value for some it can also be a defensive escape into "narcissistic emptiness" (Epstein, 1990). In other words, there can be confusion between egolessness and self-abnegation. The latter has been described as pathological de-personalisation and de-realisation, i.e. hysterical dissociation (Castillo, 1990). Meditation can be used to deny the existence of certain bodily functions and aspects of external reality, thereby increasing splits such as connoted in "mind/body" and "person/world" (i.e. subject/object) dualism. Worse still, there is the risk that the via negativa can turn into a painless form of premature self-destruction anticipating death, i.e. working more in the service of Thanatos than of Eros.

The path of meditation (silence) should not seek to destroy the embodied self, but rather to accomplish its liberation from blind allegiance to destructive instinctual impulses and from the emotional impoverishment resulting from our psychological defences. Meditation should allow ego just to be ego – neither permanently subjected to repudiation by the via negativa nor indulged with narcissistic grandiosity. The insights gained through self-reflection show us that Eros cannot stand alone without Thanatos, and that the via negativa, without the bridle of logic afforded by the via positiva, may be no more than an elaborate defence.

The value of some fecund silence in therapy, is acknowledged. There are limits to the "talking cure". Learning to put verbal form on feelings can be developmentally liberating, but can also be defensive – as with intellectualisation, mis-attribution and rationalisation – which serve to contort and reframe the truth of our emotional underworlds, and to distance ourselves from our spiritual "overworlds". Hence simplistic notions that mind is superior to body, that West is always less spiritual than East, that "abstract" is better than "concrete" or that one "causes" the other, are just dualistic fallacies! Beyond both matter and (conscious) mind, i.e. beyond body and language, lies the ineffable domain beyond symbolisation and representation – namely stillness and silence. It is largely unconscious. For Bomford (2002) God acts primarily through the unconscious. Adaptive dissociation, as fostered by meditation and prayer, may facilitate access to the unconscious domain.

In conclusion, I have argued that traditional Eastern approaches, as exemplified by the practice of meditation, can help create purpose, understandings, communion and growth, which complement knowledge emanating from the now dominant Western scientific tradition with its emphasis on logic, analysis and the thinking mind. Scientific research and meditative contemplation are both valid and appropriate methods of inquiry into the mystery of life – but at different ends of an investigative continuum, yet they are capable of creative interplay, e.g. by the interweaving of loose and tight styles of sense-making.

References

Balint, M. (1958). The three areas of the mind. *International Journal of Psycho-Analysis*, **39**, 328-340.

Bankart, C.P. (1998). Qijong in the West: Challenges, hazards and opportunities. Paper read at International Symposium entitled, "Psychotherapy and Oriental Thought", convened by Asian division of the World Council for Psychotherapy, Beijing, China.

Bankart, C.P., Koshikawa, F., Nedate, K. and Haruki, Y. (1992). When West meets East: Contributions of Eastern traditions to the future of psychotherapy. *Psychotherapy*, **29(1)**, 141-149.

Barnstone, W. (1972). *The Poems of St. John of the Cross*, New York: A New Directions Book.

Benjamin, J. (1988). The Bonds of Love: Psychoanalysis, Feminism, and the Problem of Domination. New York: Random House.

Bion, W.R. (1970). *Attention and Interpretation*, London: Tavistock..

Black, D.M. (2002). Introduction to God and the Unconscious. *British Journal of Psychotherapy*, **18(3)**: 321-324.

Bomford, R. (2002). God and the Unconscious. *British Journal of Psychotherapy*, **18(3)**: 339-348.

Capra, F. (1975). *The Tao of Physics*, New York: Fontana.

Carrington, P. & Ephron, H. (1975b). Meditation and Psychoanalysis. *Journal of the American Academy of Psychoanalysis*, **3(1)**, 43-57.

Castillo, R.J. (1990). Depersonalization and Meditation. *Psychiatry*, **53**: 158-168.

Coltart, N. (1992). *Slouching Towards Bethlehem: And Further Psychoanalytic Explorations*. London: Free Association Books.

Compte, A. (1855). The Positive Philosophy. In. *Language, Man and Society*, New York: AMS Press 1974.

Cowie, R. (1977). Religious experience and individual differences in religious commitment. British Psychological Society Annual Conference, 26th April, Dunfanaghy, County Donegal.

DelMonte, M.M. (1987). A constructivist view of meditation. *American Journal of Psychotherapy*, **41(2)**: 286-298.

DelMonte, M.M. (1989). Systems theory and psychotherapy. *Journal of Contemporary Psychotherapy*, **19(2)**: 117-135.

DelMonte, M.M. (1990). The relevance of meditation to clinical practice: An overview. *Applied Psychology: An International Review*. 39(3): 331-354.

DelMonte, M.M. (1995). Silence and emptiness in the service of healing: Lessons from Meditation *British Journal of Psychotherapy*, **11(3)**: 368-378.

DelMonte, M.M. (1996). Systems theory and psychotherapy: A constructivist perspective. In. M.G.T. Kwee and T.L. Holdstock (Eds.), *Western and Buddhist Psychology: Clinical Perspectives*, Delt: Eburon Press.

DelMonte, M.M. & Kenny, V. (1985). Models of Meditation. *British Journal of Psychotherapy*, **1(3)**: 197-214.

DeVos, G. (1986). Afterward. In. D.K. Reynolds (Ed) *The Quiet Therapies: Japanese Pathways to Personal Health.* Honolulu: University of Hawaii Press.

Doyle, B. (1983). *Meditations with Julian of Norwich.* Bear & Co., Santa Fe.

Epstein, M. (1990). Psychodynamics of meditation: Pitfalls on the spiritual path. *Journal of Transpersonal Psychology,* **22(1)**: 17-34.

Fleischman, P.R. (1995). *Vipassana Meditation: Healing the Healer. The Experience of Impermanence.* Maharashtra, India: Vipassana Research Institute.

Freeman, L. (1992). Meditation and personal identity. In. *Proceedings of the Workshop: Towards the Whole Person: Integrating Eastern and Western Approaches to Body-Mind Skills.* St. Andries Benedictine Abbey, Brugge, pp 9-15.

Freeman, L. (2002). *Christian Meditation Newsletter, Spring,* p 5.

Freud, S. (1912). *Recommendations to Physicians Practising Psycho-Analysis:* Standard Edition, 12, 111-120. Hogarth Press, London, 1955.

Freud, S. (1930). *Civilisation and its Discontents,* Standard Edition, London: Hogarth Press.

Fromm, E. (1977). An ego-psychological theory of altered states of consciousness. *International Journal of Clinical and Experimental Hypnosis,* 25(4): 372-387.

Genesis, *The Old Testament,* The Holy Bible, Cambridge.

Govinda, Lama Anagarika (1973). *Foundations of Tibetan Mysticism,* London: Rider, p.223.

Joseph, S. & Diduca, D. (1997). Schizotypy and Religiosity. British Psychological Society Annual Conference, 26th April, Dunfanaghy, County Donegal.

Jung, C. (1958). Psychological commentary on the Tibetan book of the great liberation. In. *Psychology and Religion, Vol.2 Collected Works,* New York: Pantheon Books.

Keefe, T. (1975). Meditation and the Psychotherapist. *American Journal of Orthopsychiatry,* **45(3)**: 484-489.

Kelly, G.A.(1955). *The Psychology of Personal Constructs,* New York: Norton.

Lacan, J. (1966). *Ecrits,* Senils, Paris.

Langs, R. & Badalamenti, A. (1996). *The Cosmic Circle: The Unification of Mind, Matter and Energy.* New York: Alliance Publishing Inc.

Lasch, C. (1979). *The Culture of Narcissism: American Life in an Age of Diminishing Expectations.* New York: Norton.

Lesh, T.V. (1970). Zen Meditation and the development of empathy in counsellors. *Journal of Humanistic Psychology,* **10:** 39-74.

Lewis, C.A. (1997). "Cleanliness is next to Godliness": An examination of the relationship between religiosity and obsessionality. British Psychological Society Annual Conference, 26th April, Dunfanaghy, Co. Donegal.

Louth, A. (1992). Eros and Mysticism. *Guild Lecture* **No. 241**. London: *The Guild of Pastoral Psychology.*

McDonagh, J.M. (1982). *Christian Psychology: Towards a New Synthesis.* New York: Crossroad.

Main, J. (1982). *Letters from the Heart.* New York: Crossroads.

Main, J. (1984). *Moment of Christ: The Path of Meditation.* London: Darton, Longman & Todd.

Main, J. (1989). *The Way of Unknowing.* London: Darton, Longman & Todd.

Mascaro, J. (1962). *The Bhagavad Gita,* London: Penguin Classics, p.80.

Mingyi, Q. (1998). Thoughts of Chinese philosophy and psychotherapy. Paper read at International Symposium entitled, "Psychotherapy and Oriental Thought", convened by Asian Division of the World Council for Psychotherapy, Beijing, China.

O'Brien, E. (1964). *The Essential Plotinus,* New York: Mentor.

O'Donoghue, J. (1997). Anam *Cara: Spiritual Wisdom from the Celtic World.* London: Bantam Press.

O'Donoghue, J. (1998). *Eternal Echoes: Exploring our Hunger to Belong*. London: Bantam Press.

Perls, F.S., Hefferline, R.F., & Goodman, P. (1973). *Gestalt Therapy: Excitement and Growth in the Human Personality*. London: Penguin.

Rubin, J.B. (1985). Meditation and psychoanalytic listening. *Psychoanalytic Review*, **72(4)**, 599-613.

Russell, E.W. (1986). Consciousness and the unconscious: Eastern meditative and Western therapeutic approaches. *Journal of Transpersonal Psychology*, **18(1)**, 51-72.

Shafii, M. (1973). Silence in the service of the ego: Psychoanalytic study of meditation. *International Journal of Psychoanalysis*, **54(4)**, pp.431-443.

Speeth, K.R. (1982). On therapeutic attention. *Journal of Transpersonal Psychology*, **14(2)**, 141-160.

Stace, W.T. (1960). *The Teachings of the Mystics*. New York: Mentor.

Von Bertalanffy, L. (1968). *General Systems Theory*, New York: Brazillier.

Weyens, R. (1992). Lectio Divina. In. *Proceedings of the Workshop: Towards the Whole Person: Integrating Eastern and Western Approaches to Body-Mind Skills*, St. Andries Benedictine Abbey, Brugge, 15th-17th July, pp.48-51.

Meditation: multiple effects, a unitary process?

Jean L. Kristeller
Dept. of Psychology, Indiana State University

"... meditation is incorrectly seen as an escape from reality or only a form of relaxation..." Urbanowski & Miller, 1996, p. 31.

"...nerve cells have been liberated from much of their usual irrelevant synaptic clutter." Austin, 1999, p. 658.

Is meditation an esoteric spiritual practice requiring a lifetime of effort? Or one of many useful, but somewhat interchangeable, relaxation techniques? Among the effects of meditation claimed – and supported by substantial evidence – are changes in physiology, emotion, cognition, behaviour, in sense of self, and in spiritual awareness. Yet often in reviewing the meditation literature, the focus is on a particular aspect of meditation effects: it is about transformation of the self; or producing physiological relaxation; or spiritual enlightenment. One is reminded of the story of the six blind men and the elephant. One man starts feeling the elephant's leg and declares the elephant is like a tree trunk; one goes to the tail and says it is like a small snake; the third stands at head and insists it is like a boa constrictor, etc. The point of the story, of course, is that all of these are true of the elephant. Is this also the case for meditation effects? If so, how do we make sense of multiple effects emerging from a relatively simple set of practices? While traditional meditative practice – and contemporary research – may choose to focus on one effect or another, it behooves us from the perspective of psychological application or theory, to more fully consider a broader matrix of meditation effects, as laid out in Table 1. It may then be easier to engage the underlying theoretical questions as to why such a range of effects exists.

The horizontal axis of Table 1 depicts the range of meditation effects separated into six domains of functioning: physiological, emotional, cognitive/attentional, behavioural, relationship to self and others, and spiritual. These areas map relatively well onto accepted domains of human functioning within contemporary psychology. The second aspect of the model as depicted on the vertical axis of Table 1 is the impact of practice on meditation effects across three developmental stages. For example, in the domain of physiological effects, physical relaxation is produced easily and quickly by most individuals after learning basic meditation techniques, while true physiological

Table 1: A Multi-Modal Developmental Model of Meditation Effects

Stage of Development							
		Perfect wisdom, Nirvana.....					
	Late	Extra-ordinary control of body	Pure Awareness One-pointed-ness/ Samadhi	Bliss..	Complete right action/ Moral Purity Cessation of Conditioning	Loss of self-attachment Total other love	Sense of unity Bliss...
	Intermediate (Variable)	Loss of pain ↑ Pain control Change in physiologic processes Breath Control	Samadhi Kensho/ mystical experiences ↑ Attentional flexibility ↓ Ruminative thinking ↑ Mind-fulness	↑ Sustained Equanimity ↑ Positive emotion ↑ Engagement in the moment ↑ Letting be	↑ Compassionate behaviour ↓ Addictive Behaviour ↑ Adaptive behaviour Deconditioning	Satori Suspension of sense of self ↑ Compassion Self-integration ↓Narcissism	Samadhi Kensho/mystical experiences Mystical experiences Merging with God/ "the one"
	Initial	↑ Awareness of Breath/Body Altered body sensations Relaxation Response	↑ Ability to focus ↑ Awareness of mind/ thoughts	↓ Reactivity ↑ Awareness of emotional patterns	↑ Impulse Control ↑ Awareness of behaviour patterns	↑ Self-acceptance ↑ Sense of self	(Altered perception/ states) ↑ Spirituality/awe
Area of Develop-ment		Physical	Attentional/ Cognitive	Emotional	Behavioural	Relation to Self/Others	Spiritual

control may require months, if not years of practice. Similarly, awareness of emotional reactivity is an early effect; attaining sustained emotional equanimity is the mark of a trained master. This developmental aspect of the model, therefore, depicts the range of effects that vary dependent of the level of experience of the research participants, from beginners to practiced monks. While developmental approaches to meditation effects are well represented in the literature (Brown, 1977; Goleman, 1996), they generally focus their attention on subtle distinctions of attainment in experienced meditators.

GOALS OF THIS PAPER

The goals of this paper are several fold. The paper will first present a model of meditation as an attentional/cognitive process. It will then present the implications of this model of meditation across six domains of effects in more detail, incorporating the developmental component. It will then raise the question: despite this range of effects, is there a set of unitary processes that might be operating across these domains? Despite the variety of traditional and contemporary meditation practices, it is generally agreed that the core of meditation techniques encompasses a relatively simple set of practices that engage conscious efforts at controlling and directing attention, awareness, and mental reactivity. Why should a simple set of cognitive practices have such wide ranging effects? And as significantly, what might this teach us about brain/mind functioning? Considering this question may also provide insight into the organization of neural activity, the relation of conscious experience to self-regulation and emotional regulation, and the potential for self-growth and clinical value that can emerge out of meditative practices.

These issues will be addressed by considering our current understanding of psychological processes within the traditional literature and psychology of the Asian meditative traditions. Finally, the implications for research and clinical application will be briefly examined.

MEDITATION AS AN ATTENTIONAL/COGNITIVE PROCESS

Shapiro, in 1980, stated that meditation is "...a family of techniques which have in common a conscious attempt to focus attention in a non-analytical way, and an attempt not to dwell on discursive, ruminating thought" (cited in Austin, 1999). Generally, two primary families of meditative techniques are identified: concentrative meditation and mindfulness meditation (Goleman, 1996). Concentrative techniques involve sustained attentional focus on a specific object, such as a *mantra* (a repeated sound or word), with a goal of complete absorption, whereas mindfulness meditation cultivates sustained attentive awareness to whatever may emerge into conscious experience, without reaction or analysis. Examples of concentrative techniques include focus on the breath, on a word or phrase (the mantra, a Zen koan, the Christian Jesus prayer), visualization of an object (as in Tibetan Mandala meditation), and body-focused awareness. Mindfulness techniques are most apparent in Vipassana meditation, Zen *shikantaza* ("just sitting"), some visualization techniques, and other contemplative traditions. However, awareness cannot occur without sustained attention, and sustained attention or concentration appears to cultivate awareness. Most meditative approaches, with Zen meditation as a notable example, incorporate aspects of both.

Virtually all meditative practices involve these and certain other elements, though each tradition emphasizes some aspects of practice over others. There is generally a postural centering and/or physical quiescence. There is an introduced focus of attention and repetition, often utilizing the breath. There is disengagement from usual processes of analysis, cognition and reaction. A non-judgmental attitude is sought. And there is virtually always some sense of seeking a higher level of balance, understanding, insight or awareness, which might be conceptualized as a seeking of self-regulation – or even wisdom.

The importance of experiencing silencing of thoughts altogether is often referred to in the traditional literature. Outer silence, whether by retreat from usual everyday responsibilities or literally the silence of the physical space of practice, is relatively easy to attain. Inner silence is far more difficult, and is distinct from a repression or suppression of usual cognition. Rather, it is experienced either as a suspension of thought content or a moving into a place of silence. Beginning meditators often express frustration that they cannot "silence" their thoughts, not understanding that such silence is the result of practice, and is difficult, if not impossible, to force. The occurrence of such silence may be an important marker of a shift in neuropsychological functioning.

Given this basic set of elements to meditation practice – attention, awareness, and the process of non-thinking – it becomes clearer how meditation is essentially a cognitive process, as contrasted to an emotional, physiological, or behavioural one. How, then does this simple set of elements lead to the profound changes claimed for meditation practice? The Buddha, in his first teachings, identified meditation as the most important element on the noble eightfold path to bring into existence right action, right speech, right livelihood, right effort, right understanding and right thought. These areas of effect, although not identical to those identified in Table 1, map fairly well onto how we can now construe major dimensions of human functioning and the six domains of meditation effects: physiology, cognition, emotion, behaviour, relation to self and others, and spiritual well-being.

A multidimensional model

As noted above, Table 1 outlines the multidimensional model of meditation effects. It is possible here to provide only a very brief overview of each domain. To the extent possible, this model is based on a review of the empirical literature; when that was lacking, the traditional meditation literature was given substantial weight, such as in the domain of the spiritual impact of meditative practice. It is also not intended that these domains be viewed as completely independent from each other. That would be naïve from both a psychological and neurological perspective; however, considering them separately may help us better understand how they may then link together, either due to training effects or due to the inherent integration of the mind/brain.

Six domains of meditation effects

Physical effects

Physical effects are emphasized in the yogic and Hindu traditions, with most of the research based on evidence from Transcendental Meditation (TM) and related approaches. Early effects include the "relaxation response" characterized by hypometabolic shifts in SNS/PNS activation (Benson & Wallace, 1972) and heightened awareness of breath. With practice, neurological patterns shift toward greater EEG coherence (similar patterns of EEG firing across regions of the brain); changes in patterns of activation (shifts toward alpha states and occurrence of non-descending theta) are observed (Delmonte, 1984). Late effects may include exceptional body control (e.g., *gTun-mo Yoga* (raising body temperature in cold environments)) (Benson, 1982). Clinical applications include treatment of pain (Kabat-Zinn, Lipworth & Burney, 1985), cardiovascular disease (Patel *et al.*, 1985; Wenneberg & Schneider, 1997), and panic attacks (Kabat-Zinn *et al.*, 1992).

Cognitive/attentional effects

Cognitive effects are inherent to the meditative process. Certain meditative traditions, such as Zen, emphasize training in focused attention and awareness. Early effects include heightened awareness of the flow and content of thoughts, decreases in distractibility and greater attentional awareness, and heightened attentional acuity/reduced reactivity in mindfulness meditation (Kasamatsu & Hirai, 1963; Brown *et al.*, 1984). Clinical applications may include treatment of attentional deficit disorder (Shannon, 2002).

Emotional effects

Although decreased emotional reactivity is sought, initial practice may access suppressed conflicts and greater awareness of emotional patterns. Greater affect regulation may occur with certain types of mindfulness exercises, even without formal meditation practice (Linehan, 2001). Clinical applications include improvement in anxiety disorders (Kabat-Zinn *et al.*, 1992) and depression (Teasdale *et al.*, 2000; 2002).

BEHAVIOURAL EFFECTS

Early effects include increased awareness of behavioural patterns, followed by decreases in impulsive and compulsive behaviour. There may be a sense of a general "deconditioning", of being somehow "freed" from the power of earlier patterns of avoidance or compulsions. This sense of freedom may be accompanied by increases in purposeful, focused action. Changes in addictive behaviour have been noted (O'Connell & Alexander, 1994; Brooks & Scarano, 1985), and meditation has been applied to treating binge eating disorder (Kristeller & Hallett, 1999). The degree to which such behavioural changes occur spontaneously as a function of meditation practice is not clear; for behavioural change to occur, it may be particularly important to identify such goals explicitly. For example, in our research with binge eaters, the degree of improvement was strongly related to use of eating-specific meditations (r=.66), rather than to use of general sitting meditation.

RELATION TO SELF AND OTHERS

Gaining a more substantive sense of self, with increases first in self-acceptance and then in self-actualization (Alexander *et al.*, 1991) occurs first. Following that (or in tandem) is being able to let go of self in the service of heightened empathy and compassion for others (Lesh, 1970; Kornfield, 1993), a hallmark of traditional meditative practice. An increase in altruistic choices may occur, proposed by some to be the defining criteria of heightened wisdom (Sternberg, 1990). A focus on the shift in relation to self is the framework for psychodynamic applications of meditation practice and Zen Buddhism (Epstein, 1998; Rubin, 1996).

SPIRITUAL EFFECTS

Much of the traditional literature, whether from Eastern (Buddhist and Hindu) or Western (Judeo-Christian) traditions, places spiritual goals and awakening as the primary point of meditative practice. After only limited practice, an increased sense of inner peace and a suspension of mundane concerns may occur. However, although the use of meditation as a way to heighten spiritual engagement and induce mystical experience is clearly acknowledged (Davidson, 1976; Seeman, 2003; Shapiro & Schwartz, 1998), this domain has received surprisingly little systematic investigation in which indices of spiritual experience are the primary dependent variables, rather than the other types of responses identified above.

THE RELATIONSHIP OF EFFECTS TO EACH OTHER

The order of the effects in Table 1 along the horizontal axis (physical; cognitive/attentional; emotional; behavioural; relation to self and others; and spiritual) is not arbitrary. It is intended to reflect a possible ordering of the ease by which each effect can be attained during early stages of practice. Physiological change is placed first because virtually all individuals can experience a sense of physical relaxation within those traditions that emphasize this aspect. Using meditative techniques to shift attention and awareness, to become more aware of emotional experiences, and to reduce emotional reactivity, also appears to be relatively easy. Changing behaviour or sense of self may be more challenging. Given the dominance of the spiritual domain to the tradition of meditative practice might suggest that it should be placed elsewhere – even first – in the model, but given the limited empirical work on this area, it is also not apparent how generally available this is to early meditators. An alternative model might place these domains as equally accessible, with the variation due to the different emphasis of different types of meditative training.

For example, Christian meditative or contemplative traditions place primary emphasis on spiritual experience, with virtually no focus on physical relaxation or control. In contrast, Hindu or yogic traditions, including contemporary versions such as TM, are body-centered. Other Asian traditions, including both Zen and Vipassana, place less emphasis on the body, but much more on cognitive shifts and emotional equanimity. Whether other changes are also occurring during these practices but are simply not emphasized – and the order in which they occur – is a matter of empirical investigation. Contemporary clinical use of meditative techniques initially emphasized the physical and self-actualization effects, whereas more recently the cognitive, emotional, and behavioural effects have received more systematic attention.

This model, however, does not propose that these six domains of effect are independent of each other. Nor does this model propose that these effects are unique to meditation, nor that they are yet fully validated. Rather the point is to propose a model of distinct areas of impact that may be heuristically useful and provide clarity for future research. An analogy to music may be useful. Both meditative practice and music are grounded in cultural traditions, yet it is now well recognized that the ability to understand and appreciate music is universal. Like meditation, music appears to play comparable roles within diverse human societies. Despite the marked differences between culturally specific types of music (for example, the Indian raga and the Viennese waltz), all music engages a combination of sound, tempo, and pitch, which is processed through distinct neurological capacities, which operate together to create what is considered "music". A sense of emotional connectedness to music is also always important. Understanding the range of effects that music in general, and different types of music in particular, may have on human experience contributes substantially to a psychology of music. Once these domains of experience are identified, we can then begin to consider how practice or experience within one domain creates skill and further accomplishment. This is the type of map that I am proposing in order to better understand meditation effects. Despite wide variations in meditative techniques and in levels of practice, commonalities of experience exist.

The developmental component of meditation effects

The second aspect of this model is the developmental dimension. That meditative effects change with practice is widely acknowledged in contemporary literature (Goleman, 1996), but has received little systematic empirical investigation. There is considerable confusion over what might be realistically expected during early stages of meditation practice (during the first few weeks – or even hours), what would be expected during a period of time that is realistic for therapeutic work (several months), and what is more appropriately sought in the context of personal retreats under the direction of experienced meditation masters. At the same time, the model proposed here is not intended to be a "stage" model such as proposed by Wilber (1986), in which he models types of effects in the form of layers of an onion in which one moves inward from physical effects to a core of spiritual awakening. In his model, the *domains* define developmental stage, rather than having stages of development occurring *within* each domain.

Early practice

During early meditation practice, effects across different domains might be best understood as the result of simply a quieting of attention; of bringing awareness to a single focus instead of allowing it to jump quickly from stimulus to stimulus; to the suspension of critical judgment; and to disengagement of thoughts and reactions from usual preoccupations. At this level, the clinical effects of meditation practice may be similar to those of other relaxation techniques or distracting activities. When the mind is turned away from preoccupying concerns, whether by focus on a *mantra* or by watching television, disengagement occurs and some degree of relaxation will follow. Within the domain of physiological change, there is possibly also a non-conditioned reflex brought into play related to slowing down the breath (Lehrer, Sasaki & Saito, 1999; Haruki & Takasi, 2001), introducing a simple rhythmical pattern, and a shift into a non-descending theta state (Delmonte, 1984). Within cognitive, emotional, and behavioural realms, in addition to the distracting value of the mantra, the element of mindfulness – non-judgmental awareness – is introduced. This may have the value of disrupting usual conditioned patterns of thinking, feeling and acting; of a slowing down of usual conditioned reactivity and response; and introducing a heightened sense of personal control. In the realm of relation to self, the moment-to-moment experience of being, of self-acceptance rather than judging, may be critical. Within the spiritual realm, it is the momentary disengagement from usual concerns and preoccupations that allows for consideration of higher level meaning or awareness of a space of inner quietness and awe that has impact. However, during early stages of practice, these effects may be quite subtle, and unless the person is searching for them in the context of a particular expectational set, they may escape notice or may not occur at all.

Intermediate – early practice

With somewhat extended practice, the individual tends to notice an ability to take more conscious control of attention, accompanied by an ability to bring relaxation – or directed action – into increasingly challenging situations. Thoughts may no longer seem to jump around as quickly. Attention is more easily directed at will. A critical understanding of the process may require the merging of Buddhist psychology with contemporary learning theory. What happens when usual patterns of conditioned reaction and responding occur? By the second month of daily practice (or a comparable number of hours), many individuals can experience a suspension of thought, a brief space of silence within the chattering of the mind. Something like a neurological "vacuum" is created, producing an opportunity for other levels of processing of the situation to occur. Because the results of such processing is almost always reported as of higher value, it may be appropriate to refer to this process as "wisdom functioning". A sense of enhanced behavioural control may occur. Cognitive and emotional reactivity may be substantially reduced, as evidenced in the reduction of panic or anxiety attacks. There may be an increased sense of a coherent self. Access to the spiritual may come more easily or spontaneously, particularly with use of loving kindness meditations (Kornfield, 1993). At the same time, a sense of compassion, of opening the heart to others, can be heightened. In Zen terms, the first experience of enlightenment or *kensho* may occur.

Intermediate – later practice

In continued regular and deeper personal practice, enduring changes may be occurring in neurological processing. Access to "wisdom functioning" is enhanced and more stable. Conscious control over physiological processes that are usually reflexive or automatic such as pain, sleep, dream states, or metabolic reactions becomes possible. Ability to sustain or direct attention is magnified beyond the usual. Individuals reach a state of self/no-self that allows compassion for others to infuse their life. Activities of choice or occupation may be experienced with what Csikszentmihalyi refers to as "flow" (Csikszentmihalyi, 1997). *Samadhi* experiences in Zen may occur more reliably. What is often referred to as "spiritual" or as "wisdom" may inform most activities, decisions and interactions. However, even at this highly evolved level, lapses can and do occur (note the rash of sexual and fiscal scandals tied to senior meditation leaders in the last decade in a number of spiritual settings) (Rubin, 2003).

Specific effects, or the order in which they appear, may continue to depend on the type of training in which the person engages and the particular capacities of the individual, but the underlying processes are likely to be highly similar. Again, the analogy to music may be appropriate. A highly trained opera star and an accomplished jazz musician clearly do not have identical skills – and may bring to their craft important distinct capacities (a natural voice vs. an ability to improvise) – but many of the underlying processes vis à vis heightened musical abilities are likely to be similar.

Late stage

With extended practice, probably in combination with unusual personal capabilities, the extraordinary states of physical control, pure awareness, cessation of conditioning, bliss, loss of self-attachment, and sense of sustained unity with a deity or higher realm is experienced. There is no longer a struggle with or attachment to physical or sensual pleasures. At this point, the distinction between spiritual enlightenment and optimal development in other arenas of functioning may disappear.

Understanding the underlying process

The model presented here posits that there are important distinctive and separable effects of meditation practice. Our psychological and physiological makeup consists of various dimensions of functioning (i.e., emotional, cognitive, etc.); meditation effects may occur across these domains of functioning simultaneously, or may vary dependent on expectancy effects, different emphasis in training, or differences in individual needs or capacities. The extent to which variation occurs and for what reasons is an empirical question that needs much further study. However, changes in each of these dimensions should also be understood as changes in parts of the whole. To the extent that meditation engages a shift in a general way of functioning, such a shift might then have the potential to create changes in all domains of functioning.

How do changes in the processes of attention and awareness impact such a wide range of mind-body functioning? The mind – or our perceptual processes – is inherently designed to be constantly scanning our external environment for sources of danger and for sources of gratification (punishments and rewards in Western psychology; aversions and attachments in Buddhist psychology). We now understand that such scanning includes our internal world as much as the external; in Buddhist psychology, thoughts are considered one of the "senses", comparable to sight, hearing, touch, taste and smell. Thoughts and emotional responses arise and are then observed and responded to as if they were "real". Not only are these the result of imposing meaning on the stimuli that impinge on our brain, but these responses engender further reactions, thoughts, feelings and behaviour. In fact, cognitive psychotherapy recognizes how much we construct our reality through this imposed meaning. The body then responds as if the external stimuli or the internal experiences were actual danger signals; there is a physiological preparedness that occurs marked by changes in blood pressure, heart rate, muscle tension, etc. Cognitive therapy acts directly on these meaning experiences by directing us to substitute alternative content: optimistic thoughts for pessimistic thoughts or reframing the meaning of particular experiences. Behavioural therapy works by repeatedly changing the pairing of actual triggers and responses, through extinction or by practice.

Meditation acts somewhat differently. First, it provides a way to passively disengage from whatever signal is impinging on the mind. It does this through the use of relatively meaningless repetitive stimuli. Secondly, mindfulness meditation involves the cultivation of bare attention, training the process of attention in and of itself, rather than as a function of the level of inherent interest of the object. Learning to engage bare attention, learning to attend without engaging in the usual train of thinking, creates the possibility of suspension of thought, of experiencing the silence between the thoughts. As Austin notes (1999, p.658), "the nerve cells are liberated from their usual synaptic clutter" – at least at the conscious level – and silence ensues. Finally, meditation engages a deconditioning process. Rather than distracting oneself from the thought object, the instruction is to watch it or be aware of it without reacting, responding or imposing further meaning (judgment) on it. By disengaging the stimulus from the response, over and over again, the mind becomes different in a fundamental way, much as is recognized in contemporary learning theory. One effect of the disengagement from the usual chatter of our conscious mind (for, of course, the brain is continuing to function quite actively in the background) is a sense of liberation and a sense of freedom.

This process also appears to create the opportunity for "wisdom" to occur. With the suspension of our usual, conditioned, or overly determined responses, there may be an increased emergence of more novel, creative or "wiser" perspectives on life challenges. The insights that arise may not be profound, but the realizations often are experienced as fresh and in some way unexpected. The process of "deconditioning", of disengaging the most immediate associative responses, allows a broader range of connections and perspectives. One of the challenges to understanding the neuropsychological processes underlying these effects of meditation is how or why these emergent realizations generally appear to be positive or "wise" in quality rather than simply random or novel.

It may also be that this suspension of "mind" is integrally related to changes in sense of self that are commonly associated with meditative practice. From a neurological perspective, it is hard to understand why changes in sense of self would emerge from a "simple" cognitive technique. Within Western psychology, the sense of "self" seems to encompass all conscious experience. However, Buddhist psychology views "the self" as inherently illusory and values the transformative power of being able to disengage from full personal identity with this sense of "self". If the ability to disengage from conditioned responses also promotes a loosening in attachment to "sense of self", as is asserted to accompany extended meditation practice, then studying the processes of meditation may also help in understanding the underlying neurophysiology of the experience of self.

The final arena in which research on meditation poses both a challenge and opportunity is in the underlying processes of experience of spirituality. Although the concept of spirituality as a psychological process, separate from religious belief, is by no means a new idea (James,1902/1997; Huxley, 1970), there is only recently a resurgence of interest in defining and examining the process of spirituality within contemporary psychology (Pargament, 1997; Peterman *et al.*, 2002). Others are beginning to consider how to examine the underlying neurological processes (Austin, 1999; d'Acquili & Newberg, 1998) of the meditation experience as a window into this aspect of human functioning, and meditation research may contribute to understanding the interface between the phenomenological experience and the neuropsychological mechanisms.

To review, there are three basic ways in which meditation shifts how we relate to our outer and inner world: it provides a simple, yet powerful way to disengage our senses from whatever is normally pulling at them; it provides a way, with somewhat more practice, to disengage our conditioned reactions and responses to these sense objects; finally, in the course of this disengagement, meditation allows the space for new, more creative or "wiser" levels of processing to occur. These three elements, I propose, can explain the impact of meditation on each of the domains of functioning in the model. At early levels of practice, I suggest that the impact of meditation is relatively specific to particular effects, and that specific goals, meditative techniques and expectancy may shape the observed results. However, with continued practice and as common underlying neuro-psychological processes are engaged, generalization across domains may occur.

Implications for clinical application

From the perspective of clinical application, two implications of this model are important. First, the three processes noted above are engaged relatively early during the course of practice, and therefore can be accessed and experienced by individuals for purposes of self-awareness and growth with relatively little meditation experience. I have found that both clients and students of mine experience the quieting of the mind, disengagement from conditioned reactions, and an opening up to their own sense of inner wisdom after four to eight weeks of regular daily practice. For clients, even this limited practice may have profound and enduring impact on a limited domain of functioning as illustrated by the work of Kabat-Zinn in treating individuals with anxiety disorders (Kabat-Zinn, Massion, Kristeller *et al.*, 1992). However, the effects may not be consistently available nor do they easily transfer across domains of functioning at this early point.

The issue of targeted effects is the second way in which this model may be valuable from a clinical perspective. It is not yet well understood how different domains of effect are most systematically produced. Some areas of effect, such as physiological relaxation, appear to occur relatively reliably with a wide range of meditative techniques. Other effects, such as change in a particular behaviour, may require focused meditation approaches. Generalization across multiple domains of functioning may take considerable more practice and effort than is usually offered in therapeutic settings to become reliable. *This level of practice may be outside the purview of direct clinical treatment, and is better carried on by the individual within one of the wisdom traditions.* This model may therefore contribute to creating realistic expectations for clinical impact.

The significance to meditation research

What are the implications of this model for research on meditation? More attention needs to be paid to the underlying processes involved in different types of meditation. Are there multiple underlying processes or a single higher-order process? Or both? Can changes in a single domain drive other domain shifts? What is the role of different types of training? Of expectation? How do individual differences affect progress in different domains? What is occurring neurologically during “silence”? Is the development of spiritual wisdom a separate domain or the final outcome of all paths?

Further questions that should be raised in research to consider the potential clinical applications of meditative practice, within a Multiple domain-Developmental Model, are:

- What accounts for individual variation in effect?
- Why is it that effects may appear across multiple domains?

- How can particular types of development be promoted?
- How does meditation bring about emotional regulation?
- How is it that meditation appears to promote "wisdom functioning" across all domains?
- What are the neuropsychological processes by which such a simple technique promotes spiritual growth? Are the spiritual effects pre-eminent?

Several steps to future research need to be considered. It is necessary to examine the impact of meditation across domains and across levels of practice, and to consider the effects of different meditative approaches at early stages of practice. More attention should be given to individual differences; variation in individual capacities may shed light on variation in underlying processes, as called for by Kosslyn and his colleagues (2002). Doing so will be facilitated by further development of measures of individual response. Within the experimental context, use of neurological imaging (fMRI) may prove useful, not only with advanced meditators (d'Aquili & Newberg, 1998) but at different stages of practice.

Within the clinical realm, documenting responses to different types of meditation experience is needed. Virtually no comparisons across meditative techniques have been carried out. Matching of meditative approaches to treatment of specific disorders would be valuable. And increased clinical trial research using sophisticated mixed design models may be able to tease apart the relationship between different types of clinical impact and individual differences.

In summary

Over thirty years of research on the psychological and physiological effects of meditation has produced a substantial foundation for future work and even for clinical application. However, the models informing meditation research have failed to consider the range of effects, particularly in the context of contemporary models of human cognition and a growing recognition of how the thinking, feeling, and processing mind creates the reality in which we conduct our lives. Meditation as a clinical tool has tended to remain marginalized as an esoteric and exotic approach. This may be attributed both to overly narrow identification of meditation with particular effects – and to exaggerated claims of "being good for what ails you". The elephant is more than the sum of its parts – and understanding this sum may provide surprising answers about how we function in general.

REFERENCES

Alexander, C.N., Rainforth, M., & Gelderloos, P. (1991). Transcendental Meditation, self-actualization, and psychological health: A conceptual overview and statistical meta-analysis. Special Issue: Handbook of Self-Actualization. *Journal of Social Behavior and Personality*, **6(5)**:189-248.

Austin, J H. (1999). *Zen and the brain.* Cambridge, MA: The MIT Press.

Benson, H. (1975). *The relaxation response.* New York: William Morrow.

Benson, H. (1982). Body temperature changes during the practice of gTum-mo Yoga (matters arising). *Nature,* **298**:402.

Benson, H., & Wallace, R. (1972). Decreased blood pressure in hypertensive subjects who practiced meditation. *Circulation*, **46(1)**:130.

Brooks, J S., & Scarano, T. (1985). Transcendental Meditation in the treatment of post-Vietnam adjustment. *Journal of Counseling and Development,* **64**:212-215.

Brown, D., & Engler, J. (1984). A Rorschach study of the stages of mindfulness meditation. In D. Shapiro & R. N. Walsh (Eds.), *Meditation: Classic and Contemporary Perspectives.* New York: Aldine.

Brown, D.A. (1977). A model for the levels of concentrative meditation. *International Journal of Clinical and Experimental Hypnosis,* **25(4)**:236-273.

Csikszentmihalyi, M. (1997). *Creativity: Flow and the psychology of discovery and invention.* New York: Harper Perennial.

D'Aquili,E G., & B., N. A. (1998). The neuropsychological basis of religions; or, why god won't go away. *Zygon: Journal of Religion and Science,* **33(2)**:187-201.

Davidson, J. (1976). Physiology of meditation and mystical states of consciousness. *Perspectives in Biology and Medicine,* **19**:345-380.

Delmonte, M. M. (1984). Electrocortical activity and related phenomena associated with meditation practice: A literature review. *International journal of neuroscience,* **24(3-4)**:217-231.

Delmonte, M. M. (1987). Constructivist view of meditation. *American Journal of Psychotherapy,* **41**:286-298.

Easterlin, B.L., & Cardena, E. (1998). Cognitive and emotional differences between short and long term Vipassana meditation. *Imagination, Cognition & Personality,* **18**:69-81.

Eppley, K. R., Abrams, A. I., & Shear, J. (1989). Differential effects of relaxation techniques on trait anxiety: A meta-analysis. *Journal of Clinical Psychology,* **45**:957-974.

Epstein, M. (1998). *Going to pieces without falling apart: A Buddhist perspective on wholeness.* New York: Broadway Books.

Gelderloos, P., Walton, D., Orme-Johnson, D., & Alexander, C. (1991). Effectiveness of the Transcendental Meditation program in preventing and treating substance misuse: A review. *International Journal of the Addictions,* **26**:293-325.

Goleman, D. (1996). *The meditative mind.* New York: J.P. Tarcher.

Haruki, Y., & Takase, H. (2001). Effects of the eastern art of breathing. In Y. Haruki, I. Homma, A. Umezawa & Y. Masaoka (Eds.), *Respiration and Emotion*, Tokyo: Springer-Verlag.

Huxley, A. (1970). *The perennial philosophy.* New York: Harper and Row.

James, W. (1997). *The varieties of religious experience.* New York: Touchstone Books.

Kabat-Zinn, J. (1990). *Full catastrophe living.* New York: Delacorte Press.

Kabat-Zinn, J., Lipworth, L., & Burney, R. (1985). The clinical use of mindfulness meditation for the self-regulation of chronic pain. *Journal of Behavioral Medicine,* **8(2)**.

Kabat-Zinn, J., Massion, A.O., Kristeller, J.L., Peterson, L.G., Fletcher, K.E.P.L., Lenderking, W.R., *et al.* (1992). Effectiveness of a meditation-based stress reduction program in the treatment of anxiety disorders. *American Journal of Psychiatry,* **149(7)**:936-943.

Kasamatsu, A., & Hirai, T. (1963). Science of Zazen. *Psychologia,* **6**:86-91.

Kornfield, J. (1993). *A path with heart.* New York: Bantam Books.

Kosslyn, S.M., Cacioppo, J.T., Davidson, R.J., Hugdahl, K., Lovallo, W.R., Spiegel, D., *et al.* (2002). Bridging psychology and biology: The analysis of individuals in groups. *American Psychologist,* **57(5)**.

Kristeller, J.L., & Hallett, B. (1999). Effects of meditation-based intervention in the treatment of binge eating. *Journal of Health Psychology,* **4**:357-363.

Kristeller, J.L., Schwartz, G.E., & Black, H. (1982). The use of Restricted Environmental Stimulation Therapy (REST) in the treatment of essential hypertension: Two case studies. *Behavior Research and Therapy,* **20**:561-566.

Lehrer, P., Sasaki, Y., & Saito, Y. (1999). Zazen and cardiac variability. *Psychosomatic Medicine,* **61(6)**:812-821.

Lesh, T.V. (1970). Zen meditation and the development of empathy in counselors. *Journal of Humanistic Psychology,* **10**:39-74.

Linehan, M. M., & Schmidt, H., III. (1995). The dialectics of effective treatment of borderline personality disorder. In W. T. O'Donohue & L. Krasner (Eds.), *Theories of behavior therapy: Exploring behavior change* (pp.553-584). Washington DC: American Psychological Association.

Marlatt, G.A., & Kristeller, J.L. (1999). Mindfulness and meditation. In W.R. Miller (Ed.), *Integrating Spirituality In Treatment: Resources for Practitioners* (pp. 67-84). Washington DC: American Psychological Association.

O'Connell, D., & Alexander, C. (Eds.). (1994). *Self recovery: Treating addictions using Transcendental Meditation and Maharashi Ayur Veda.* Binghamton, NY: Hawroth Press.

Pargament, K.I. (1997). *The psychology of religion and coping.* New York: Guilford Press.

Patel, C., Marmot, M.G., Terry, D.J., Carruthers, M., Hunt, B., & Patel, M. (1985). Trial of relaxation in reducing coronary risk: four year follow up. *British Medical Journal (Clin Res Ed),* **290(6475)**:1103-1106.

Peterman, A.H., Fitchett, G., Brady, M.J., Hernandez, L., & Cella, D. (2002). Measuring spiritual well-being in people with cancer: The Functional Assessment of Chronic Illness Therapy-Spiritual Well-Being Scale (FACIT-Sp). *Annals of Behavioral Medicine,* **24(1)**:49-58.

Rubin, J. (1996). *Psychotherapy and Buddhism: Toward an Integration.* New York: Plenum Press.

Rubin, J. (2003). Close encounters of a new kind: Toward an integration of psychoanalysis and Buddhism. In R. Segall (Ed.), *Encountering Buddhism* (pp. 31-60). Albany, NY: State University Of New York Press.

Schwartz, G.E. (1979). The brain as a health care system: A psychobiological framework for biofeedback and health psychology. In G. Stone, N. Adler & F. Cohen (Eds.), *Health Psychology.* San Francisco: Jossey-Bass.

Seeman, T.E., Dubin, L., & Seeman, M. (2003). Religiosity/Spirituality and health: A critical review of the evidence for biological pathways. *American Psychologist,* **58(1)**:53-63.

Shannon, S. (Ed.). (2002). *Handbook of complementary and alternative therapies in mental health.* San Diego, CA: Academic Press.

Shapiro, S.L., Schwartz, G.E., & Bonner, G. (1998). Effects of mindfulness-based stress reduction on medical and pre-medical students. *Journal of Behavioral Medicine,* **21**:581-599.

Sternberg, R.J. (Ed.). (1990). *Wisdom. Its nature, origins, and development.* Cambridge: Cambridge University Press.

Suedfeld, P., & Kristeller, J.L. (1982). Stimulus reduction as a technique in health psychology. *Health Psychology,* **1**:337-357.

Teasdale, J. D., Moore, R. G., Hayhurst, H., Pope, M., Williams, S., & Segal, Z. V. (2002). Metacognitive awareness and prevention of relapse in depression: Empirical evidence. *Journal of Consulting and Clinical Psychology,* **70**:275-287.

Teasdale, J.D., Segal, Z.V., Williams, J.M.G., Ridgeway, V.A., Sousby, J.M., & Lau, M.A. (2000). Prevention of relapse/ recurrence in major depression by mindfulness-based cognitive therapy. *Journal of Consulting and Clinical Psychology,* **69**:615-623.

Urbanowski, F. B., & Miller, J. J. (1996). Trauma, psychotherapy, and meditation. *Journal of Transpersonal Psychology,* **28(1)**:31-48.

Wenneberg, S. R., & Schneider, R. H. (1997). A controlled study of the effects of the Transcendental Meditation(R) program on cardiovascular reactivity and ambulatory blood pressure. *International Journal of Neuroscience,* **89(1/2)**:15-29.

Wilbur, K., Engler, J., & Brown, D. (1986). *Transformations of consciousness.* Boulder, CO: Shambhala.

Old wine in new bottles: the relevance of the wisdom traditions to cutting edge psychotherapies

C. Peter Bankart
Wabash College

Abstract

The focus of this paper is an exploration of the direct and immediate relevance of the wisdom traditions to cutting edge approaches to psychotherapy in the West. We focus on two emerging contemporary Western paradigms. Acceptance and Commitment therapy is a powerful new approach to self-directed behavioural change; and Narrative Therapy, an approach that focuses on reforming the meaning structures in individuals' lives. While neither of these approaches appears to have been developed with any direct foundation in Eastern psychology, both, in fact, are deeply enriched by an understanding of traditional Buddhist teachings and practices. As Western psychologists increasingly give greater recognition to the power of human consciousness to clarify, guide, and direct human wellbeing the careful study of Eastern teachings will almost certainly assume a central place in the basic education of future practitioners.

One of the principal functions of purposeful human endeavor is the enhancement of human wellbeing and happiness. In the wisdom traditions, as in much of the natural and biological sciences and in virtually all of clinical psychology, the key to enhancing wellbeing is the elimination or at least the reduction of suffering. As I have learned more about the traditional teachings of the wisdom traditions I have increasingly come to think that Western psychology can move significantly beyond its customary focus on helping people, as B.F. Skinner put it several years ago, "feel more free" by rearranging aversive contingencies in the environment. Most specifically, I am convinced we can learn a great deal about the quest for happiness and wellbeing from the teachings of Buddhism on mindfulness; teachings that locate the source of human suffering within ourselves.

It is something of a philosophical commonplace that the essence of freedom lies between the presentation of the stimulus and the beginning of the sensory-motor response that is occasioned by the brain's registering of that stimulus. In working with violent and angry offenders, for example, the counsellor attempts to demonstrate to the client that he (or she) can slow down the emotional chain reaction triggered by a perceived insult. He can exercise choice, and by doing so he can experience greater control over his own actions and therefore his environment. By developing effective self-control strategies the client, in effect, becomes more successful in mastering and controlling his world, which in turn increases his emotional wellbeing. The freedom the abusive husband or parent now experiences is not the product of his greater control over his wife or children, but of his greater control over his own psychological and emotional processes. Moreover it is reasonable to expect that as he manages a greater measure of control over these processes the people he interacts with will expend significantly less energy exerting aversive counter-control over him. Everyone wins.

The million-dollar question, of course, is how do we gain this sort of control? Perhaps the next miracle drug from Eli Lilly will be a "smart pill" that will build an automatic time delay into all neural circuits that pass through the amygdala. Or perhaps Merck will come out with a magic substance that will double the processing power of our right frontal lobes. That would seem to be the future many of our colleagues in the scientific community are counting on. Indeed, in more than 30 years of teaching I have yet to convince more than a small minority of my students that there is anything more profound about human suffering than a temporary and fixable "chemical imbalance." My frustration with the hegemony of pharmaceutical reductionism is probably the main reason I am with you here today.

I am, indeed, much more comfortable putting my faith in the exercise of human reason than I am in the promise of better living through chemistry. Of course people can forget to think just as they can forget to take their medicine, but we are pretty much guaranteed to have access to our minds, even if we forgot to restock our pharmaceutical suitcase before leaving for the airport. Talking with students and clients about the application of human reason is a fundamentally sound endeavor – and one that I am certain will not be disproved in a double-blind active-placebo control. I also like the company it puts me in contact with.

My investigation begins with the experience of self, and particularly with the idea developed by Jack Engler that the self

> is conceived as something which is not innate in personality, not inherent in our psychological or spiritual makeup, but as evolving developmentally out of our experience of objects and the kinds of interactions we have with them. In other words, the "self" is literally constructed out of our experience with the object world. This "self" which we take to be "me" and which feels so present and real to us is actually an internalized image, a composite representation, constructed by a selective and imaginative "remembering" of past encounters with significant

> objects in our world ... [and] *is actually being constructed anew from moment to moment.* [Engler,1984:29, emphases in the original]

Engler's definition of self is an excellent bridge to the ways in which the self is conceptualized and understood in the wisdom traditions. The doctrine of no-self or anatta only makes sense once you get past the Western, more or less Christian, definition of self which considers each of us to be a sort of essential chip off the old block of an all-powerful God. As Gay Watson (2000) reminds us, psychologists since the time of William James have challenged this Lockean view of self-as-Being, but Western culture has clung tenaciously to the idolatrous idea of self as an isolated, independent essential essence.

In Buddhist psychology, however, this perceived separateness/alienation of the self is recognized and warned against as a harmful and dangerous illusion. This idea is the intellectual and spiritual center of the Mahayanan doctrine of dependent origination.

> When one no longer sees in this way and things are seen as they really are, such desires and the traces they leave on mental processes will cease since they are the result of thinking in terms of the separateness or selfhood of oneself and all phenomena. As one lets go of this grasping of separateness compassion will arise, a concern for that from which one is not separate (Watson, 2000:35).

Why is this an important distinction? Because it lies close to the heart of the network of illusion that perpetuates the endless cycle of human suffering. And this is where I have found much of great interest in the philosophical discourse of Michel Foucault.

A few years ago I confessed to Professor Haruki that I was starting to spend more time reading Continental philosophy than I was perusing the publications of the American Psychological Association. Although the Japanese are notably famous for their ability to not give themselves away nonverbally, I could not miss the look of deep professional concern that flickered across my colleague's face. The rest of my talk today is devoted to trying to convince him and everyone else that I have not taken leave of my senses or my scientific sensibilities. In fact, and in deference to my friend Mark Blows, I hope to show you that adding a little bit of Foucault to the Eastern wisdom in our wheelbarrows can deeply enrich the soil of our professional practice. It may, in fact, require a small measure of French philosophy to properly tune the Western mind to the possibilities embedded in Eastern wisdom practices.

Foucault is specifically concerned with the human cost of objectifying the self in the Western philosophical tradition. The problem that Foucault calls us to address is the insistence that Western science, culture, and politics inculcates in us to classify and objectify the self (Foucault, 1982).

According to Foucault an objective analysis of discourse reveals the essential workings of this process – the ways in which interpretations and thus understandings of behaviour are often imposed from without by sources of authority. For Foucault these "dominant discourses" impose their interpretations of reality by shaping the language that creates and is the source of self-knowledge. Language is thus the ultimate power of socializing agents, and, of course, language is the primary medium through which therapists attempt to bring change to their clients' troubled lives.

This peculiarly Western objectification of self leads a person to say, to understand, and ultimately to be a black man, an alcoholic, gay, poor, angry, middle class, learning disabled, too fat, stupid – and ultimately, under capitalism, an employee who is represented by a resume, a transcript, or in Foucault's terms, a 'file'. He joins the rest of the world in praising, condemning, judging, classifying and fearing his "true self" as a thing that exists in science and in nature – all according to the tidy conceptual schemas of the forces that control and benefit from the exercise of power (Foucault, 1980).

Foucault (1982) argues that this pervasive objectification is a life long process which is accomplished primarily through "internalized personal discourse" (Madigan, 1992). Leading the cultural parade of those who tutor us in this thing-ifying of the self are those of us who practice and promulgate psychotherapy. Foucault describes the psychotherapist as chief among those who disqualify and overwhelm authentic "local" knowledge of our selves. As Rollo May (1979) wrote, Western psychology has bought into this objectification so thoroughly that, as therapists, we have become its chief acolytes:

> When man was tragic [we] made him trivial. When he suffered passively [we] described him as simpering; and when he drummed up enough courage to act, [we] called it stimulus and response. Man had passion, and [we] called it "the satisfaction of basic needs." (p. 5)

The result of this relentless objectification has been the development[1] of multi-level consciousness, consisting both of internalized culturally scripted and sanctioned hegemonic knowledge, and unconscious and preconscious inklings of private self-knowledge. This totalitarian construction of reality is everywhere around us – it is stable, widely shared, and by and large its truth claims are undisputed. Teenage American girls universally know that they are "fat" and teenage American boys universally know that any sign of vulnerability or weakness is evidence of their inadequacy as men. According to recent news reports, Israeli teenagers unconditionally endorse and internalize the conviction that any young man who expresses a desire for peace is a coward and a sissy. Every African American young man I have known believes in the absolute non-negotiable importance of being shown "respect."

The real therapeutic issue is that virtually no teenagers recognize these rules to be either problematic or alien to the developing self. The rules are not just obvious, clear, and self-evident – they are internalized as necessary dimensions of a socially acceptable and successful self. Returning to the example of our anger-ridden violent offenders, the necessity of violence in the face of "provocation" is self-evident – and essential to our client's view of himself as a competent and successful human male. The idea that one can turn a deaf ear to provocation, or to walk away from a fight is virtually unimaginable. As one of my students told me last semester, the best thing to do as an American adolescent in high school is to beat up one or two other boys at the beginning of every school year; that way people will know to leave you alone.

And yet, and still – there is another voice. This is the voice of what Deikman (1982) memorably called "the observing self." This is the self that possesses what Foucault called local knowledge; it is the knower of secret truths. For Deikman it is the source of all mystical experience. For Madigan (1992) this knowledge is the wellspring for the power of "subjectification" – the reclaiming of authorship over one's self; the source of our resistance to being defined by a hegemonic alliance of psychiatric, political and economic labels.

Let me preface the next section of my paper with an assertion that you are free to accept or reject according to your own empirical experience. I believe that the great power of the wisdom traditions in the West is that they offer us our nearly unlimited opportunity to begin the process of identifying and sorting out all of the fragments, memories, sense impressions, dreams, fantasies and hallucinations that continue to challenge the hegemony of the objectified, thing-ified self. As Engler (1984) put it, the wisdom traditions facilitate psychological growth by empowering the practitioner to "renounce outworn, infantile, ties to objects and to give up or modify self-representations that have become restrictive, maladaptive or outgrown." (p. 26)

This is the key to both the power and the subversiveness of the wisdom traditions. Take for example the threefold aim of meditation identified by Engler (1984):

1. To come to know one's own mental processes
2. To gain the power to shape and control them
3. To gain freedom from ignorance of authentic self-processes

Application to narrative therapy

Narrative Therapy was developed by an Australian, Michael White, and a New Zealander, David Epson, in the 1980s. Consistent with the theme of this presentation, I believe that the core ideas and practices that inform the heart of narrative therapy are enriched and deepened when they are viewed through the lens of non-Western approaches to human behaviour and suffering. Central to this thesis is the observation common to both narrative therapy and the wisdom traditions that who and what we are is in a constant state of flux, determined by an impermanent reality, a dynamic process of being, not something essential about our unique existence

According To Monk (1997) Narrative Therapy is a journey of exploration in search of talents or abilities (dimensions of the self?) that are hidden or veiled by a life problem. You can think of it as an exploration for a more optimistic alternative interpretation or evaluation of the client's current situation or long-term circumstances. This alternative is grounded in the life-experience of the client, but it is not necessarily within the perceptual frame of the client's current experience. The subtitle of the book Narrative Therapy in Practice written and edited by Gerald Monk and his colleagues is "The Archeology of Hope," a phrase that eloquently gives expression to the process that narrative therapists lead their clients through to help them discover alternative constructions of their personal histories.

The goal of the therapist engaged with clients in the process of narrative therapy is to help them recover and reintegrate aspects of experience that have been disowned or discredited in order to enable them to forge new meaning in their lives. This can be something as fundamental yet profound as recasting a history of childhood abuse from a narrative of one's self as the victim of physical or sexual predation to tale of being a battered but wiser survivor. Or it may entail the revision of a great range of interrelated meanings, some of which may reflect dramatic changes in the construction of the self.

The point, as Drewery and Winslade (1997) point out, is that narrative therapy recognizes that human beings construct meaning, and that the construction of meaning is always in a social context – where many different, often partially or largely conflicting discourses operate. This means that several competing interpretations of self and of experience can be in competition for authority. The client's experience of self, then, is a matter of some struggle – a struggle for claim to authenticity; a struggle that takes place in a "cultural soup" of social, cultural, and political significance (Monk, 1997).

The idea that the definition of self is at least partially arbitrary, subject to power relations, and at the very least the product of multivocal and inconsistent worldviews is alien to the Western mind trained in reductionist science and logical positivism under the beneficent eye of a singular deity. As a Western psychologist I received a bare minimum of exposure to "wisdom" – I was trained to know my client and her problems in ways that she was probably incapable of doing for herself. Indeed even the Rogerian dimension of my professional mind "knew" truths about my client that she was too confused or afraid to know. There was, after all, a real and true and unique "Gloria" whose "cure" was in coming to know and accept her very Gloria "self." At no point in my training as a Western self or a Western therapist did I really consider the possibility of investigating the possibilities for exploring multiple dimensions of the experience of being. Rather I was urged to firmly secure my own identity and then devote my career to helping others to reify, affirm, and own their own stable uniqueness.

Narrative therapy challenges these assumptions in every possible way. Memory is explored as an archeological record revealing a series of chance encounters: a third grade teacher who rewarded curiosity; of curious verbal conventions, a fifth grade teacher who taught that boys who showed emotion were called “sissies”; and direct primary reinforcement, a high school coach who affirmed one’s emerging masculinity through competition and violence. Thus was an identity built brick by brick, often on a swamp of uncertainty, conflict, and fear of disapproval. The self was snipped and stretched and folded and stapled to fit a Procrustean bed that required girls to be ever and ever thinner and boys to be ever and ever more stoic. This process goes on and on without pause until in the end, as Donald Meichenbaum (2002) remarked at a workshop I attended a few months ago, for the life of us nobody can understand how that perfect newborn child could end up a few years later drowning her babies in the bathtub, or taking his guns to school to teach the bastards a lesson.

Thus the dominant 20th Century Western discourse convinces us that each of us is the prime mover in our own lives. As counsellors and therapists we are charged with “curing the sick” and “reforming” the nonconformists. Little attention is paid in Western discourse to the human struggle to live one’s life with dignity and courage. The person is an object, and all of us are little more than billiard balls bumping up against each other – responding to our environments and to each other according to the laws of physics (Drewery & Winslade, 1997). Each isolated self is responsible for the outcome – credit for success, blame for failure – defined according to standards appropriate to advanced capitalism. Each of us struggles, more or less on our own, to achieve rational control over self, others, and the world. The greater part of wisdom, in the end, is surrender to what is imposed, given, and minimally disruptive.

In a significant demonstration of the therapeutic significance of challenging the power of the dominant discourse, Harker (1997) described how narrative therapy challenges the prevailing view that young men whose lives have been interrupted by sexual abuse must remain eternal “victims” who have somehow been robbed of their essential masculinity. The task confronting these men is to recover and redefine their lives by accessing the courage, determination, resourcefulness, and dignity that characterized their recovery from the abuse. They must, in short, seize the opportunity to redefine their very core idea of themselves as human beings and men, by constructing alternative narratives of their experience.

The task of the therapist is to get beyond the dominant cultural discourse of victimization that portrays these men as irreversibly damaged and broken, and to help these men discover alternative truths about themselves and their experiences. The job of the therapist is to create safe space, a scaffold, in

Mahoney's (1991) formulation, in the client's life to give him the psychological breathing room necessary for a reconsideration of what is essential and truthful about his experience.

In a similar vein, Winslade and Smith (1997) explore the dilemmas inherent in our professional discourse about our clients' struggles with alcohol and other chemicals. The language of victimization conceptualizes the "disease" of "addiction" from which there is no possibility of "cure." The person whose life is controlled by alcohol is an object of a culturally specific mixture of pity and contempt, transforming her from a responsible conscious agent to a victim of a disease and disability, an object subjected to some form of medical practice. We can imagine the same discourse expressing a feckless concern for the pre-enlightenment Siddartha's "anorexia nervosa" during his fast under the bhodi tree.

In their writing about narrative therapy McKenzie and Monk (1997) describe how difficult it is for most Western counsellors, especially those in training, to abandon the object-patient metaphor of human suffering inherent in the Western medical model in favour of the constructionist approach. Even when Western therapists are in philosophical sympathy with the post-modern constructionism implicit in narrative approaches, they seem reluctant and perhaps even unable to give up the language of disease, disability, and disorder when considering the difficulties their clients are facing. My belief is that education in the wisdom traditions, and especially those of Mahayana Buddhism would go a long way toward helping to resolve these dilemmas.

APPLICATION TO ACCEPTANCE AND COMMITMENT THERAPY

As a young scholar I was trained in the most rigorous forms of functional analysis and became a journeyer on Skinner's (1975) "steep and thorny road" of radical behaviourism. One of the hallmarks of that training was that we eschewed all forms of psychological theorizing, and vowed to renounce any efforts to claim to know or to make efforts to reform or modify the inner worlds of human beings. To enforce these commitments we had to work primarily with rodents and pigeons. Because I was granted special exemption I was given license to conduct my Ph.D. dissertation on male undergraduates – but only after I swore to regard them as somewhat oversized pigeons and rats.

So, as I wandered the warrens of psychology in search of intellectual sustenance whenever I veered too far from my Skinnerian intellectual roots I found that my response strength reflexively weakened. New responses were often weak, poorly generalized, not under appropriate stimulus control, and prone to extinction if reward was not promptly forthcoming. You can imagine the sudden increase in my response curve, therefore, when I discovered a form of radical behaviourism that made sense without violating the rest of my worldview and personal experience.

This wonderful discovery was called Acceptance and Commitment Therapy, sometimes referred to with the acronym "ACT" which is short for "Accept, Choose, and Take Action." ACT has been under development for the past fifteen years by Steven Hayes and his colleagues at the University of Nevada at Reno. Simply put, the goal of ACT is to increase the effectiveness of human beings at reaching their most valued goals. I would like to think that the Buddha would have recommended Acceptance and Commitment Therapy to those of his followers whose MMPI scale scores were excessively elevated.

ACT is not, technically, a form of cognitive behaviour modification, since at no time in the course of therapy does the counsellor make any efforts to challenge, modify, or adjust a client's cognitions. In fact most of the time the ACT therapist behaves more like a Zen master than a Western trained psychotherapist.

Basic assumptions

- Goal of healthy living is not to feel good – but to FEEL what is there to be felt. To feel emotions honestly and without defense.
- Emotional avoidance is self-defeating and dehumanizing
- The psychologically healthy person is one who can: Accept, Choose, and Take Action.

ACCEPT – what? Acceptance is the cornerstone of ACT, just as it is the bedrock of Mindfulness training. Acceptance is the opposite pole to AVOIDANCE – avoidance of reality.

- ACCEPT that there is a problem
- that previous efforts to change – directed by dysfunctional beliefs, strategies, and change agendas have FAILED
- ACCEPT that feelings are [JUST] feelings; thoughts are [JUST] thoughts, and Memories are [JUST] Memories
- ACCEPT that excuse systems aren't capable of getting the job done.
- ACCEPT that some of life is unpleasant, AND you can tolerate it
- ACCEPT that you must accept the necessity of change.

Choose – Being able to choose how to respond in the current situation requires developing an understanding of the real nature of the problem. This requires answering an important question: What is the main problem that stands between you and the valued direction in which you want your life to go at this point? What sort of world you will have? This is the central dilemma that both William James addressed in his writing on pragmatism, and that Alfred Adler addressed in describing the importance of strengthening the will.

The central idea of being able to make significant choices about one's own life is where the essential Confucian nature of ACT becomes apparent. Tweed and Lehman (2002) have described Confucian learning as characterized by several will-strengthening traditions, including:

- Effortful learning accomplished through practical and single-minded effort
- Pervasive behavioural reform rooted in deep internal transformation that aimed at the development of virtue, character, and the development of the "good person"
- A practical and empirical application of the fruits of one's learning to real world problems and dilemmas

The essence of this transformation from a person buffeted by past experience to a person of character who can actively choose his or her own behaviour is rooted in the core notion of the self. As we saw in Narrative Therapy, the real and substantial work in ACT is, as the Buddhists have taught for millennia, wrapped up in the nature of the self, though much of the time it would be more accurate to say, the ILLUSION of the self.

ACT calls on people to "voluntarily and repeatedly engage in a kind of conceptual suicide in which the boundaries of the conceptualized self are torn down" (Hayes, Strosahl & Wilson, 1999, p. 181) to make room for whatever experiences are actively present in the person's history. This deliberate confronting of empirical reality potentiates what ACT theorists call "the Observing Self" – which also happens to be the core phenomenon that is at the heart of human spirituality (Hayes, 1984). The result is the recovered ability to experience the world from the core of conscious awareness and being that Buddhists call Mind – a pure central consciousness – an unchanging Self that is not threatened by difficult psychological content – a self that experiences continuity, wholeness, transcendence, and presence. To which Buddhists would add compassion and wisdom.

An example will perhaps help to clarify the distinctions I have been trying to draw between these different constituencies of the self. Some years ago my family and I stayed at a minshuku, a sort of Japanese Bed & Breakfast, in a coastal village south of Tokyo. According to the guidebook, the speciality of this particular minshuku was the extra-cost special breakfast prepared to order by the proprietress, if one took care to order the night before. When the dish was presented to us the next morning it proved to be a teaming cauldron of morsels of ingredients that our 10-year-old son immediately identified as "awful slimy things that have been scraped from the bottom of the sea."

The experience proved to be as unbearable as it was unforgettable. We struggled to ingest at least those bits and pieces that looked vaguely more or less like recognizable food, while the cook scrutinized us for the first evidence of the sure signs of delight that she had come to expect from her patrons. We failed miserably and she was deeply disappointed.

But imagine now that a kindly therapist has asked us to recollect the experience in the hope of curing the anorexia that emerged in the wake of our gustatory trauma. In reply to the seemingly simple question, “On that fateful morning, what did you have for breakfast?” A range of possible answers comes to mind, depending on which dimension of the self was enlisted to answer the question.

The Conceptualized self: The “I am a person who always...” self. This is the aspect of the self that is usually the source of our most important resistance to change. It actively distorts memory, and is a source of self-stabilizing self-deception. The conceptualized self, knowing that “breakfast” is “the most important meal of the day” and that “breakfast” means corn flakes with milk and bananas, would reply: “I didn't eat breakfast. I suffered terribly.” This is the conceptualized self as catastrophic victim.

The Self-Aware self: This is the aspect of my self-awareness that has been trained to describe my being in object-terms. This is the self that is the possessor of “objective” information. Its answer to the question becomes: “I ate disgusting totally unidentifiable boiled parts of various sea creatures and plants.” This is the self that still believes it is a wonder that he didn't die a horrible painful death after ingesting “awful slimy things that have been scraped from the bottom of the sea.”

The Observer self: The conscious self, the self of MIND, the self of metaphor and of acceptance and thus of change might answer the question with: “I swallowed my revulsion. I became a little bit Japanese for breakfast.”

This self-as-perspective, this ‘pure consciousness” forms the primary foundation that supports therapeutic movement in ACT. According to ACT suffering occurs because of needless struggles with the world that we have structured by insisting on everything having literal meaning. The therapeutic art lies in teaching the client how to be aware of the content, to be aware of the awareness of the content, and yet NOT to be preoccupied with content or attached to it as a matter of his or her personal identity. In other words, we have to teach the client how to notice when thoughts and feelings are present from the perspective of the Observer Self, without objectifying these events in such a way that we mistake them for the actual experience of the self. Another way to put this is that we have to help clients learn how not to take themselves so damned seriously. The use of humor, irony, and paradox in ACT is strongly reminiscent of the use of koans and slapstick teaching stories in Zen (Kwee, 1996).

TAKE ACTION – Taking effective action is the ultimate test of the effectiveness of ACT. It reflects the client's answer to the question: What do you want your life to stand for? It is a reflection of a person's renewed ability to make affirmative choices and to express their innermost values as a human being. It is the ability to revel in the struggle of living one's life without excuses and with a sense of purpose and commitment. As Hayes *et al.* (1999:241)) note:

> There is a Zen saying, "you cannot jump a canyon in two steps." Willingness [to take action] is like that. You can limit willingness by limiting context or situation. You get to choose the magnitude of your jump. What you can't do is limit the nature of your action and still have it work.

Liberation, freedom, happiness, awakening; these are the cornerstones of the promise of the wisdom traditions. They are also the possibilities inherent in the practice of Western psychotherapy. I believe that both our "new bottles," Narrative Therapy and Acceptance and Commitment Therapy reflect the great quality still left in the "old wine" passed down through the wisdom traditions' teachings about the nature of self and reality.

The challenge before our profession is to face and to overcome the source of our greatest and most persistent ignorance as scholars and as practitioners, the hegemony of head (or intellect) over body (and feeling). This goes to the very heart of our dis-ease as a profession, a dis-ease that prevents us from addressing our failure "in a number of essential respects in offering humankind the necessary guidelines to address the tremendous problems in living we are faced with" (Holdstock, 1996:15). Thus I join with Mikulas (1996:317) in endorsing the view that "a comprehensive integrated psychology must draw from all of the world's psychologies" The wisdom traditions have much to teach us about the nature of human suffering and the great resources of the human spirit.

As we are reminded by the Dalai Lama the basic sources of happiness and a fulfilling life are a good heart, compassion, and love. Moreover "when we examine different states of mind within ourselves, we can cultivate and develop those that are positive and beneficial and avoid and eliminate those that are negative and destructive" (1996:5). I believe that both Narrative Therapy and Acceptance and Commitment Therapy can be valuable tools in this pursuit, and thus aid in the quest for increased human happiness and wellbeing.

ENDNOTE

1 Interestingly, Engler (1984) criticizes Eastern psychology for neglecting the developmental aspects of consciousness and thus not acknowledging an important source of human conflict and confusion.

REFERENCES

Dalai Lama (1996). Cultivating altruism, In A. Kotler (Ed.) *Engaged Buddhist Reader* (pp. 3-9). Berkeley: Parallax Press.

Deikman, A. J. (1982). The observing self: Mysticism and psychotherapy. Boston: Beacon Press.

Drewery, W. & Winslade, J. (1997). The theoretical story of narrative therapy. In G. Monk, J. Winslad, K. Crocket, & D. Epston (Eds.) *Narrative therapy in practice: The archeology of hope* (pp.32-52). San Francisco: Jossey-Bass.

Engler, J. (1984). Therapeutic aims in psychotherapy and meditation: Developmental stages in the representation of self. *The Journal of Transpersonal Psychology, 16,* 25-61.

Foucault, M. (1980). *Power/knowledge: Selected interviews and writings.* New York: Pantheon Books.

Foucault, M. (1982). The subject and power. In H. Dreyfus & P. Rabinow (Eds.), *Michel Foucault: Beyond structuralism and hermeneutics* (pp. 208-226). Chicago: University of Chicago Press.

Harker, T. (1997). Therapy with male sexual abuse survivors: Contesting oppressive life stories. In G. Monk, J. Winslad, K. Crocket, & D. Epston (Eds.) *Narrative therapy in practice: The archeology of hope* (pp. 193-214). San Francisco: Jossey-Bass.

Hayes, S. C. (1984). Making sense of spirituality. *Behaviourism, 12,* 99-110.

Hayes, S. C., Strosahl, K. D., & Wilson, K. G. (1999). *Acceptance and commitment therapy: An experiential approach to change.* New York: Guilford Press.

Holdstock, L. (1996) Dis-ease in psychology: The basis for a new beginning? In M. G. T. Kwee & T. L. Holdstock (Eds.) *Western and Buddhist psychology: Clinical Perspectives* (pp. 15-43). Delft, The Netherlands: Eburon.

Kwee, M. (1996). Travelling in the footsteps of Hotei towards the 21st Century. In M. G. T. Kwee & T. L. Holdstock (Eds.) *Western and Buddhist psychology: Clinical Perspectives* (pp. 175-213). Delft, The Netherlands: Eburon.

Madigan, S. P. (1992). The application of Michel Foucault's philosophy in the problem externalizing discourse of Michael White. *Journal of Family Therapy, 14,* 265-279.

Mahoney, M. J. (1991). Human change processes: The scientific foundations of psychotherapy. New York: Basic Books.

May, R. (1979). *Psychology and the human dilemma.* New York: W. W. Norton.

McKenzie, W. & Monk, G. (1997). Learning and teaching narrative ideas. In G. Monk, J. Winslad, K. Crocket, & D. Epston (Eds.) *Narrative therapy in practice: The archeology of hope* (pp. 82-117). San Francisco: Jossey-Bass.

Meichenbaum, D. (2002). Personal communication.

Mikulas, W. (1996). Towards a conjuunctive psychology: Happiness and levels of being.. In M. G. T. Kwee & T. L. Holdstock (Eds.) *Western and Buddhist psychology: Clinical Perspectives* (pp. 295-320). Delft, The Netherlands: Eburon.

Monk, G. (1997). How narrative therapy works. In G. Monk, J. Winslad, K. Crocket, & D. Epston (Eds.) *Narrative therapy in practice: The archeology of hope* (pp. 3-31). San Francisco: Jossey-Bass.

Skinner, B. F. (1975). The steep and thorny way to a science of behaviour. *American Psychologist, 30,* 42-49.

Tweed, R. G. & Lehman, D. R. (2002). Learning considered within a cultural context: Confucian and Socratic approaches. *American Psychologist, 57,*89-99.

Watson, G. (2000). I, mine, and views of the self. In G. Watson, S. Batchelor, & G. Claxton (Eds.), *The Psychology of awakening: Buddhism, science, and our day to day lives* (pp. 30-39). York Beach, Maine: Samuel Weiser.

Winslade, J. & Smith, L. (1997). Countering alcoholic narratives. In G. Monk, J. Winslad, K. Crocket, & D. Epston (Eds.) *Narrative therapy in practice: The archeology of hope* (pp. 158-192). San Francisco: Jossey-Bass

Compassion in our day: learning from Shantideva

Mark Blows
Member of the Australian College of Clinical Psychologists, Associate Fellow of the British Psychological Society

Abstract

The eighth century work of Shantideva is, in many ways, as fresh and as relevant today as it was when written. In this work, he used various psychological methods to inculcate Buddhist principles. These methods are of interest but the essence of his work lies in philosophy and ethics, including the madhyamika philosophy, which is taught today by the Dalai Lama. Shantideva's treatise on compassion, based on a view of interdependence rather than individual competition, takes us beyond the boundaries of psychology. His work is worth serious study for those interested in comparative religion. The ideal of the way of the Bodhisattva resonates with Christian teaching. Psychologists have much to gain from a study of works like this, if taken as inspiration beyond or supplementary to their own subject rather than trying to colonise or appropriate.

Acknowledgments

In writing this paper, I acknowledge the invitation given to everyone by the Dalai Lama, to study Buddhism so that we may understand our own religion better. I acknowledge the inspiration from Buddhist teachers who helped me follow up that invitation, as well as my Christian teachers and those who tried to teach me the secular discipline of psychology.

In his original work, *Bodhisattvacharyavatara*, translated by Stephen Bachelor as "A guide to the Bodhissatva's Way of Life", Shantideva points to central features of Mahayana Buddhism which are as challenging and as relevant to modern life as they were in the eighth century when he presented his treatise. The subject of compassion invites comparison with the teaching of Christianity and the methods of education described by Shantideva invite comparison with modern psychology. Where possible I cite my references but much of the material has been absorbed through talks, written works, workshops and retreats, so that it is not possible to cite all of my sources in detail. Very frequently, recollections arise at appropriate times long after the time of ingestion. Time and place recede in memory while the teaching may stay, hopefully undistorted.

THE SETTING AND THE LEGEND SURROUNDING SHANTIDEVA'S TREATISE

In the great eighth century Buddhist University in Northern India, Nalanda, they had a problem with apathetic students. In order to sort out the sheep from the goats they set an examination, in the form of a dissertation. Because he was seen as one of the unproductive layabouts, taking advantage of the food and shelter of the university, which was also a monastery, it was thought that Shantideva would fail. Much to everyone's surprise, Shantideva gave the best dissertation; so much so that his dissertation became one of the standard works in the library of Mahayana Buddhist texts.

The part of the story I like most is what he did after he delivered his dissertation. According to legend, he levitated, levitated right out and above the monastic precincts, disappeared from sight and landed somewhere to the North. What he did there is uncertain but reports of *siddhis*, works of a great master, were sometimes heard of. One of the interesting rumours is that he settled down with a woman, doing the ordinary things that a houseman does. If so, he could have had some serious problems for the reason that I shall shortly reveal.

THE PLACING OF SHANTIDEVA'S TREATISE IN THE CONTEXT OF BUDDHISM

Shantideva's treatise falls easily into place within Buddhist teaching, following on from the four noble truths and the eight fold path which are the basis of Buddhism. The four noble truths are 1) The fact of suffering. 2) The causes of suffering. 3) The cessation of suffering and 4) The means of cessation.

The word "suffering", a short one word translation of the Tibetan word *dukka*, refers to the unsatisfactory nature of existence. We are talking about discontent that follows sickness, aging, loss through death, hurt and loss though disputes, the effects of excess desire and attachment, the effects of fear and anger. Attachments and our lack of knowledge reinforced by psychological defences lie behind the discontent and disequilibrium. We are talking about everyday experiences, not psychopathology, except in Freud's sense of the psychopathology of everyday life. According to Han de Wit (2000), it is *existential suffering* rather than more severe or convoluted *neurotic suffering*, which arises from the former, that is the subject of Buddhism. This does not mean that Buddhist methods are not relevant in treatment programmes for psychopathology, only that they are primarily a psychology for everyday living, normal psychology.

The fourth noble truth gives rise to the educative steps of the eight fold path (Silananda 1990). This is the substratum of Shantideva's treatise, particularly an explication of compassion, as is characteristic of Mahayana teaching. In Early Buddhism, right concentration or mindfulness is emphasised. With mindfulness, one rolls back ignorance or lack of awareness of one's *kleshas* or habits of mind that lead to false solutions to our suffering. Thus liberation is achieved for the individual, the *Arhat,* who is consistently mindful of what he does. This is the foundation. Mahayana schools draw out the principle of compassion that is inherent in Early Buddhism; that is the attentive or mindful attitude applied to relationships. A method for the cultivation of loving kindness (*metta*), in Early Buddhism, is described by de Silva (1996). That method is used in most schools of Buddhism to this day. *Metta* involves guided imagery using the association of our experience of being nurtured by our mother. Even more fundamental as a method, as psychologists would probably agree, is that of modelling. The Buddha was moved and distressed by the suffering he saw about him after his escape from his father's palace; and after his experience of enlightenment under the bodhi tree, he made it his business to assist others in the relief of their suffering. That is a model of compassion and the meaning of it. It involves devotion, service and responsibility as well as feeling for others. The model, as psychologists would recognise, is more powerful than wordy dissertation or doctrine. In my personal view, this emphasis on compassion reveals the Buddhist tradition to be a cousin of Christianity. The accompanying mythology is different but the purpose, the way of the contemplatives, who realise the principle of compassion within themselves in both traditions, is similar.

Relationship to other religions

It may be argued that when the Early Christian bishops tidied up their act to exclude gnostics and women with unruly subjective interpretations, they substituted verbal formulae for attention to the path. The Athanasian Creed is a very dense knot of verbal formula, some of it of indeterminate meaning. Yet reformers such as St. Benedict reminded Christians that Christ was "in the face of the other", that is the tradition has a social purpose, devotion through compassion. Viewed in this way, Christianity may be seen as the cousin of Mahayana Buddhism, as the Vedanta tradition in Hinduism may also be seen. Cousins, of course, are quite different from identical twins and it is not my intention to confuse commonality with identity. I have had no formal teaching within the Muslim tradition, but my Muslim friends give me many examples of the same orientation, of practical love within relationships.

Reincarnation and the ideal of the bodhisattva

As well as the four noble truths, there is another aspect of Buddhism that should be borne in mind. The Eastern traditions accept reincarnation, whereas Western Christian traditions tend to reject it. Although reincarnation was accepted by the Chinese Christian church, introduced into China by Aluoben, 635 CE, during the Tang dynasty, at the emperor's invitation, it was rejected by the Western church based in Rome (Palmer 2001). In Buddhism, the aim is to be released from the perpetual and involuntary cycle of reincarnation. This attainment is called *moksha* or *nirvana*. According to the Vaibhashika school of Buddhism, this means cessation of existence, the end of body/mind experience. However, according to Mahayana thought, this is not so. In Shantideva's path of the Bodhisattva the aim is to be able to direct one's rebirth to continue the work of benefiting human and other sentient beings. As repeatedly pointed out by the Dalai Lama, one does not have to be a believer to appreciate and to practice this path of compassion. It is possible to have an atheistic version of the path. Thus the guide to the Bodhisattva's way of life is a very inspiring ideal for those who do believe in continuity after death, not necessarily reincarnation specifically, and becomes a very practical psychology for those who do not but who have a similar ethical orientation.

Some grist mill psychology; reciprocal inhibition[1]

My colleague and friend, Padmal de Silva, has drawn attention to the similarities between the techniques of modern psychology and those used by the Buddha (1985, 1986, 1990, 1993, 1996). His papers are very much recommended for students interested in Buddhist psychology. One of the techniques, known also in the Patanjali Sutras in Hindu Yoga, is that of reciprocal inhibition. In the Buddhist tradition this is done through imagery rather than in overt behaviour. Although the technique is familiar, the context in which it was frequently used is strange to modern men and women. Religion has, for many centuries, been primarily men's business, regardless of the tradition. In one way or another men have tried to restrict the influence of women. Our greatest attraction, however, as men, is to women. This is particularly problematical for monasticism, at least in some instances. Therefore there used to be a very hard headed programme of reciprocal inhibition to remove temptation; Shantideva describes the body as "a cage of filth", both in respect of one's own body and of another body which is the object of desire. The technique is one of analytical deconstruction of the body, visualising the component parts, bone, blood, bile, faeces and so on. This is not quite the same as but is similar to sitting in a grave yard, watching the vultures eat the flesh of the dead, a Tibetan technique to reduce attachment to the body in general but also to drive home the temporary nature of existence. The effect of the technique in this particular context must be one of aversion. That is why I said that Shantideva could have had some difficulty if he did actually settle down into married life.

The same problems in the monastic setting were encountered in the early Christian church. One of the *Conferences* of Cassian, the forerunner of St Benedict, is about sex. The ideal is the complete extinction of desire. Of course there is a better way of dealing with this same desire, if you happen to be troubled by it. The tradition of analytical contemplation is very important in Mahayana Buddhism but in modern writing it is not directed in such a macabre way. Instead of destructive analysis of the body into its parts, we may simply accept the suchness of life, using everyday knowledge of biology. Human beings in general, whether men or women, unlike stationary forms of biological life, like trees and plants, carry our energy exchange systems around with us, the respiratory and the digestive systems. It may well be that the waste products, useful though they might be in ecological systems, subjectively have unpleasant olfactory effects. Realising something like this, Krushchev, the Russian statesman, once said, appropriately: "We are all much the same in the bath". With realistic observation of such things, undue idealisation is reduced. Yet at the same time, beauty may be appreciated, beauty of appearance, movement or speech. It is ego-centric possessiveness that causes difficulty, not pleasant effects. Our individual perception of beauty may be offered to the benefit of all, in Mahayana terms to the Dharmakaya. Or as put by Hildegard of Bingen, the Christian nun, praise God for the neatness and beauty of the body even in its elementary functioning. The rather grist mill technique described by Shantideva may be replaced with something better.[2] Of course there is some value in Shantideva's approach. While not perhaps going all the way in the use of his recommended technique, I have, I confess, used something of it. For instance, with women approaching my age it is easy to focus on the signs of transience of the body such as veins on the legs or slight excrescences on the skin of their faces. Unfortunately, when that is done, a flicker of disconcertion may be observed in the lady and then a ripple of doubt about my own compassion may arise within if not a measure of remorse. Of course it is better to accept the suchness of things as they are and to laugh. There is no need to take the monkey mind seriously.

"As rain does not penetrate a well-thatched house, so lust does not penetrate a cultivated mind" (from the *Dhammmapada*, quoted by de Silva, 1998). This statement from the Buddha recorded soon after his death, may be read as supporting Shantideva's attitude to the body and to "copulation". But the Buddha's statement is ambiguous and from the viewpoint of modern psychology, it is dangerous, not to use some of the rain. For a very different perspective on the subject, I recommend a book by a rebel, Gedun Chopel, *Tibetan Arts of Love: Sex, Orgasm & Spiritual Healing*, translated by the eminent scholar of Tibetan Buddhism, Jeffrey Hopkins. This issue is found in Hindu Yoga. In Patanjali's well known yoga *sutras*, one of the eight steps is *brahmacarya*, highest conduct. In the nineteenth century editions this was interpreted as sexual abstinence. Karambelkar introduced a more rational interpretation in his 1985 edition, that of highest conduct including responsible sexual conduct. This is a more helpful focus for most people as well as a better translation of the Sanskrit.

This discussion of the inhibition of sexual impulses would have less point if it were restricted to monastic living. Throughout the ages, the puritanical attitude has been extended to the laity. Further it is assumed in the Mahayana tradition, but not only there, that the life of the professed is preferable, if not superior, to that of a layman or woman. The attitude flows over well beyond the monastic wall. A similar attitude may be traced in the history of music, within Christianity and Islam. Plato and Pope Gregory the Great were but two main proponents of restriction. Early Christian religious singing is more sensual than Pope Gregory thought appropriate. In my opinion, the rejection of *eros* in any of its forms is problematical. It is one of God's greatest gifts, but like rain, its abundance is not always easy to deal with gracefully.

A derivation of reciprocal inhibition is used by the Dalai Lama. It is called using *an antidote*. It is a more subtle and fluid cognitive approach and is used in a variety of contexts. Examples of this approach may be found in his book, *The Art of Happiness*, based on a dialogue with an American psychiatrist, Howard Cutler. Tantric practices offer many opportunities for antidotes. Shantideva does not discuss tantra but his teaching may be seen as preparation for it, especially the later sections on emptiness and wisdom. At a public meeting in Sydney some years ago, the Dalai Lama said that the tantra practice of Tara was "good for men". He did not elaborate on that occasion. Tara is regarded as the consort or feminine form of Buddha mind. This is like working with the Virgin Mary, the Catholic symbol of non-attached love. There is one essential difference between Tara and the Virgin Mary, apart from the side issue of concentrating on prayers of petition. Sexuality in the images of Tara is not subdued or denied but enhanced. There is no gross sexual component here, just the use of sexuality to raise energy (*Kundalini*). Incorporation of the feminine, one's anima, is an antidote for the aggressiveness of men. Tantra does not work as reciprocal inhibition but rather uses the so called "poisons" or passions for sublimation. Essential for tantra is the realisation of *emptiness* or non-inherent existence. Mental tendencies may be transformed with the understanding that the constructions of our mind have no substantial existence.

I have been intrigued by a statement at the end of the apocryphal gospel of St. Thomas, where it says that in order to enter the "kingdom of heaven", Jesus's expression, corresponding to that of *moksha* or enlightenment, Mary must become a man. Is this mere male chauvinism or is it a tantric reference, for it has been thought that Jesus was possibly not unfamiliar with such methods in his esoteric teaching? I like to think that this is a corruption of the text and what it means is that Mary should absorb her animus, the reverse of the Tara practice. It may just be an expression of masculine bias.

Some psychology on a higher plane

Mahayana Buddhism focuses on relationship with the other, especially the generation of compassion. This may be viewed as having its implicate form in the early Indian idea of *ahimsa* or doing no harm. Shantideva, as indicated at the beginning of this article, was a scallywag with a good sense of humour. So in drawing out what a compassionate attitude might be like, he used a kind of reverse role play technique, a heightened dramatic experience of the opposite. This is as fresh and as relevant today as it was when it was given in his dissertation. Here is an example:

> "By all means I shall make clear to the entire world
> All the good qualities I have
> But I shall not let anyone hear
> Of any good qualities he may have"

and further:

> "It is said that this deluded one
> Is trying to compete with me,
> But how can he be equal with me
> In learning, intelligence, form, class or wealth?
>
> Thus upon hearing of my good qualities
> That have been made well-known to all
> I shall thoroughly enjoy the satisfaction
> Of the pleasant tingling-sensation that occurs.
>
> Even though he has some possessions,
> If he is working for me,
> I shall give him just enough to live on
> And by force I'll take the rest."

I thought capitalism was a modern trend, maybe not. This statement of exploitation was written by Shantideva as an exercise in role reversal. The invitation is to share the experience of the underdog who receives such messages. He goes on to make a very important distinction. The point is not that the person is at fault in having the aggressive, competitive attitudes but that these attitudes are examples of misconception. The phrase used in the translation is "disturbing conceptions", which is correct but misleading unless you are familiar with the theory of yoga, where the primeval, uncluttered state of mind, is still and "undisturbed". Unless you are familiar with that background, it may be better to use the word "misconception". Misconception is, in the Buddhist literature, according to my understanding, much the same as what is called "ignorance".

The passage indicates a competitive, exploitative attitude, one that may also be described as egocentric and authoritarian. By authoritarian I mean seeing relationships in terms of ascendancy and submission. It shows a tendency to use other people as a means for one's own egocentric ends. The passage could have been written today, just as easily as in the eighth century. At the level of practical psychology, we know that non-authoritarian, co-operative attitudes work best in the class room and in the work place. Distress in the work place is closely related to the lack of individual control over decision making (Campbell & Singer, 1983). At a more macro level, there is a whole range of events in the field of international relations that are based on alienation of the other, punishment and manipulation, rather than respect and authentic recognition of the value of the other. I have but given a sample of Shantideva's work about engendering compassion. The serious student may want to read the whole of his work.

Shantideva's view on compassion is very applicable to daily life. This is as useful for non-believers as it is for the followers of religion. The promise of the spiritual attainment of being a bodhisattva is not essential to the principles of compassion, although it inspires.

Optimism and comparison with Christianity

In some respects, but not all, there is more optimism in Buddhism than in mainstream Christianity, at least as it is known to many people. In Shantideva's treatise, errors of attitude or misconception may be remedied with the appropriate methods. There is not the heavy emphasis on *sin* we find in the Christian literature. There is a lighter confidence in the underlying goodness of human nature which is obscured by errors of conception. In the early Christian church, sin was more a matter of "missing the mark"[3], rather than a bias towards evil which has caused unproductive guilt in many. St Augustine and many after him reinforced the more pessimistic view of bias towards evil. This was not the view of the Middle Eastern church that entered China in the Tang dynasty (Palmer, 2001). Goodness was regarded as the essential feature of human nature, even if this goodness is frequently clouded. Unfortunately this Eastern version of the Christian tradition all but died out because of cultural purging in China. The tolerance of Emperor Gaozum who invited Aluoben was not sustained. In neighbouring countries many of these Christians converted to Islam, which may be viewed as a reformation of Christianity, incorporating much of Jesus's teaching but rejecting the doctrine of the Trinity.

There is no mystical salvation from misconception, in Shantideva's treatise. The faulty attitude is highlighted by dramatising it. Jesus used the rhetorical technique of hyperbole to awaken his student with a degree of shock but role reversal as such was not used by him, at least not according to the accounts given in the Gospels. Shantideva provides many models of ways of considering others, from the details of ordinary social manners, for instance, how to eat, how to avoid excessive noise and so on to vital matters of motivation and intention.

Compassion is not, as many so called tough minded persons say, 'namby pamby' softness. Rather it involves wisdom, patience, persistence, being firm if necessary but in a mindful, attentive, not reactive or hostile way. In other words it requires personal discipline. The attainment of compassion is made easier by the realisation of *emptiness* or lack of inherent existence. His discussion of that is a vital part of Shantideva's treatise. Before introducing that topic, a comment on meditation:

Meditation as a way of transforming the mind

Shantideva has a section on meditation but in a form that psychologists, who appropriate meditation as a technique, may not recognise. Meditation, in Buddhism has two broad forms and many finer divisions. The first form is analytical meditation, which is contemplation, letting the ideas sink in, subtle reflection. The whole of Shantideva's treatise is meditation in this sense, if it is used as intended. The other sense is via concentrating on a single object, mantra or mental picture – merely repeating a mantra or staying with an image is not meditation but a route to it. This produces better capacity to concentrate and produces the necessary distance from our ordinary preoccupations, which is what is required for deep tranquillity. Without tranquillity, introspective self examination of any value is difficult, perhaps hardly possible. The same general division is found in traditional Christian contemplation, albeit with different terminology, such as in the classic text by an anonymous English monk, The Cloud of Unknowing. In the view of the Dalai Lama, of the two forms of meditation, analytical or vipassana and concentrative, the former is regarded as the more important. Of the various possible contents of analytical meditation, emptiness or interdependence is regarded as the most important. This not quite the emphasis given in contemporary Christian meditation, as taught by Laurence Freeman (1986, 1989, 2000) which places emphasis on a type of concentrative meditation. However, there is no essential difference if the total context is taken into account. Psychologists who want to use forms of so called meditation should consider the fact that in the Wisdom traditions, meditation is embedded in particular contexts of teaching and methods, such as, for instance, analytical reading and thinking, discussion, *lectio divina* (or dwelling with phrases or sections of scripture) in the case of the Benedictine Christian tradition, ceremonies and rites etc. The event of meditation and its meaning is influenced by these contexts. The experience of meditation is primed by various events, events in life, and the preparation for meditating on a given occasion. In my opinion, if psychologists want to use a technique in therapy, derived from meditation, they should call it something else, such as relaxation, cognitive reduction or attention control, not meditation, which in the religious context, usually means a form of prayer.

Digressing for a moment from Shantideva, I had the pleasure of meeting my old friend, Fr. Laurence Freeman, recently at the Catholic University in North Sydney. He gave a talk there. One of his statements puzzled me at first. He said that meditation is the Holy Spirit within us turning to the Father. Well, as a small boy, desiring empirical confirmation of my Christian education, I confided to my best friend in the infants' school, over lunch, that if you go very quiet and still, you can hear the Holy Spirit within. I said this pointing to just below the navel. "Don't be silly", said my friend, "That's your tummy rumbling". Unfortunately, my friend had not the benefit of a religious education! After meditating on Fr. Laurence's statement, I appreciated it. It has the virtue of pointing to the transcendence of the individual self. While no simple verbal formula is sufficient for the experience, as distinct from the verbal instruction on how to start meditating, there is a lot of similarity across the different traditions, about the direction of the journey through practice. With recognition of this, the Dalai Lama warmly embraced the Christian teacher, Bede Griffiths, (1994) at their meeting in Perth, Western Australia, shorty before Fr. Bede's death. It is nice when cousins meet.

Interdependence, sunyata, emptiness of inherent existence

This is the most critical part of Shantideva's treatise. At least some realisation of the principle of *emptiness* is necessary for meditation in both the Mahayana traditions and in the Christian one. Incidentally Mahayana Buddhism includes Zen, which may be described as an austere or stripped down version, related to the early *Chan* movement in China and the Tibetan *Dzogchen* which flourishes today in Australia through the teaching of Sogyal Rinpoche (1992) and Chogyal Namkhai Norbu (1989). All of the Mahayana traditions rely on realisation of *emptiness*.

One of the main texts, the one from which Shantideva drew his argument is that of Nagarjuna, a second century sage, whose teaching was well known at the Nalanda monastery. He was a voluminous writer about all aspects of the path of the Buddha but the section of his work of concern here is the *Madhyamika* philosophy attributed to him. In teaching a rather materialistic king, Nagarjuna took, as his example, a (horse drawn) coach. We could just as easily take a motor car or a locomotive. Let us take a locomotive, for all boys, including old ones like myself, love these machines. The arguments runs like this: In what is the identity of the locomotive? It has wheels, it has pistons, it has levers, it has a funnel, but in none of these parts does one find the essential identity of a locomotive. The weakness of the argument is that it fails to see that the identity of the locomotive lies in the coherent system.

We know that if we drive the locomotive from station A to station B, it will arrive in one piece. We do not find it at station B before it leaves station A, although a very small portion of it may remain at station A, after it has moved to station B, as detected by the smell of burnt steel. Although we can conceive of the locomotive as a dance of subatomic particles, those particles have been, to a point, tamed and rendered ruly, organised into a bounded coherent pattern. We have to grease and oil the machine, paint it and so on – treat it with affection or it will disintegrate before its time. *Impermanence* or the limited integrity of any integrated system may be understood. Few of these machines last more than a few score years.

The human body is another example of a system. In considering the body, *interdependence* is obvious. Without oxygen exchange, life is very short. If we ascend or descend to environments where the air or water pressure is too slight or too great, the body system simply ceases. We have to eat, drink water and so on. This system is very vulnerable. The argument is more subtle if we examine the "ego" or mental system of the body/mind complex.

If we return to the locomotive, we see that it has no 'executive ego'. It requires a driver to make it go. There has been much argument in psychology about whether people really have executive egos. Guy Claxton thinks not as shown by the catchy title of one of his essays, *The Light's on but there's Nobody Home* (Claxton 1986). There is not space to argue this here but I think that there is an executive "I", however it may arise. It is easy to demonstrate individual power of decision making. Nevertheless we do know that this executive I, which may be preferred to the ambiguous word "ego", is not as independent as we would like to think. Studies of people with split brains, where the interconnection between the two hemispheres is broken, show that the left hemisphere or dominant side of the brain is a bit of a con artist. If something happens which was not registered there, it will present a verbalised rationalisation to maintain the appearance of control. Examples abound in everyday life. Much of what we attribute to our own initiative is like this. My wife is clever at thinking of ad hoc hypothetical interpretations of events to suit her own convenience. Of course, I never do that! If we look further afield than the executive I, into our thinking, cognitive frames of reference and so on, it becomes obvious that we are the result of our cultural influences, even if we do adopt selective assimilation sets or programmes based on what has been meaningful to us in past years. The cognitive mind is only partly independent. It is also an open ended interactive system.

Shantideva, together with Nagurjuna, appears to go too far with his argument but it can well be appreciated, as formulated in the *Madhyamika* philosophy, that entities are not inherently existent from their own side, totally independently. This does not deny that entities exist altogether. The Dalai Lama puts it well in the phrase: “You cannot put your finger on it”. In the last analysis, there is only relative existence. Entities are interdependent. This is particularly important in respect of our concept of self. This philosophy helps to penetrate Jesus's dictum: “Love your neighbour as yourself” and similar principles taught by Jesus' Jewish contemporary, Hillel. Both the other and one's self are included in this love. It is not *selfless*, as sometimes interpreted. St. Benedict said: “Christ is in the face of the other” and Muslim sufi poets celebrate their perception of our neighbour being, in an absolute sense, ourself. In Buddhism, it is said that the emergence of a Buddha mind will not happen without favourable conditions in the community. So, while Buddhist training places a lot of emphasis on individual effort, enthusiasm and commitment, as Shantideva points out, nothing happens without a suitable social context.

It takes time to realise within oneself the full implications of interdependence. The thrust of Mahayana teaching, of which Shantideva's treatise is a fine example, is this principle of interdependence. My objections are not critical. I have my doubts about the verbal logical arguments of Nagarjuna. Verbal logic is perhaps more suited to demolishing arguments than in establishing positive principles. There are many other routes to arriving at appreciation of the principle. Despite the forceful statements of those who hold exclusivist views, those who are so quick to label others with tags that alienate, the view of interdependence seems self evident. We work hard to deny it. Recognition of our interdependence leads to the establishment of a co-operative society or community, based on consideration of others, not on aggressive ego-centric competition, like that highlighted by Shantideva's role play.

For further reflection on interdependence, studies of some American Indian communities may be recommended, such as the chapter in this book by Chris Rybak, and also studies of the Australian indigenous people such as that by Johanna Blows (1995). There is recognition of interdependence between the individual and the community and with nature in these communities. Their understanding, which can inspire us, was solidified through myth and tradition. We have to find our own route.

Loose ends

I have commented on some of the salient features of Shantideva's treatise. There is much more in it than can be dealt with here. The underlying feature is consideration of others.

Buddhist monks can often give vivid descriptions of suffering in hell after death. In my experience, they can outdo Christian priests quite easily in these horror tales. I have not included that here even though Shantideva gives the usual gruesome entertainment on this theme. It seems altogether unnecessary to use this bully technique when the positive approach in his work is more than sufficient to inspire the reader. The description of hell was possibly expected in the equivalent to a PhD thesis at Nalanda, as was the deconstructive imagery of the body. Hopefully, if he went to live with a woman, that reciprocal inhibition did not succeed in his case. He also shows some unfortunate cultural prejudice. He tells us that it is no use trying to teach people who wear bandages around their heads as if they had an injury or people who carry sticks and umbrellas. Muslims and Englishmen need not apply!

Evaluation/relationship to psychology

I think it imperative to maintain the value that we as Westerners give to independent rational evaluation. Every person is his/her own philosopher as stated by George Kelly. This is very important. Many Western students of Mahayana Buddhism take *guru yoga* far too seriously and suspend their own reflective thought for too long. There is a time to get up from sitting at the feet of the master. The *external guru* is not always right. In my opinion, we have to achieve a balance between introjecting the ways of our teacher and thinking for ourselves. It is almost impossible to argue with some Buddhist monks because of their belief that the fault of non-acceptance must lie in the student. I hope that I have shown a reasonable balance in discussing the work of Shantideva. The Buddha himself advocated selection, taking the teachings that are useful to one. The Dalai Lama sometimes says: "According to Buddhism (such and such) but personally I think (such and such)". There is no need to lose our Western heritage of critical thinking. Unfortunately in many Western nations that is attenuated because of the prevailing trend of secular materialism. Subjects that encourage reflection on values such as history, philosophy, language, the history and philosophy of music and art and the study of quality literature are receiving diminishing funds in educational institutions in favour of subject that bring in money, such as business studies, IT and economics.

Despite my criticisms, I believe that Shantideva's treatise is most relevant to the problems that we face today. Re-orientation towards compassion based on realisation of interdependence could lead to a very much better harmony across the widening circles of ourself, our family, our work place, our local communities to international communities, and our relationship as human beings to other sentient beings and perhaps the earth itself. The principles have many applications. It is a view favoured by many contemporary thinkers, in response to September the 11th and the invasion of Iraq. For instance, Bishop Jack Spong has spoken about understanding what lies behind criminality and terrorism. Without condoning reactive violence in any of its forms, it is very important to see the broad context of interdependence, the causes that produce such actions and thus our responsibility (Spong 2003).

Psychology does not encompass ethics as do the wisdom traditions. Psychology can be used to beat the other fellow in business, in competitive sport, in warfare and so on as much as improve some aspects of his health. The wisdom traditions are broader in theoretical scope and in application than is psychology. A central notion such as compassion is difficult to render into the form of an operational definition suitable for experimentation. Such broad sweeping notions that have many different contextual manifestations may lead to incomplete experimental analogues. They do have some usefulness but do not cover the full picture.

Rather than try to displace the wisdom traditions, as some psychologists profess to do, or colonise them, we should, in my opinion, function in relation to them. Many psychologists use techniques found in the wisdom traditions, perhaps in a modified form. We help people through crises because we can teach something of the view that arises from the wisdom traditions. But we cannot claim equivalence.

The Dalai Lama gave the wonderful non-proselytising, open invitation to study Buddhism so that one might understand our own religion better. There is a little difference between Buddhists and Christians. Some of the latter are a little like Mr Doolittle in the musical "My Fair Lady" based on Bernard Shaw's play "Pygmalion". Buddhists tend to work on themselves, sometimes too seriously, but Christians hope that "Someone else will do the bloomin' work". They rely too much on help from ineffable sources. The best learning arises from dialogue not lectures and a dialogue implies a relationship into which we put effort.

Let us hope that we can continue to dialogue with mutual respect across the different wisdom traditions and psychology, without exclusiveness, proselytising or colonising, with good humour and mutual respect.

ENDNOTES

1 For readers who are not psychologists, reciprocal inhibition is a type of conditioning technique whereby an unwanted response to a situation or stimulus is replaced by one that is incompatible with that unwanted one and forms an alternative habit.

2 This is not an argument against monasticism. In the 1970's I was a consultant to a monastery of Benedictine nuns and I greatly respect the work that they do, as well as the work of a number of monks, whom I count among my friends. That work, preserving the Christian tradition and the expression of that tradition in the general community is of great value. In my experience monks and nuns tend to be realistic about most aspects of life including the vagaries of the sexual impulse, and to joke about it. Renunciation is not the same for everyone.

3 The phrase "missing the mark" was brought to notice by Fr. Michael Kelly of the Monastery of St. Benedict, Arcadia, NSW, Australia, in talks about the work of Cassian and other early church fathers.

References

Blows, Johanna, M. *Eagle and Crow: An Exploration of an Australian Aboriginal Myth*. New York: Garland.

Campbell, F. and Singer, G. (1983). *Stress, Drugs and Health*. Sydney: Pergamon.

Claxton, G. (1986). The light's on but there's Nobody Home. In *Beyond Therapy: The Impact of Eastern Religions on Psychological Practice*. Guy Claxton (ed.). London: Wisdom Publications.

The Cloud of Unknowing and Other Works. Tr. Wolters. (1978). London: Penguin Classics.

Dalai Lama, (1998), *The Art of Happiness*, Sydney: Hodder & Stroughton.

de Wit, H. (2000). Working with existential and 'neurotic' suffering. In: *Meditation as Health Promotion: A Life Style Modification Approach*. ed. K.T. Kaku. Delft: Eburon.

de Silva, P. (1984). Buddhism and behaviour modification. *Behaviour Research and Therapy*, **22**, 661-678.

de Silva, P. (1985). Early Buddhism and modern behavioural strategies for the control of unwanted intrusive cognitions. *The Psychological Record*, **35**: *437-443*.

de Silva, P. (1990). Self management strategies in Early Buddhism: A behavioural perspective. In *Space In Mind: East-West Psychology & Contemporary Buddhism*, John Crook & David Fontana (Eds.). Shaftesbury: Elewen Books.

de Silva, P. (1990). Buddhist psychology: A therapeutic perspective. *Current Psychology: Research and Reviews*, **9**: 236-254.

de Silva, P. (1993). Buddhist psychology: A therapeutic perspective. In U. Kim & J.W. Berry, Eds.) *Indigenous Psychologies*. Newbury Park: Sage Publications.

de Silva, P. (1996). Early Buddhist meditation and mental health. In *Comparative and psychological Study on Meditation*. Y. Haruki, Y. Ishii & M. Suzuki (Eds.). Delft: Eburon.

de Silva, P. (1998). The primacy of mind in Early Buddhist psychology. In *The Embodiment of Mind: Eastern and Western Perspectives*. M.M. DelMonte & Y. Haruki (Eds.). Delft: Eburon.

Freeman, L. (1986). *Light Within: The Inner Path of Meditation*. London: Darton, Longman and Todd.

Freeman, L. (1989). *The Selfless Self*. London: Darton, Longman and Todd.

Freeman, L. (2000). *Jesus: the Teacher Within*. London: Continuum.

Gedun Chopel, (1992). *Tibetan Arts of Love, Sex, Orgasm & Spiritual Healing*. New York: Snow Publications.

Griffiths, B. (1994). *Universal Wisdom: A Journey Through The Wisdom Of The World*. London: Harper Collins (Fount).

Karambelkar, P.V. (1985-1987). The serialised text: Patanjali Yoga, In, *Yoga Mimamsa, Kaivalyadhama*, **24(1)**: 137-176, **(2)**: 177-216, **(3)**: 217-156, **(4)**: 275-296, **26(1 & 2)**: 297-432, **(3 & 4)**: 433-546.

Norbu, Chogyal Namkhai. (1996). *Dzogchen: The Self-Perfected State*. New York: Snow Lion Publications.

Palmer, M. (2001). *The Jesus Sutras: Rediscovering the lost religion of Taoist Christianity*. London: Judy Piathus, London.

Shantideva Acharya. (1979). *A Guide To The Bodhisattva's Way Of Life*. Stephen Batchelor (Tr.). Dharmsala, India: Library of Tibetan Works and Archives.

Silananda, U. (1990). *The Four Foundations of Mindfulness*. Boston: Wisdom Publications.

Sogyal. (1992). *The Tibetan Book of Living and Dying*. London: Rider.

Spong, J. (2003). *Radio Interview with Margaret Throsby*, F.M. Australian Broadcasting Commission, Australia, 13th October 2003.

Psychology of niratman (non-self) and sunyata (void, non-substance)

Shoji Nakamura
Emeritus Professor of Komazawa University

1. The objective selves that Buddhism denies

The main purpose of this study is to clarify the character and features of *Nirātman* (non-self) and *Śūnyatā* (void), which are the goals of Zen ascetics, from the standpoint of *Pratitiya Samulpada* (arising from causation).

In the West, great importance is attached to the establishment and reinforcement of ego, self or ego-identity, etc. In the East, on the contrary, we lay emphasis on *Nirātman* and *Śūnyatā*. However, ego and self can be recognized in Buddhism as well. For instance, we can see the following precept in the *Dhamma-pada*, "A master of oneself is nothing but oneself, one could not find it out anywhere. If one could control oneself, one would gain a master not easily obtainable", and in "A work on Analects of Lin-Chi", we can also see a precept, "To behave oneself always with perfect freedom like a master". These precepts are nothing but a recognition of the importance of ego as the subject for adaptation. We usually divide ego into subjective ego and objective self. What Buddhism denies is a part of objective self identified with targets of desires. We think, for example, body, talent, face, family, role, status, fortune, honor, etc. have same meanings as self and are attached to it.

2. The idea of *Anitya* (things are impermanent) and *Nirâtman* (non-self)

Buddhism denies the idea that all things in this world, no matter if it is a self, or things that surround a self, stay the same permanently and are immortal. This can be referred to as *Anitya*, and means that all things including the self change, are born and die constantly. The following teachings refer to the relation between *Anitya* and *Nirātman*. "In our experience, all things including self change, be born and die constantly (*Anitya*). But, to those who do not understand *Anitya*, these phenomena are regarded as *Duhkha* (suffering). There is no self that is stable and does not change. Therefore, the self is a *Nirātman*. (Samprayoga Sutra 4.1.1)

3. "*PRATITYA-SAMUTPADA*" (TO RISE FROM CAUSATION)

(1) Precedence of relationship (interaction)

The nature or characteristics of things are determined by interactions between each other, and are not peculiar to their own nature. A rock is considered hard only when it is rubbed against something soft and the object is flawed, and "hardness" is not a nature peculiar to a rock. Fussiness of a wife is a nature made out of interaction with an indecisive husband, and is not a peculiar nature of a wife. If a husband starts to assert himself, his wife may quiet down. Husbands and wives do not exist from the beginning. Husbands become husbands only when they have a wife, and vice versa. When they get a divorce, they both still exist as persons, but no longer as a husband or a wife. Therefore, *Pratitya-samutpada* means one waits for the other, and the other waits for one for existence. One and the other come into existence depending on each other. Both one and the other wait for each other and exist with the presence of each other. This kind of existence is called *Nihsvabhāva* (having no peculiar nature of its own). On the contrary, when a thing exist depending only upon itself is called *svabhava*.

(2) *Nihsvabhāva* (having no peculiar nature of its own) and *Samsraya* (place to depend on)

When a thing depends on and waits for the other for its existence, it is *Nihsvabhāva*. *Nihsvabhāva* is that a thing has no peculiar nature of its own. Even if a thing is present, it could not exist by itself. *Pratitya-samutpada* means that one waits for the other, and the other depends upon the one for existence. But in order for this relationship to become realized, one and the other must be distinguished. Each has to have its own nature, as oneself and otherself. If by any chance, either or both of them do not have a peculiar nature of its own, it is impossible to realize a relation such as one depends on the other, and the other waits for one. In order for one to wait and to depend on the other, it has to be responsible for one. The concept of *Samsraya*, which appears in the theory of *Vijnapti-mātratā* (Yuishiki), takes this role. Let us go on to consider *Samsraya* using Yamanouchi's ideas. *Samsraya* is a boundary, and the boundary is the limit for a thing to exist, or be able to work. *Samsraya* is a not only a boundary which divides the limit of two worlds, but, first of all, has to be a horizon that establishes one territory. For example, a ranch is an area of land surrounded by a fence. Wild nature has no boundary, but when it is divided with a fence, a territory such as a ranch or a farm is established. *Samsraya* is such a boundary and a limit. An elder brother is qualified as elder by the existence of a younger brother, and the younger brother is qualified as younger by the existence of an elder brother. But if both of them do not have peculiar nature of their own, what will be the basis of their relationship of elder brother and younger brother? In order for things to be *Nihsvabhāva* and still have the relationship of *Pratitya-samutpada*, one has to be the *Samsraya* of the other. Toshima (1998)) compares the boundary brought by *Samsraya* to the relationship of figure and ground in Gestalt Psychology, and states as follows; "In a homogeneous visual world, we cannot perceive anything. By bringing difference into a homogeneous visual world, figure and ground are segregated and figure-ground articulation is created. This difference creates the figure-ground relationship in Gestalt Psychology." When certain conditions are fulfilled, a figure appears from a ground. The boundary between figure and ground is the same as the boundary brought about by *Samsraya*. "It is said that *Samsraya* is neither *Svabhava* nor *Nihsvabhāva*. When communication is compared to playing catch, a receiver who catches the ball, which is thrown and throws it back is needed. Relationship is the same as this and needs a point to reach and to stop. *Samsraya* means a nature of work that gives a point to depend on and fulfill that relationship. Therefore, *Samsraya* is the regulation theory of dependence where being as boundary becomes the point of relationship and makes itself as it is. Both self and the other are being *sunyata*, but being *Samsraya* of each other creates the relations of *Pratitya-samutpada*. Furthermore, he continued that *Samsraya* itself does not have *Svabhava*, and is only a boundary. Therefore, it is the same as the boundary line between figure and ground (in figure-ground reversible figure). A boundary line itself does not have figure. Its figure is decided by of which outline of the figure it becomes."

(3) Pratitya-samutpada and Nirātman

The relation of *Pratitya-samutpada* was that one depends on and waits for the other, and the other depends on and waits for one for their existence. The same thing can be said with the ego. Ego depends on something that is not ego, and together exist as ego. Therefore it is *Nihsvabhāva*. Ego which is *Nihsvabhāva* is called *Nirātman* (non-self). Okano (1990) states: "When one thinks of now, here, and self, it cannot exist without the presence of the desk which the reader is placing the book on, the chair he is sitting on, the carpet of the room, the floor, the house, and the family members. Which means there is no independent nature of "self". In other words, I cannot exist by myself. Rather, I am not existing by myself. In order for me to be present, I need a relationship with something that is not myself. To put it in other words, I am a temporary phenomenon that ties myself to those that it is not." He states that ego is a knot that ties itself to many other things that are not itself, and it changes constantly between other objects, and there is no such thing as myself as permanent presence. The relationship between myself and those that I am not can be thought of as a current of information. Bateson (1979) states: "Where is the boundary of the ego of a blind person with a stick? Is it between the skin and the handle, the middle of a stick, or the tip? Questions like that makes no sense. When we think of the walking of a blind person, we have to think of the whole information circuit that the hand, the stick, and the road create. But this blind person may stop walking and start eating something the next second. Then, an information circuit of a food, fork, and hand is created." Like this, self-consciousness as an information circuit changes constantly and does not keep its original shape. In this way, it is *Nirātman*.

(4) *Śūnyatā* (void, non-substance) and Tetra-Lemma

Sadakata (1990) explains the difference between *Śūnyatā* and *Abhāba* (nothingness) as follows:"I enter a classroom, stand behind the podium and place my bag underneath, where the students cannot see it. After half an hour into my lecture, I bend down, take my bag, place it on the podium, and say nothing for a while. The students stare at my bag, expecting something to happen. After seeing the students' reactions, I place my bag under the podium again. And then, I start to explain. All of you must be staring consciously at the space of the podium thinking, "The bag doesn't exist", that is to say, connecting this space with a kind of "doesn't exist". By the way, this space above the podium is the same as that of 30 minutes after the class had begun. During those 30 minutes, you did not have the consciousness of "doesn't exist". In other words, this place was in the preceding stage of existence – non-existence state to you. All of you were looking at this space with mind free of captivity. These two kinds of attitudes of yours to this same space correspond to the difference between *Śūnyatā* and *Abhāba*. As can be seen, *Śūnyatā* exists where existence transcends rather than in the existence – non-existence state.

In Buddhism, *Śūnyatā* is usually explained in four phrases. The relation between the four phrases and *Śūnyatā* can be explained using Hirakawa's (1975) explanation. "Nothingness can be divided into "discontinuing nothingness" and "continuing nothingness". A good example of "continuing nothingness" is that of imagining meeting your friend whom you haven't seen for 20 years. It is hard to find a trace of the past. If you say, "You have changed", it means that he has grown old, and there are no trace of the past left in his body. But, since "You are still You", it means that self-identification has continued unchanged. Therefore, it is contradicting. In other words, it means that while "You are being", "You are not being" at the same time.

Expressions like this are logically contradicting, but we have many experiences like this in our daily lives. Buddhism explains this using the four phrases, which reflect four types of decision about existence. They are
(1) Affirmation
(2) Negation
(3) Either Affirmation or Negation
(4) Neither Affirmation nor Negation (This is the decision of *Śūnyatā*).

When these types are applied to the example of an old friend, it can be stated as
(1) It is you
(2) It is not you
(3) It is either you or not you

(4) It is neither you nor not you.

Yamanouchi (1974) reversed (3) and (4), placing the theory of double negation in the third position, and double affirmation in the fourth. He placed the position of double negation at center of all theories. He states that this is the theory of "Tetra-Lemma", which originates the Oriental thought and the basis of logic of *Śūnyatā*.
(1) Affirmation
(2) Negation
(3) Neither affirmation nor negation
(4) Therefore, either affirmation or negation

(1) and (2) are bivalence, they are logic of the West. The logics of (3) double negation and (4) double affirmation make the characteristics of the Eastern lemma. (3) logic of double negation is said to be not only negation of affirmation, but also the absolute negation which negates negation. This absolute negation is referred to as *Śūnyatā*. Being *Śūnyatā* becomes the basis of all presence, and leads the logic of (4) double affirmation. Since it is neither affirmation nor negation, it is *Śūnyatā*, and since it is *Śūnyatā*, it is affirmation and negation as well. The former example can be said as
(1) It is you
(2) It is not you
(3) Neither is it you nor is it not you, therefore
(4) It is you and at the same time, it is not you.

In 'it is you' and 'it is not you', the relation between you and not you is fixed and limited. Therefore, there is no place for another relation to be established. 'It can be you or not be you' can only be said when both the proposition of affirmation and of negation are negated, is there room for any kind of relation to be established. Therefore, with this absolute negation, a basis of establishing an unprejudiced, flexible relation full of plasticity can be obtained.

After all, to become *Śūnyatā* is to transcend 'all kinds of confrontation like ego and non-ego, life and death, good and evil, beauty and ugliness, large and small, and doubt and *Satori* (enlightenment). By transcending the confrontation, various attachments can be cleared, each moment can be lived to the full. At the same time, one's doubts can produce free movement that lead to *Satori*, making one aware of a kind of life that transcends good and evil.

According to Ciompi (1982), "'difference' leads to 'differentiation', and 'differentiation' leads to 'structure'. The structure and the system are substantially the same, and are generally the products made from invariant and variable". This principle can be applied to the structure of the ego. Ego is constructed and operated as a system by invariant and variable. It is said that in Buddhism, as stated before, "Ego waits for what is not Ego, and by it finally becomes Ego". Therefore, it is *Nirātman* (non-self) and is *Śūnyatā* (void, non-substance) also. This can be explained by the concepts of invariant and variable. In other words, in the given condition, Ego adjusts itself to it and changes itself rapidly using the variable part. However, there is a total unity within the person's diversity, and it is due to the invariable part of oneself. Toshima (1993) divides ego into universality (depth ego) and individuality (surface ego). He also states that with universality and individuality, the surface ego is able to keep the unity while able to change in relation to others according to a situation. That ego is not one's own nature (*Svabhava*), but has no peculiar nature of its own (being *Śūnyatā*) and also arises from causation (*Pratitya-samutpāda*). He called those kinds of free, unprejudiced group of transformations outputted by surface ego in relation with others as *Śūnyatā* (void) in all.

SUMMARY

The main purpose of this study is to clarify psychologically the character and feature of *Nirātman* (non-self) and *Śūnyatā* (void, non-substance), which are the goals of Zen ascetics. The basic idea of Buddhism is that everything including ego changes, is born and dies constantly, and there is nothing permanent eternally, and that everything in this world exists in a relation of interdependency. Therefore, it is *Nihsvabhāva* (having no peculiar nature of its own). But here a question rises which asks whether a thing that does not have peculiar nature of its own is able to form a relationship of interdependency. To be able to do so, each has to have something which accepts each other. This is the concept of *Samsraya* (place to depend on). It was made clear psychologically that it is equal to the boundary between figure and ground in figure-ground relationships. Also, the concept of *Śūnyatā was explained with "Tetra Lemma", which form the basis of the Eastern ideas, an*d it was explained that its characteristic is the third logic of double negation and through its absolute negation, the basis of establishing unprejudiced and flexible relationship full of plasticity can be obtained. Lastly, the author made some comments about *Nirātman* and *Śūnyatā* from the aspect of System Theory.

REFERENCES

Bateson, G. (1979). *Mind and Nature: A Necessary Unity.* New York: E P Dulton.

Ciompi, L. (1982). *Affektlogik. Uber die Struktur der Psyche und ihre Enwicklung.* Ein Beitrage zur Schizophrenieforschung, 2. Auflage, Klett-cota, Stuttgart.

Hirakawa, A. (1975). Several Features of Meditation on Sunyata. *Koza Bukkyoushiso,* 3: *165-202.* Risousha.

Okano, M. (1990). *Psychology of Yuishiki (Consiousness only),* Seidosha.

Sadakata, A. (1990). *Śūnyatā and Nirātman.* Kodansha

Toshima, Y. (1993). Ego, Nirātman and Śūnyatā —Presence within Existiotional Relationship. *Psychological Monograph in Memory of Professor Yoshiharu Akishige Yoshiharu Akishige*, pp: 299-314. The Group for Recollecting the Memory of Professor Akishige.

Toshima, Y. (1989). *To live in Kuga (Śūnyatā)*. Nakanishiya Shuppan.

Yamanouchi, T. (1974). *Logos and Lemma*. Iwanami Shoten.

The process of cultural translation: untying the knots that bind

Integrating the Essence of Wisdom

Elisabeth A Stutchbury
Social and Cultural Anthropologist, Buddhist Practitioner and Assistant Teacher, *Dzogchen* Lineage

Abstract

Cutting edge mind-science research draws on the dialogue developing between western scientific neuroscience and the "technologies of consciousness" of Tibetan Buddhism. It is becoming increasingly clear that first person accounts of meditative experiences will inform the direction of future research. The implications of the process of cultural translation provide a reflective perspective on the challenges encountered exploring the essence of the Tibetan Buddhist wisdom tradition.[1]

The frontiers of research

Buddhism: from India to Tibet, to the "west"

The process through which Buddhism was integrated into Tibetan culture, giving rise to what we now call Tibetan Buddhism, took at least four centuries. Even before the late 8th century, when King Trisong Detsen (*khri srong lde'u btsan* Tib.) and his successors attempted to establish Buddhism as the state religion, and the huge task of translating the Indian Sanskrit texts was begun, there had been Buddhist influence with some Buddhist temples built in Tibet. By the 12th century, the various waves of contact and translation of Buddhist texts and religious practices from India into Tibet are regarded as being complete. The Gelugpa Order, of which the Dalai Lama is the leader, did not emerge until the 15th century. Despite the colonial expansionist efforts and interest of several countries, the high isolated plateaux of central Asia afforded Tibet geographical isolation until the beginning of the 20th century.[2]

This year, 2004, is a full one hundred years since the British army, led by Younghusband, marched into Lhasa, and the Potala, the residence of the Dalai Lamas, the temporal and spiritual ruler of a previously isolated realm in Central Asia. This 'began' the process that has led to the numerous Tibetan teachers, refugees in the diaspora, who fly around the world, teaching Vajrayana Buddhism in the globalised post-modern world. Tibet was drawn into the politics of the wider world and subsequently, in the middle of the 20th century the domination of the troops of the People's Republic of China in Tibet began a period of forced subordination to the modern Chinese state with the associated escape of refugees. This situation continues to this day (Goldstein, 1997).

Tibetan Buddhism is still practised within Chinese controlled Tibet, despite continued suppression[3] and is also actively engaged in by the thousands of Tibetan refugees scattered throughout the world. Tens, if not hundreds, of thousands of Westerners have become followers of Tibetan Buddhism in the last forty-five years, and recently this form of Vajrayana Buddhism has been reintroduced into previously politically repressed regions within central Asia, including Mongolia and the Russian Federation.[4] Tibetan Buddhism itself will change, perhaps quite radically, in these western contexts, where several other forms of Buddhism from various other countries, including Vietnam, Thailand and Sri Lanka, are encountered.[5] In Australia, Buddhism, one of the great world religions, is the fastest growing religion and the second largest religion after Christianity, according to the last census (2001) with nearly 358,000 followers.[6]

Research into the emergent forms of Buddhism, a result of cultural translation into many divergent "western" countries, the effects of globalisation, and the contribution that Tibetan Buddhism might make to the development of a world cultural system is still in its infancy. Some significant contributions include the discourse focussed on Tibetan Buddhism and western feminism (eg Campbell, 1996; Gross, 1993; and Klein, 1995) and the discourse exploring western perceptions of Tibet and Tibetan Buddhism (eg Bishop, 1989; Lopez, 1998; Schell, 2000). The following discussion reflects on another significant area of dialogue, that between Tibetan Buddhism and western neuroscience, and offers some speculative comments on the process of cultural translation.

The nature of consciousness and the function of brain

Neurosciences, the study of the way the brain functions, play a central role in the study of mind, cognition, related mental phenomena, emotion and action. Furthermore, the study of mind as a scientific object now entails interdisciplinary research not only from the neurosciences, but from molecular genetics, experimental psychology, linguistics and artificial intelligence. Consciousness itself has become the focus of scientific study, and with that research into the relationship between consciousness and mental abilities which are brain focussed, such as vision, smell, emotion and memory (Varela, 2004).

In order to study the brain, and its many complex functions, and the way these effect behaviour, scientists now realise the necessity of developing precise ways of researching human experience – the conscious perception of the embodied experience. It is only in this way that we can approach a greater understanding of human consciousness, exploring the frontiers of the relationship between brain and its functions and mind itself, research which looks beyond the functioning of the mind into the very nature of mind.

FROM THE DECADE OF THE BRAIN TO THE DECADE OF BEHAVIOUR

In a recent *Scientific American*, a Special issue exploring *"Better Brains – How Neuroscience Will Enhance You"*, I learnt that since the millennium we have been in the "Decade of Behaviour", and that the 1990's was the "Decade of the Brain" – a time which was intended to raise public awareness and research into the functioning of the brain (September 2003: 26). Perhaps it is not surprising that I was not previously aware of this designation for research for these decades, given that my training is in anthropology, a discipline which is already a hybrid of all of the social sciences, with a consequent focus on human society, culture and behaviour. On the other hand, an important strand of my research during the 90's was focussed not only on the human brain, but on the much larger questions of human consciousness, the relation between mind/body, the relationship between mind, or consciousness, and the brain, and the functioning of the immune system; research which I have previously presented to the Transnational Network (Stutchbury, 1998: 103-127).[7] So although this focus of scientific research was not known to me, I have not missed the boat at all, and perhaps I am riding on the crest of the wave, as this decade focuses on behaviour!

The impetus for my involvement in this discourse on the mind, its function and nature, and on the workings of the brain, can be seen as serendipitous. Some of the yogic practitioners who were the focus of my anthropological fieldwork were recommended by HH the Dalai Lama to the Harvard scientist Herbert Benson, for some of the very early scientific tests into the physiological effects of a particular advanced meditation practice, that of Tummo (*gtum mo* Tib.), or "inner heat" (Benson, 1982a, 1982b).[8] Consequently I was well placed to explore and provide a critique of the gulf between the Buddhist and western scientific perspectives in the early research in this arena. It is this material which is the focus of my earlier studies. However, the strength of my analysis derives not only from the anthropological field work I conducted in the western Himalaya, but significantly on insights and understanding gained through my own involvement with Tibetan meditation practices. Through combining these different perspectives, the "objective" anthropologist and the "subjective" meditator,[11] I was able to contextualise and articulate my appreciation of the knowledge and wisdom embedded in Tibetan Buddhist technologies of consciousness.[10] This combining of perspectives seems critical in a process of cultural translation, or in the process of exploring the convergence between two different paradigms.

On being a "halfie"

Back in the early 80's, when I did my initial anthropological fieldwork, the predominant perception of how to do research was, that in order to maintain an unbiased perspective, one should not get too involved with the people that one was studying. To have a personal agenda of wanting to find a spiritual teacher was not something to be discussed openly with colleagues and professors! The "other" was the object of the scrutinising gaze of the impartial observer. Although it was accepted that as an anthropologist, one also became a participant/observer, learning to live in the "others'" culture, one clearly maintained the framework of the superiority of one's cultural framework, and used this filter to evaluate the "other". [11]

This established view was challenged in the academic discourse, with a discontent that had grown since the 70's. Lila Abu-Lughod clearly articulated the dilemma and the necessity of re-evaluating the fundamental distinction between self and other, introducing the descriptive "halfie" to the anthropological literature: *"people whose national or cultural identity is mixed by virtue of migration, overseas education, or parentage...and the indigenous anthropologists to whom they are related"* (1991: 137). Her writing helped me to crystallise my thinking about several issues I faced in writing ethnography. The phenomenon is just that which Saroja Srinivasan is talking about when she presented her "hybrid's" view at the Seventh International Conference, at Wollongong, 2002.[12]

In the closing years of last century, my life changed in a significant way, and I retired from the academy. Continuing ill-health combined with the restructuring of tertiary education in Australia led me to decide to relocate to a quiet and clean environment by the sea. Subsequently, I have continued to develop as a "halfie". Upon completing my doctoral dissertation I had thought, with considerable relief, that I would never have to undergo such a rigorous examination process again. However, two years ago my hybrid tendencies led me to be examined by a leading international Tibetan Buddhist master, in an oral "training" in front of my master, and my peers.[13] This was a tremendous challenge – presenting a discussion of some of the finer points of Buddhist philosophical viewpoints in an hour-long talk, with no time for preparation – totally on the spot. A humbling experience in which I clearly discovered, and revealed, how little I know!

This assessment took place according to the criteria of the "others' cultural framework, and is part of the ongoing process through which Tibetan Buddhism is making a translation, a communication from its own basis with our Western cultural framework. Increasingly I am becoming a "subject" in the process of the development of Buddhism, and in my case, particularly Tibetan Buddhism, in the West.[14]

The challenge of the 21st century

In this post-modern, globalised world, we are experiencing a meeting of several different cultures, and witnessing the slow change and transformation to all involved, as well as huge eruptions of violence and aggression as the people of various countries, cultures and religions involve themselves in power play, in order to establish their control and dominance in this process. We are also at the same time gaining access to the insights and understanding of several wisdom traditions, through which we may be able to develop a way of understanding how things are, that is beyond the strictures or framework of any particular culture.

Through this we may also reach a balance with each other, and our natural environment that will enable us to coexist together peacefully. In short, we are challenged to develop a world culture and create a new sacred balance.[15] The theme of the Wollongong conference addressed some of these issues, "The Relevance of Wisdom Traditions in Contemporary Society," with a particular focus on the challenge the wisdom traditions make to psychology. Through reflecting on this theme, the question is mirrored, "what is the challenge of psychology to the wisdom traditions?"

This question has been raised on numerous occasions.[16] It is all a matter of perspective. With a particular focus on Buddhism, the dual aspects of the challenge have led to a dialogue in mind-sciences, between scientists and Buddhists, fostered and actively encouraged by HH the Dalai Lama. The numerous publications, proceedings of the various symposia that have been held over the past 15 years or so, attest to the wealth of understanding to be gained from this dialogue.

Before turning to a brief presentation of the most recent developments within that dialogue, which looks beyond the brain into the mind, I briefly review some of the recent neuroscientific research, and continue exploring the reflections of my own involvement.

How the brain functions – neuroscientific research

The research focus during the 90's has without doubt improved our understanding of how the brain works, unravelling critical chemical and electrical pathways involved in memory and emotion, and clearly demonstrating scientifically the plasticity of the brain. Not only does it seem from the hard scientific data available from recent research that neurogenesis occurs even in adults, with the formation of new cells from stem cells, but that the brain also has the ability to re-configure itself (Stix, 2003; Gage, 2003; Holloway, 2003). Moreover we now know that memory also is a very fluid process (McCrone, 2003), evidence which supports an understanding that has been well appreciated by researchers in the "soft sciences", although people often think that their memory is valid and factual.

Insights from anthropology

In my anthropological fieldwork I collected oral histories from many people about how a small Tibetan gonpa or meditation hermitage was established in 1912, and traced the history of that hermitage from the events leading to its founding to the time of my research (Stutchbury, 1991; 1994). The people with whom I lived do not have an orthography for their language, and so the transmission of culture, including the stories that I collected, are all passed on orally, rather than in written histories. In order to make sense of the different stories, and the varying individual versions of past events, I had to develop an appreciation for the way the past is remembered, and recounted. The narrative of past events is coloured by present concerns and possible future interests. Clearly memory is fluid, and changes, and people's individual stories are more like myths rather than hard facts. Not only that, the people with whom I lived appreciated that there is something quite illusory and dream-like about the past, not to mention the present! That was one of the many aspects of their understanding, in a Tibetan Buddhist cultural milieux, which challenged my culturally derived construction of reality.

By engaging in some of the meditation practices taught in that small Himalayan hermitage, I embraced that challenge to my world-view. I embarked on a journey of healing, a road that I continue to travel, for I have had several chronic and debilitating illnesses and injuries. Through the meditation practices that I have learnt I have developed a great respect and confidence in the various Buddhist meditations, and their efficacy in changing things, changing me, changing my habitual emotional patterns and temperament, and in assisting my mind/body in its healing process. I realised that what I was doing with the various meditation practices was learning to "re-program" my emotionally based responses, as well as change the way I thought about myself in relation to others.

By necessity, as writing my doctoral dissertation remained an important endeavour, I also embraced the challenge of developing a voice in the academic discourse which attempted to give genuine epistemic status to these technologies of consciousness (for instance in the Network article mentioned above). I did this through emphasising the voice of the practitioners themselves, Tibetan yogis and yoginis, informed by my own first-hand experience and emergent understanding of the potentiality of these technologies of consciousness.

At the same time that I was endeavouring to integrate my fledgling understanding of the effects of meditation practise into the discourse on Tummo, a much more significant and productive dialogue was developing on the interface between Tibetan Buddhism and western scientific perspectives. Daniel Goleman reports in *Destructive Emotions* that the late Tibetan master, Chogyam Trungpa Rinpoche, back in 1974 declared that *"Buddhism will come to the West as a Psychology"* (Goleman, 2003:72). At that time, Buddhism was regarded as a religion, or perhaps, as there was no belief in God, as a philosophy. It was not well appreciated that Buddhism has a very precise understanding of the mind – the functioning of the mind, and its potentiality, developed through centuries of contemplative practice.

The dialogue between Tibetan Buddhism and the neurosciences

During the 90's several symposiums were held exploring the science of mind, in which psychologists, neuroscientists, cognitive scientists and the like entered into a dialogue with exponents of Tibetan Buddhism, notably with the Fourteenth Dalai Lama, ably assisted by translators well skilled in Buddhist philosophy and psychology, as well as scientific disciplines.[17] While each of the symposiums held under the auspices of the Mind and Life Institute, and subsequent publications, have shed great insight, in the nineties this discourse was still very much in its infancy. (eg. Goleman, 1997; Hayward & Varela, 1992; Houshmand, Livingstone & Wallace, 1999; Varela, 1997; Davidson & Harrington, 2002, Zajonc, 2003.)[18]

Daniel Goleman, author of several recently published books with quite broad public appeal, such as *Emotional Intelligence* (1996) and *Destructive Emotions* (2003), in the Symposium *Mind Science: A Dialogue between East and West*, in March 1991, under the joint auspices of Harvard's Mind/Body Medical Institute and Tibet House New York (Goleman & Thurman [Eds.], 1991: ix), in the early days of the "Decade of the Brain", raised two very interesting questions: '*What if [William] James had studied* gTum-mo? *Where would psychology be today? Where would cognitive science be today!*' (Goleman,1991: 98). While I'm not presuming to answer Goleman's questions in this discussion, I raise them again, as they indicate the arena of this discourse, the convergences between two paradigms, one Western and the other Tibetan, and the challenges which are encountered in exploring understandings derived from those paradigms.

The context of these queries is relevant to the present discussion. Goleman suggests that James' study of religion did not include the study of the technologies of religion, the inner psychology: *"In the chapter on attention in his classic textbook on psychology of 1910, he said that he had tried to keep his mind on one thing for more than a few moments and found it impossible. And that has been the assumption of Western cognitive science ever since"* (Goleman, 1991: 98). We can reasonably speculate that if James had known basic mindfulness/ awareness meditations from the Buddhist tradition, he would have been able to focus his attention for more than a few moments, and the assumptions made in western cognitive science would have been different.[19] Like Goleman, we can only wonder about the development of western psychology and cognitive science if James had any inkling of the advanced meditation or yogic practices of inner heat, or Tummo, and the way such practice enables the meditator to learn to differentiate between the *functioning* of the brain, and the *nature* of consciousness itself, questions that remain a compelling drive in the first decade of the mind-science discourse of the 21st century.

In their reflexivity these speculative questions also pre-empt an important understanding that has emerged from this extensive dialogue in the first year of this "Decade of Behaviour", that will greatly enhance future research. The 2000 Mind and Life Symposium, held in Dharamsala, India, where HH the Dalai Lama resides, explored the neuroscience of destructive emotions and is a watershed in this discourse. The theme of this symposium was suggested by the Dalai Lama, who took a very active part throughout (Goleman, 2003: esp. xvii-xxiii; 28-42). Goleman gathered together several eminent Buddhists as well as several very capable scientists including Richard Davidson, the late Francisco Varela, the psychologist Paul Ekman, philosopher Owen Flanagan and Buddhist photographer, author and meditator Matthieu Ricard, with B. Alan Wallace and Thupten Jinpa translating.

The breadth of this exchange over several days, and the depth and detail of some of the discussions without doubt indicates that there is much to be gained by this genuine dialogue.[20] HH the Dalai Lama's agenda is to develop an understanding of emotions and how they can be eased, which is not based on religion, but can benefit anyone (Goleman, 2003 xviii, xxii, 166-68, 220-21, 223, 254-55). He is also clear that if through this collaboration between scientific researchers and Buddhists, it is proven that any aspects of the views held in Buddhist psychology on the functioning of the mind is proven to be incorrect, that Buddhism will need to change (Goleman, 2003: 41). However, the dialogue thus far suggest that much of the Buddhist understanding derived from the Abidharma (an important Buddhist epistemology presenting mind and the nature of reality) can be substantiated, even in quite subtle detail. For instance one of the principal points of Buddhist epistemology that offers a key to realisation for the meditator is the assertion that there is a difference between bare perception, which is non-conceptual, and the subsequent conceptual engagement of the mind which then categorises and judges that bare perception. The discussion on this topic between HH the Dalai Lama and the neuroscientists is awe-inspiring. There is a small gap of 35-40 milliseconds between activity in the brainstem before there is involvement in the cerebral cortex a very brief, normally undetectable moment (Goleman, 2003: 320-326). The recognition of this moment in turn suggests particular ways in which scientific research can be developed which will further allow the nature of consciousness to be revealed.

The late Francisco Varela was able to attend the meeting in Dharamsala, despite his illness. His suggestions regarding future research, and the experiments that resulted a few months later with a skilled meditator (Matthieu Ricard) in his lab in Paris are a wonderful legacy. In order to really penetrate beneath the surface of the brain, meditation and mind, and in order to formulate more incisive research projects which will enable greater scientific breakthroughs, it is necessary to give particular attention to the experiences of the meditators and their first hand reports. With this focus on experience that is paramount in the Buddhist systems of epistemology there are some parallels with Husserlian phenomenology (Goleman, 2003: 328-329). In this way a far more precise and detailed framework can be developed which will enable meticulous matching of the results of scientific tests with the experience of the meditator. This is a crucial step in giving full epistemic status to the Buddhist system of knowledge, which has developed over centuries through the insights gained by meditation practitioners examining their own minds.

Working with Davidson, Varela had developed a methodology for investigating moments of consciousness. This detailed schema of the possibilities require three different ways of validating data, which then becomes intersubjective knowledge, rather than just someone's private idea. In first person accounts, the report or account from the person having the experience is recorded. A skilled meditator who is accustomed to examining in minute detail his or her experience will provide a much richer account than someone not trained to examine their mind and its workings. A second person account made by a skilled interviewer is also used to corroborate this first person report. The quality of this account will also depend on the depth of experience and the skill of the interviewer. The objective methods of science, such as functional Magnetic Resonance Imaging (fMRI)[21], EEG's, PET, etc provide the third person accounts (Goleman, 2003: 326-333). Varela suggests that, *"in the future...the mind sciences will evolve into a form of experiential neuroscience, bridging the gap between external and internal descriptions."* (Varela, 2004).

This methodology for future research into the functioning of the mind and the nature of consciousness converges with my work, as an anthropologist, giving primacy to the accounts of their meditative experiences given by the meditators, and developing a frame of understanding that bridges both paradigms. Perhaps there will be a further collaboration and interdisciplinary studies, in which researchers trained in interviewing the "other" can make a genuine contribution to this dialogue.

In 2003 *Destructive Emotions and How We Can Overcome Them, A Dialogue with the Dalai Lama*, narrated by Daniel Goleman, was published. The reading public learnt of the new research directions born out of that symposium. Included along with Goleman's narration of the symposium is an account of research in four different areas carried out by Davidson and Ekman on "Lama Oser" (the name Matthieu Ricard used to protect his anonymity in these experiments), a result of the collaboration between the Buddhist science of mind, and cutting edge neuroscience. The detailed data available through the use of current technology such as use of fMRI scanning combined with 256 sensor EEG[22] greatly surpasses the earlier attempts at observing physiological changes, brain waves and so on made by Benson.

Goleman suggests that this is the first time someone at "Oser's" level of training has been tested (Goleman, 2003: 3). I think the significant point is that "Oser" is a highly educated "halfie", a westerner who was a molecular biologist with a PhD in cell genetics from the Institut Pasteur in Paris before he embarked on 30 years of training as a Buddhist monk (Revel & Ricard, 1998; Zetter, 2003). Therefore his capacity to articulate details of his meditative experience is better than an accomplished Tibetan yogi with little or no English. I am sure that some of the meditators previously tested were just as accomplished as "Oser".[23] However, their appreciation of the scientific method, the aims and benefits from having the tests, and what is appropriate and meaningful to communicate about their meditation is lacking. Furthermore, out of the respect they have for their own tradition, and the precise requirements regarding transmission and divulgence of esoteric information, the communication about the technologies of consciousness has been limited (Stutchbury, 1998).

The popular press has been quick to pick up on the findings of this cutting edge neuroscience. For instance, results of this and other recent research have also been published in the *Good Weekend, The Sydney Morning Herald Magazine* (Zetter, August 30, 2003: 23-26), an indication of the high level of public interest in the possible benefits of meditation.[24] *Time* featured "The Science of Meditation" just three weeks before (August 4th, 2003), including a photo of Matthieu Ricard (Lama Oser) undergoing an MRI, and providing succinct coverage of the recent research findings.[25] Here Joel Stein, the journalist, talks of "*gtum-mo,* a technique practiced by Tibetan monks in eight-hour sessions that allows them to drive their core body temperature high enough to overcome earthly defilements or – even cooler – to dry wet sheets on their backs in the freezing temperatures of the Himalayas." (Stein, 2003: 52). Such representations of Tummo continue the mystification of these practices, and come no closer to crediting them with genuine epistemic status. Even if the goal of such advanced yoga can metaphorically be said to be "to overcome earthly defilements" we really are not well-informed by such a statement. Until the dialogue in the academic literature overcomes these obstacles, the popular accounts will continue to reflect the deficiencies.

The journalistic representations of the more recent research in this article reflect the greater skill of the scientific researchers and their presentation of this material for a broader reading public. Indeed, it seems that these scientists are actively engaging in a communication with a wider public. Davidson and Goleman have contributed significantly to a three part documentary series, *Primal Instincts* (*Primal Instincts*, 2004). Segments of the second part, on "Happiness" include filmed sequences of the fMRI tests carried out on Matthieu Ricard, and clear presentations of the implications of the same. As Davidson comments: *"If the scientific research helps people to take that message (about the value of meditation in assuaging anger and increasing happiness) more seriously, and suggests to them that there is some real substance to this, and if as a consequence they then show an interest in learning about these kinds of methods to train their mind, then I think that we will have made...a positive difference which may ultimately help individuals to lead a happier life."*

Davidson's fMRI and EEG examination of "Osel" provided clear evidence of very high left prefrontal cortex activity, which is associated with positive emotions and a happier temperament. (Goleman, 2003: 3-13, Davidson & Goleman, 2004). Davidson, collaborating with Kabat-Zinn, has also conducted an eight week meditation study with a group of workers from a biotech firm, measuring results against a control group who initially were not taught meditation. He reported the results of this research at the 2000 Mind and life Symposium. Kabat-Zinn has developed a secular mindfulness meditation practice, that is not tied to Buddhism (see eg. Kabat-Zinn, 1996: 161-170). These tests confirmed that there is an increase in left prefrontal cortex activity brought about by using simple mindfulness meditation techniques. Furthermore, there was a significantly better response in immunity to flu vaccinations associated with the effects of mindfulness meditation (Goleman, 2003: 342-345; Davidson, R. J. *et al.*, in press; Davidson & Goleman, 2004). While more research is needed, these preliminary results suggest that meditation does effect the emotions in a significant way, and can increase people's feelings of wellbeing, as well as their immune response and actual health.[26] Moreover, it seems that neuroscience is working towards substantiating that there may be a significant change to the way the brain works, even when not meditating, as a result of some sustained and regular meditation practice.

Varela, Davidson and Ekman all carried out independent tests on "Oser" as a consequence of the 2000 Mind and Life Symposium. Ekman's findings on the startle response, and recognition of emotional states in facial expression, emotional states in confrontational discussions with another, and his emotional response to 2 well-tested film clips were extraordinary, producing ..."findings that in thirty-five years of research I have never seen before (Ekman in Goleman, 2003: 19, & 13-21).

So, the meditator's experience of being "re-programmed" through meditation may well be substantiated scientifically. Ideally, this will involve long term studies of people, begun before they begin meditation, and continued over several years. The potential for future research is considerable.[27]

THE WAY MEDITATION CHANGES US – A FIRST PERSON ACCOUNT

DIFFERENT AIMS

When we meditate, we re-program our habitual way of thinking and feeling, we change the way our mind works. This affects our feelings of well-being, and our health. Working with a psychologist, or a psychoanalyst, we might also intend to change our behaviour, to ease our experience of our self in the world, our self and the way we interact with others. However, when we engage in meditation and spiritual practice as a Buddhist, our goal is not only to change aspects of our behaviour – although as we change our minds and develop our understanding our behaviour will change.

As a Buddhist, we undertake a journey that leads to our realisation, a realisation that is an understanding beyond the dualistic way of thinking that separates self from other, subject from object. We learn to distinguish between the function of the mind – the way the brain works and the way we think, feel and behave – and the nature of mind (Chögyal Namkhai Norbu, 1994: esp. 12-13). We separate our ordinary mind from the very subtle state of consciousness, which is called the 'innate mind' and is luminous in nature. Thus 'enlightenment' is the embodied process whereby we discover this continuous luminosity. That is what we realise.

Not only is the aim of Buddhist practice different from the aim of psychology, but the methods employed and the assumptions that frame understanding about the embodied states, the relation between consciousness, mind, body and brain are significantly different.

Those engaged in western cognitive neurosciences do not consider that there may be something that is beyond the neural constituents, beyond the brain, and so their frame of enquiry is limited. This is one area in which HH the Dalai Lama is very interested in pushing the boundaries, through the deeper study of meditative states, particularly the state of "abiding in the clear light" after death. (Goleman, 2003: 206; Varela, 1997; Stutchbury; 1998: 115-123).

DIFFERENT METHODS

In general in Buddhism, it is explained that there are three main paths, three main methods that we can employ to lead us to our realisation. When we follow the **path of renunciation** we give up all the stuff that causes us problems – for instance relationships, particularly involved sexual relationships and also having children and parenting; we also refrain from inebriants of all sorts, as these addle the mind and can lead to irresponsible damaging behaviours. Of course there are degrees of renunciation and different requirements depending on the social context; monasticism would be one of the more restrictive contexts. However, the general principle here is that by placing these restrictions on our behaviour we also limit our capacity to harm others.

On the **path of transformation**, we work directly transforming our energy into its positive qualities. We transform our ignorance, anger, desire, jealousy and pride into associated energetic qualities that are beneficial and positive. For instance, rather than being stuck feeling jealous about other people, we free up our energy, appreciating the good qualities and circumstances of others, thereby allowing us to use our energy to move ahead and get things done. We don't waste our time caught in our negative emotions. Indeed the more negative energy we have the greater the capacity for positive. We actually transform our way of seeing things. Instead of seeing things in a negative, depressed or down way that causes us problems, we transform our view and understanding so that we see things positively. Things are much less problematic this way.

On the **path of self-liberation**, we don't have to change or transform anything. Actually there is nothing to be liberated, nothing to be transformed, or changed – things simply are as they are. However, this requires a very clear and particular understanding of just how things are, and integrating our behaviour with this knowledge in a real sense, otherwise we still have difficulties and problems in our life. The teachings of Dzogchen explain this, and these you must receive from a qualified master.

Coloured threads and methods

Over the past twenty or so years that I have been actively engaged in Buddhist meditation, I have developed a way of describing and comparing some of the different methods of meditation, painting a visual image or making a symbolic representation. These images came to me emerging with my understanding of the use of these technologies of mind. In general there are some very specific symbols that are used to convey meaning in Buddhist teachings, particularly in *Dzogchen*. This is not such a teaching, rather it is a simple layperson's understanding, arising out of a tendency to think visually. I am going to share these images with you, and contrast them with an image of the method generally employed in psycho-analysis.

So, let us imagine our life as being a mixed up mass of threads of all different colours, all knotted together. As things have happened and people have had influence, events have occurred, we have had experiences, many different threads of different colours have entangled together – so we have a big pile or ball of coloured threads. We are holding all these threads in our hands, having a look at how we are.

When we use the method of renunciation we try to minimise the things that cause the tangles and knots to form in the first place. In this way we try to minimise our confusion and our pain. We also minimise the knots and tangles we create for others, and the pain we cause them. Typically we use simple mindfulness meditations in which we quieten the mind, and then develop insight meditation. We turn our minds inward, rather than continuing to keep our attention focussed out on the things around us. We discover how things are connected, how one thing leads to another. Following our teacher's instructions, we investigate how things are, discovering that things are not nearly as solid and concrete as we think. In this way, over time, our knots and tangles become less intense, and we are less stressed. Pursuing this path and applying this method, we may finally discover that the knots and tangles have dissolved and are not re-created – we are realised.

How we do things is rather different on the path of transformation. Where we begin is much the same, we are confused, in pain. We take our life, imaging it as a tangled mess of coloured threads, perhaps so tangled and knotted that it seems we could never sort it out. We must understand the fundamental principles of the path of renunciation, even if we have not spent a lot of time using that method and the associated meditations. We understand how all things are connected and *seem* to have resulted in such a solid mess of multi-coloured tangled threads. In our meditation we use our energy to visualise and see things differently. We actually reprogram the way we see things so that rather than seeing our lives as this tangled, knotted mess of colour, we create a pattern that is pure and ordered, like making a mandala out of our lives and all our experiences. So we take our uptight and confused energy, and we repattern it, reprogram it, bit by bit, using the techniques of meditation. If we progress to the advanced types of transformation practice we might engage in Tummo, or inner heat practices, as did the yogis with whom I did my fieldwork. Then, through a lot of training and practice using these technologies of consciousness, we become enlightened.

In path of self-liberation or *Dzogchen*, our approach is again very different, although our starting position is the same. We experience many problems, our life is stressed and confused. Even if in general we have everything we want, we are still not satisfied. Again we see our life as a tangled knotted mess of multi-coloured threads caused by all our actions and interactions with others. Perhaps we have previously worked with the other two methods, or perhaps we directly encounter this method of self-liberation.

Now we hold that pile of threads in our hands and throw it about a bit, pack it together so that it becomes more compact, like a ball. We say to ourselves, "OK, this it it, this is what my life is like!" Through the process of acceptance, and a communication from the master that explains and shows us how things really are – what the nature of our mind is – and through applying the different meditative techniques that help us to really enter into that understanding and stabilise it, we learn to differentiate between the activity of the mind, the way it functions, and it's innate nature. Automatically, things are freed, they self-liberate, and we realise our enlightened nature. Then it does not matter if there are knots or confusion, or tangles – because in the nature of light these knotted tangles simply dissolve – they are not solid anymore. Instead our lives are a pulsating energetic mass of rainbow colour.

Now when we examine the methods used in general in our western psychological approach, what do we do with the tangled knotted mess of coloured threads that is our lives? In this case, through a process of counselling, we engage in a journey that is aimed to help us to see how and when the many knots and tangles were formed. We think that if we can understand the history of our knots and tangles that we can lessen the pain and confusion and slowly untangle our lives. In the end we are left with the many coloured threads, which now make sense, perhaps laid out in strands, or woven together harmoniously like a tapestry, rather than a knotted and tangled ball of coloured thread. We realise we can never untie all the knots, but because we have an idea about the process through which we developed our confusion and pain, we also have an idea about how to avoid continually creating more tangles, through modifying our behaviour, for instance. This result contrasts significantly with the results achieved by the three related but different methods of Buddhist practice.

Hegemony in a globalising world

Secularisation and the wisdom traditions

How are we to understand the real challenge to psychology that arises from the slow process of integrating the wisdom traditions into contemporary society? How are we to understand the real challenge that psychology makes to the wisdom traditions? Clearly, as I have indicated in the above discussion, psychology has a different aim from that of Buddhism. Furthermore, research agendas driven by a western scientific framework are limited.

The goal of Buddhism, enlightenment, the realisation that arises when cognisant mind recognises the empty essence of its own functioning and of all phenomena, is beyond the scope of western scientific research, as the very analytical frameworks used cannot accommodate this potential. Scientific research thus endeavours to discover what aspects of Buddhist (and other) meditations and yoga practices can benefit people, increasing their overall happiness, health and well-being, but in the process divests it of its essential wisdom and understanding. Meditation methods are secularised, integrated into the dominant scientific western cultural framework, and utilised by psychologists who endeavour to assist people in changing their behaviour so that they can live better lives.

This is an important process, and one that offers the possibility of bettering human existence and lessening worldwide conflict. Indeed, this goal and scope is something that HH the Dalai Lama encourages, as discussed above.

Nevertheless, this is a process in which the dominant western culture appropriates some of the methods of meditation, derived from the mind-science or the technologies of consciousness of another culture, into their own. The methods are validated through scientific research, incorporated and the dominant cultural paradigm prevails.

From the perspective of the various Buddhist cultures whose methods are thus appropriated, albeit willingly, there emerges a question about the authenticity and validity of some of the appropriations that are made. This particularly pertains when the appropriated methods are integrated into less scientifically rigorous "New Age" modalities, in which case "enlightenment" may remain a goal, although the meaning may not be at all clearly understood.

The integrity of Buddhist teachings and mind-sciences, which have been passed on through centuries, and may not be reliant upon written text, relies upon precise methods of communication from master to student. For instance, the practice of Tummo, one of the so-called Six Yogas of Naropa, was taught in the 11th Century by the Indian Siddha Naropa to Marpa, a Tibetan responsible for translating several texts and introducing these Buddhist practices to Tibet. They have been passed on through unbroken oral teaching and transmission lineages to the present (Stutchbury, 1994; 1998). Although there is scope in this process for cultural change, this process of teaching and transmission also ensures that the essence of the understanding, the core of the wisdom revealed through the technologies of consciousness, is not altered.

The frontiers of research...

If we consider the process of cultural translation, particularly the translation of Tibetan Buddhism into a globalised western Buddhism, we can appreciate that the scientific investigation and secularisation of meditation methods is beneficial. But like HH the Dalai Lama, we can offer a challenge to the dominant paradigm to open and broaden its scope in order to investigate something that, according to current scientific theory, is beyond its scope.

Indeed the potential for a real integration between cultural paradigms brings us to the frontiers of scientific research and offers the greatest rewards. Pursuing this, the outcome may well be that the practitioners within the discipline of psychology find that their discipline falls short of the emergent potential of the integration of the wisdom traditions.

Significantly, this is a process in which the essence of the wisdom traditions is truly understood and appreciated, and is completely unhindered by limited cultural trappings of any kind, including those of the derivative tradition. But neither is it a simple appropriation of some aspects by a dominant culture. Indeed, if we grant that it is the truth that we seek, an understanding of "how it is, really" we must acknowledge that this cannot possibly be the dominion of any culture, but rather beyond the limits of any limited cultural understanding.

ENDNOTES

1 My master Chögyal Namkhai Norbu is a constant inspiration, as are the teachers and practitioners with whom I conducted my fieldwork. Sogyal Rinpoche's encouragement in the field of mind-science is also greatly appreciated. Heartfelt thanks to Ann M. Pickering whose generous gifts of books and extensive loans from her library over the past several years have enabled me to continue my reading in the topics covered in this paper. I would also like to acknowledge the support received from the Tibetan and Hindu Dharma Trust, Perpetual Trustees.

2 For the reader requiring more detail than this very brief sketch can offer, I recommend Geoffrey Samuel's historical and cultural overview of Buddhism in Tibetan societies, *Civilized Shamans* (1993).

3 See for instance Goldstein and Kapstein (1998). Germano reports on the large teaching "encampment" of over 9000 monks, nuns and other practitioners who gathered around Khenpo Jigme Phuntsok Rinpoche in the Larung valley, Sichuan Province, P.R.C. (Germano, 1998). In 2001, the majority of the houses and buildings were destroyed by the Chinese, with continued demolitions occurring through 2002. The majority of his followers were expelled from the area. Early in January 2004 this master died, aged 56, in a Chinese military hospital, after a period of ill health.

4 Chögyal Namkhai Norbu has established Kunsangar near Lesnichestvo, a few hours from Moscow, providing a focus for teaching in the Russian Federation and Central Asia, and now has well over a thousand followers.

5 In the case of Vietnamese Mahayana Buddhism, this has also largely been through a refugee diaspora, although this is not the case in with Theravadin Thai and Sri Lankan Buddhism, for instance.

6 When HH the Dalai Lama visits Australia, a greater proportion of Australia's population attends his lectures than in any other western country (personal communication, Tour organisers).

7 I apologise for the formatting problems with my article in this publication, including the scrambling of the Sanskrit diacritics and the loss of footnotes. I trust that if this edition is reprinted that these difficulties will have been resolved.

8 A photograph of these particular yogis demonstrating Tummo is produced in *The Heart of Healing* (The Institute of Noetic Sciences with William Poole, 1993: 59), along with another practitioner being tested in Dharamsala for respiration etc (p. 58).

9 Throughout this discussion I use the analytic categories of "self" and "other", "subject" and "object", distinctions used in the anthropological discourse. I am also here pointing to the understanding of these key concepts derived from a Buddhist perspective. The impact on these categories of analysis by the implications arising from quantum physics are also relevant to reaching an experiential position which overcomes the limitations of these distinctions. See also Wallace (2000).

10 I first used this term, arising from discussions with Geoffrey Samuel, who has worked on the mind-body complex (see eg. 1989; 1990) in a paper presented in 1991 (Stutchbury, 1991 ms). Compare with Goleman's 'technologies of religion', see below in text.

11 This perspective and judgement can be understood as a legacy of colonialism. There has been considerable debate about Anthropology's role in the colonial endeavour, and its disciplinary focus. See for instance Hymes (1972), Said (1979).

12 Paper presented at Conference "Exploring the Science of Spiritualty – a hybrid's view" and published in this volume under that title.

13 Chögyal Namkhai Norbu has developed *Santi Maha Sangha*, a 10 level course that covers the full gamut of Buddhist and Dzogchen knowledge, including philosophical views and meditation practices. 10 people (surprisingly including me) passed the initial level of this training, which bestows upon us the significant responsibility of assisting in teaching this initial level of the program. For more information please see www.dzogchen.org.au.

14 There are many other players in this process with much greater significance than me, including several western born individuals who have been recognised as reincarnations of Tibetan Buddhist masters. Moreover, there are numerous western teachers in all the traditions of Buddhism who now have large followings.

15 David Sazuki's recent 4 part documentary called *Sacred Balance* eloquently addresses some of the issues involved.

16 For instance, there is a growing and significant interest in Engaged Buddhism, with a concurrent assessment of the many ways Buddhism is influencing western society including welfare, charity work, education, peace initiatives, correctional work, ideas on health and wellbeing, hospice practices and care for the dying. See recent conference "Engaging Buddhism in Australia", 20th-22nd February 2004 – details www.vicnet.net.au/~austbud. There is a clear appreciation that it is necessary for Buddhism to maintain its authenticity in the process of adapting to the Australian context, a topic addressed by Kyabgon Traleg Rinpoche, a Tibetan Buddhist teacher who has been resident in Australia since 1980.

17 Special mention is made of B. Alan Wallace's contribution as a translator, and to his published works including *Choosing Reality: A Buddhist View of Physics and the Mind* (1996); and *The Taboo of Subjectivity: Toward a New Science of Consciousness* (2000). Wallace, as well as Matthieu Ricard, and Geshe Thupten Jinpa are all exemplary "halfies", with extensive training in Buddhist philosophy, psychology and meditation as well as PhDs.

18 Please see www.mindandlife.org; and www.investigatingthemind.org. for more details. See also Goleman (2003: 385-391). Unpublished symposiums to date: Mind and Life IX, May 2001 explored how to best use fMRI and other technologies in research on neural plasticity and meditation etc; Mind and Life X, held in October 2002 focussed on "The Nature of Matter, the Nature of Life"; Mind and Life XI, held in September 2003 was entitled "Investigating the Mind: Exchanges between Buddhism and the Biobehavioural Sciences on How the Mind Works." Other significant publications in this field include eg. Varela, Thompson & Rosch (1993).

19 See recent article from a recent Smithsonian print and on-line magazine which reports on the recent conferences and lectures by HH Dalai Lama held in the USA (Brown, 2004: 3 of 4).

20 Recent discussion on the western and Buddhist understandings of emotions and whether they should be conceptualised as " destructive" and in what way(s), attest to the challenges this dialogue presents to deeply held constructs (Mind and Life Research Network discussion list, March 2004). These issues are addressed on Goleman (2003). Significantly, very little research in western science has been carried out on what "happiness" actually is. A survey of thirty years of psychology publications counted 46,000 papers on depression and only 400 on joy (Brown, 2004).

21 The fMRI provides video sequences of the brain's activity, rather than the static images provided by MRI imaging.

22 Most EEG's use 126 sensors. The 256 sensor EEG was used to gain results that were read synergistically with the fMRI (Goleman, 2003: 9).

23 Several of the other meditators tested used different meditative techniques from those used by "Oser", who includes in his repertoire "the open state" which is how he describes the state of Rigpa, using the method of Dzogchen. Those yogis tested for Tummo, or inner heat, use a different method of meditation that of Chagchen (Tib.) or Mahamudra (Skt.). The results of these two methods are the same – realisation of the nature of mind. However, the methods employed, over time, to reach that understanding, are different. There are other neuroscientists currently conducting research on other well known western Tibetan Buddhist meditators, including for instance Lehmann *et al.* on Lama Olé Nyerdahl, "Brain sources of EEG gamma frequency during volitionally meditation-induced, altered states of consciousness, and experience of the self."

24 Owen Flanagan who was at the 2000 meeting has also published a brief summary of the research and it's implications in the Special Issue of *New Scientist* on Human Nature (Part 2, 24 May 2003:44). An article containing excerpts from *Destructive Emotions,* on some of the key issues, as narrated by HH the Dalai Lama, also appears in that issue (Dalai Lama, 2003: 42-43). See also HH Dalai Lama in the Canberra Times (Tenzin Gyatso, 2003)

25 TBS television in USA screened a series on "The Heart of Healing", publishing the accompanying book in 1993 (I've not seen the documentary). The book, for the general public, also includes a presentation of Benson's material, with the photographs of yogis doing Tummo, mentioned above

26 The scientific exploration of the effects of different meditations on immunity is an exciting area of research, still very much in its infancy. There are numerous accounts of the effects of "white light" meditation and the increase of T-cells in AIDS patients. In my earlier paper (Stutchbury, 1998) I suggested a correlation between meditation and immune response, based in part on my

personal experience and research with a chronic B lymphocyte deficiency and meditation. To my knowledge there is no scientific research published on this part of the immune response. There is no indication from Davidson's research published to date as to what neurobiological aspect(s) of the immune response is enhanced by mindfulness meditation.

27 See www.mindandlife.org/Collaborative Research Among Buddhists and Western Scientists; and Cultivating Emotional Balance.

References

Abu-Lughod, Lila (1991), 'Writing Against Culture', in Fox, Richard G. (ed.), *Recapturing Anthropology: Working in the Present*. New Mexico: School of American Research Press.

Benson, Herbert *et al.* (1982a) (J.W. Lehmann, M.S. Malhotra, R.F. Goldman, P.J. Hopkins, & M.D. Epstein), 'Body temperature changes during the practice of gtum-mo yoga', in *Nature 295*: 234-236.

Benson, Herbert (1982b), 'Body temperature changes during the practice of gtum-mo yoga', in *Nature 298*: 402.

Bishop, Peter (1989), The Myth of Shangri-la: Tibet, Travel Writing and the Western Creation of Sacred Landscape. Berkeley & Los Angeles, University of California Press.

Brown, Chip (May, 2004), 'The (Scientific) Pursuit of Happiness: What does the Dalai Lama have to teach psychologists about joy and contentment?' in *The Smithsonain Magazine*, (www.smithsonianmag.si.edu/smithsonian/issues04/).

Campbell, June (1996), Traveller in Space: In Search of Female Identity in Tibetan Buddhism. New York: George Braziller.

Dalai Lama (2003), 'On the luminosity of being', in *New Scientist, 24 May*: 42-43.

Davidson, Richard J. *et al.* (in press), "Alterations in Brain and Immune Function Produced by Mindfulness Meditation" in *Psychosomatic Medicine*.

Davidson, Richard J. and Anne Harrington (Eds.) (2002), *Visions of Compassion: Western Scientists and Tibetan Buddhists Examine Human Nature*. New York: Oxford University Press.

DelMonte, M. M. and Y. Haruki (1998), The Embodiment of Mind: Eastern and Western Perspectives. Delft, Eburon.

Flanagan, Owen (2003), 'The colour of happiness', in *New Scientist*, 24 May: 44.

Gage, Fred H. (2003), 'Brain, Repair Yourself', in *Scientific American, September*, 28-35.

Germano, David (1998), 'Re-membering the Dismembered Body of Tibet: Contemporary Tibetan Visionary movements in the People's Republic of China', in Goldstein & Kapstein (Eds.): 53- 94.

Goldstein, Melvyn C. (1997), *The Snow Lion and the Dragon: China Tibet and the Dalai Lama*. Berkeley, Los Angeles & London: University of California Press.

Goldstein, Melvyn C. and Matthew T. Kapstein (Eds.) (1998), *Buddhism in Contemporary Tibet: Religious Revival and Cultural Identity*. Berkeley, Los Angeles & London: The University of California Press.

Goleman, Daniel (ed.) (1997), *Healing Emotions: Conversations With the Dalai Lama on Mindfulness, Emotions, and Health*. Boston & London: Shambhala Publications.

Goleman, Daniel and Robert A.F. Thurman (Eds.) (1991), *MindScience: An East – West Dialogue*. The Dalai Lama, Herbert Benson, Robert A.F. Thurman, Daniel Goleman, Howard E Gardner *et al.* Proceedings of a Symposium sponsored by the Mind/Body Medical Institute of Harvard Medical School & New England Deaconess Hospital and Tibet House New York. Boston: Wisdom Publications.

Goleman, Daniel (1991), 'Tibetan and Western Models of Mental Health', in Goleman, Daniel and Robert A. F. Thurman (Eds.): 90 – 102.

Goleman, Daniel (narrator) (2003), *Destructive Emotions and How We Can Overcome Them: A Dialogue With the Dalai Lama*. London: Bantam.

Gross, Rita M. (1993), *Buddhism After Patriarchy: A Feminist History, Analysis and Reconstruction of Buddhism*. Albany N.Y: State University of New York Press.

Hayward, Jeremy W. & Francesco Varela (Eds.) (1992), *Gentle Bridges: Conversation with the Dalai Lama on the Sciences of Mind*. Boston & London: Shambhala Publications.

Holloway, Margeurite (2003), 'The Mutable Brain', in *Scientific American, September,* 58-65.

Houshmand, Zara, Robert B. Livingston and B. Alan Wallace (Eds.) (1999), *Consciousness at the Crossroads: Conversations with the Dalai Lama on Brain Science and Buddhism*. Ithaca NY: Snow Lion Publications.

Hymes, Dell (ed.) (1972), *Reinventing Anthropology*, New York: Vintage Books Random House.

Kabat-Zinn, Jon. (1996), 'Mindfulness Meditation: What It Is, What It Isn't, and Its Role in Health Care and Medicine', in Haruki, Y., Y. Ishhii & M. Sazuki (Eds.), *Comparative and Psychological Study on Meditation*. Deflt: Eburon.

Klein, Anne Carolyn. (1995), *Meeting the Great Bliss Queen: Buddhists, Feminists and the Art of Self.* Boston: Beacon Press.

Lopez, David S. Jr. (1998), *Prisoners of Shangri-la: Tibetan Buddhism and the West*. Chicago & London: University of Chicago Press.

McCrone, John. (2003), 'Not So Total Recall', in *New Scientist*, 3 May, 26-29.

Norbu, Chögyal Namkhai. (1994), *Buddhism and Psychology*. Arcidosso Italy: Shang Shung Edizioni.

Primal Instincts (2004), Co produced by the Australian Broadcasting Commission & The Canadian Broadcasting Commission in association with Discovery Networks International. Screened on Australian ABC television February-March 2004.

Revel, Jean-François and Matthieu Ricard. (1998), *The Monk and The Philosopher: A Father and Son Discuss the Meaning of Life*. New York: Schocken Books.

Said, Edward W. (1979), *Orientalism*. New York, Pantheon Books.

Samuel, Geoffrey B. (1990), *Mind, Body and Culture: Anthropology and the Biological Interface*. Cambridge: Cambridge University Press.

Samuel, Geoffrey B. (1989), 'The body in Buddhist and Hindu Tantra', in *Religion, 19,* 97-210.

Samuel, Geoffrey B. (1993), *Civilized Shamans: Buddhism in Tibetan Societies*. Washington & London: Smithsonian Institute Press.

Sazuki, David. (2002), *Sacred Balance*. 4 part television documentary. Based on book by David Sazuki and Amanda McConnell. Canadian Broadcasting Corporation. Screened on Australian SBS in February, 2004.

Schell, Orville. (2000), *Virtual Tibet: Searching for Shangri-la from the Himalayas to Hollywood*. New York: Metropolitan Books Henry Holt & Company.

Scientific American, a Special edition (2003), 'Better Brains – How Neuroscience Will Enhance You", September.

Srinivasan, Soroja. (2004), Exploring the Science of Spirituality. In *The Relevance of the Wisdom Traditions in Contemporary Society: The Challenge to Psychology*. Blows, M., Srinivasan, S.,Bankhart, P., DelMonte, M., Blows, J. & Haruki, Y. (Eds.), Eburon: Delft.

Stix, Gary (2003), 'Ultimate Self-Improvement', in *Scientific American,* September 2003: 26-27.

Stutchbury, Elisabeth A. (1991 unpub.), *Rediscovering Western Tibet: Gonpa, Chorten and the Continuity of Practice with a Buddhist Community in the Indian Himalaya*. PhD dissertation, R.S.Pac.S. ANU.

Stutchbury, Elisabeth A. (1991 ms.), 'The Six Yogas of Naropa: A Tibetan System of Meditation.' Paper presented, Invited Session, *Functions and variations in states of Consciousness in Cultural Perspective*, 90th Meeting of the American Anthropological Association, Chicago, USA. Also presented, Département d'anthropologie, Université de Montréal, Québec, Canada.

Stutchbury, Elisabeth A. (1994), 'The Making of Gonpa: Norbu Rinpoche from Kardang and Kunga Rinpoche from Lama Gonpa', in Samuel, G.B., H. Gregor and E. Stutchbury (Eds.), *Tantra and Popular Religion in Tibet, 376*, 155-204. New Delhi: International Academy of Indian Culture and Aditya Prakashan. Sata-Pitaka Series Indo-Asian Literatures.

Stutchbury, Elisabeth A. (1998), 'Tibetan Meditation. Yoga and Healing Practices: Mind-Body Interconnections', in DelMonte, M.M. and Y. Haruki: 103-127.

Tenzin Gyatso. (2003), 'Scientific support for the healing power of positive thinking', in *The Canberra Times, Thursday 19th June.*

Varela, Francesco J., Evan Thompson & Eleanor Rosch (1993), *The Embodied Mind: Cognitive Science and Human Experience*. Cambridge Ma. & London. The MIT Press.

Varela, Francisco J. (1997), Sleeping, Dreaming and Dying: An Exploration of Consciousness with the Dalai Lama. Boston Ma.: Wisdom Publications.

Varela, Francisco J. (2004), 'The Importance of the Encounter with Buddhism for Modern Science', www.mindandlife.org/Buddhism and Modern Science (February).

Wallace B. Alan (2000), *The Taboo of Subjectivity: Toward a New Science of Consciousness*. New York: Oxford University Press.

Wallace, B. Alan (1996), *Choosing Reality: A Buddhist View of Physics and the Mind.* Ithaca N.Y: Snow Lion Publications.

Zajonc, Arthur (ed.) (2003), *The New Physics and Cosmology: Dialogues with the Dalai Lama*. New York: Oxford University Press.

Zetter, Kim (2003), 'Keep Taking the Meditation' in *Good Weekend: The Sydney Morning Herald Magazine. August 30*, 22-26.

Concepts of self regulation in the east and the west

Yutaka Haruki
Waseda University, Japan

1. Concepts of self in psychology

The concept of "self" is defined in different ways by different psychologists. The theory advanced by James (1890), though old, forms the basis of the subsequently developed theories. He analyzes "self" by dividing it into two categories. One category of "self" is defined as "I" characterized as "self as knower." In other words, this self is a principal and subjective self. The other is defined as "me" characterized as "self as known." In other words, this is an objective self. According to James' theory, a person has a subjective self which tries to know about himself when he is conscious of himself, and an objective self which is known by himself ("I") and others. The objective self, says James, has the sides of "material me," "social me," and "spiritual me." On the other hand, from a metaphysical point of view, the subjective self is considered the soul and transcendental ego as immutable entities against the backdrop of an objective self each person experiences. However, James, claiming it unnecessary to make an issue of such entities, considers the subjective self as consciousness itself.

On the basis of James' theory, Mead (1934) advanced his own theory that the objective self develops socially and that "me" reacts as if to respond to the expectations of others. According to Mead, the reactions of "I" are personal and not generated in response to the expectations of others. Mead says that "I" would not exist without "me," but that it would be difficult to grasp "I" correctly by experience.

Freud's concept of "ego" may be different from the concept of "self." However, from the point of view of his personality theory (id, ego, super-ego) it needs to be discussed here. "Ego" balances the two powers "super-ego" and "id" so that they will adjust themselves to the outside world. It is the function of "ego" to exercise control so that "instinctive id" will conform to social norms (super ego). Assuming that Freud's personality theory is "self theory," "ego" may correspond to "I" as characterized by James.

Jung's concepts of "ego" and "self" differ from Freud's. Simply put, "ego" is the hub of one's consciousness and "self" is the hub of the whole including consciousness and unconsciousness or the hub which integrates the binomial confrontational factors. Ordinarily "ego" has the function of consolidating and stabilizing the consciousness process. Though "ego" experiences instability when an activity aimed at a higher level of integration occurs within "self," "ego" and "self" necessarily work together toward self-realization either through interactions or confrontations. Using James' terms, "ego" could be described as "I" and "self" as "me."

Rogers' theory on "self" is interesting too. Each one of us has the concept of our own self. It is a stereotyped unconscious perception of "self." Through a process, it forms a specific substance which varies from one occasion to another. Meanwhile, each individual has gone through experiences. It is generally understood that in the case of good adjustment the concept of "self" and the relevant experience are at one, and that in the case of mal-adjustment, they are not at one. In the case of mal-adjustment, "self" denies the relevant experience or falsifies "itself". Psychotherapy aims at the unification of these two factors.

Skinner's behaviour theory does not make an issue of the concept of "self." However, Skinner (1953) discusses the matter of self-control. In other words, self-control is to reinforce one's actions on his own. This was referred to as "self-reinforcement." According to Skinner, self-control in this case means the same as in the case where a person is controlled by another and that this is only a special case where the controlling person and the controlled person are the same. The controlling agent was referred to as "controlling response" and the controlled agent as "controlled response." One's own controlling response is the same as another's controlling response. The controlling response per se is acquired from society and is controlled by society. In the light of James' concept of "self" referred to earlier, "controlling response" may be equated with "I" and "controlled response" with "me."

2. TEN BULLS PICTURES

The ten bulls pictures were drawn by Kuoan, a zen priest who lived in Liangshan, Dingzhou in China (currently Hunansheng Changdexian) in the Zong period (in the 1100s). These pictures were introduced in Japan practically at the same time as in China and they have been well known in Japan as pictures conveying Zen ideas. Zen is said to be a religion of self-awareness. Zen practices (Zazen) are intended to make a person aware of himself. These pictures are known to depict the process very skillfully.

1st Picture *Jingyu* (Searching for the lost bull)

A person sets out to look for a lost bull. Zen priests explain that the bull is a true self, a natural self. A person who becomes aware that he has lost his own true self in his day to day life sets out to look for the lost self. (The person in each picture will hereinafter be referred to as "I.")

2nd Picture *Kenseki* (Finding the traces)
I have not found the lost bull yet except for its footprints. Seeing the bull's footprints, I know that I have gained an intellectual understanding about myself and acquired knowledge of myself through reading and the teachings of my teachers.

3rd Picture *Kengyu* (Finding the bull)
Gradually I have come to see part of my true self. I also hear a voice which makes it all the more real. It helps me understand my "self' as such, but I am doing nothing other than just watching (understanding) across the river.

4th Picture *Tokugyu* (Catching of the bull)
Not only am I watching the bull, but I have also got hold of it. I could get my hand on my true self. However, the bull does not act the way I want him to. He has gone wild and it looks as if is going to run away and go out of my sight. I have not got hold of my true self yet.

5th Picture *Bokugyu* (Gentling the bull)
At last I could tame the bull. There is no longer discord between me and the bull. I and my true self have come to terms. The bull is coming with me as I lead him by the bridle. Though the reins are slackened, I must hold them firmly.

6th Picture *Kigyukike* (Returning home on the back of the bull)
The bull no longer needs the bridle. I and the bull have become one. There is no discord between "I" and my true self. I do not have to give directions and I and the bull are headed toward the place for us to return to as willed by the true self. However, here I am riding the bull, that is, I and the bull are two separate beings.

7th Picture *Bogyuzonjin* (Bull forgotten – man remains)
We reached our destination (home) and the bull was no longer needed. The true self has become mine and there is nothing I want. I am completely relaxed in a sanctuary (home). There is a house in which I am.

8th Picture *Jingyugubo* (Both bull and man forgotten)
There are no longer me, the bull and the house. Everything is gone. I was the last person to go. I have been seeking something but I am gone and the mind has become blank.

9th Picture *Henponkangen* (Return to the origin, back to the source)
The world as it is jumps into my totally blank mind. As long as I am seeking something, my mind becomes biased and it keeps my mind from seeking the

truth. With the mind freed of my "self' I can clearly see red flowers and green willows as such. It is in such a world that we are living.

10th Picture *Nittensuishu* (Entering the market-place with bliss-bestowing hands)
I come to the market-place with my hands dangling. After gaining the insight into the truth, 1 return to the market place relaxed and looking different from what I did before.

Psychological interpretations of ten bulls pictures

I would like to interpret the ten bulls pictures described in Section 2 by making reference to the various explanations rendered in Section 1 from a psychological point of view with respect to "self."

The ten bulls pictures are understood to describe the mind of a person who is going through Zen practices or the growing process of a man. Needless to say, the accounts of the process of such Zen practices or its interpretation are based on Zen thought. The aim of the pictures is to get Zen thought across in a simple way. They dramatically depict processes of self or self regulation.

The message of these pictures is that I (the person in the picture) set out to look for the bull to tame it. Incidentally, what is "I" and what is the "bull"? If we assume "self' and "self regulation" to be the theme of these pictures, the application of James' theory on "self' would be useful in rendering a psychological interpretation, one which is the easiest to understand. Namely, "I" is a "subjective self' and the "bull" is an "objective self."

It may be understood that the pictures from 1 to 3 show the beginning of the search for self-identification. The search for self identification (who am I) has begun. Zen teaches that a bull is one's true self or one's natural self and that one is to recognize his true self (bull). However, when the ten pictures are taken as a whole, I would rather think that "I" and the "bull" together represent "self' and it is the search for such "self."

The pictures from 1 to 3 show that the "subjective self' is trying to understand the "objective self' and the former has reached the stage of "finding" the latter. What is important here is that "I" and the "bull" are separated and not tied. In other words, the subjective self has come to gain an objective understanding of the objective self.

"Self' as discussed and understood by psychologists does not go beyond a subjective self and an objective self. It is against Zen teachings to stay at the level of understanding. Zen exhorts the practical application of a theory on what to do with "self". The main issue here is how "I" will get related to the "bull." From this perspective, the theme of the pictures from 4 to 6 may be "self regulation." As stated earlier, if "I" (the person in the ten bulls pictures) and the "bull" are taken to mean the subjective self and the objective self respectively, it may be understood that the pictures from 4 to 6 show the process of the subjective self controlling the objective self. If we apply Skinner's theory on control, "I" could mean controlling response and the "bull' controlled response. If we apply Freud's theory, the point of the pictures could be that "I" (ego) controls "id" (instinctive desire represented by the "bull"). The relationship between these two can be seen by the extent to which the rope is stretched. Picture 4 shows the rope tightly stretched meaning that there is feud between the two (strained relationship). Picture 5 shows "id" ending up being controlled by "ego" (the rope is no longer stretched). Picture 6 shows an ideal state of "self." It shows a state of complete harmony (no rope is used) between the subjective self and the objective self with the strained relationship gone. "Id" seen as controlled in Picture 5 may in fact have been suppressed, but Picture 6 shows the victory of "ego" striking a spectacular balance between "id" and "super ego" or the energy of "id" may have turned into a beautiful sound after going through the process of sublimation. In the light of Rogers' theory, this state may be described as an ideal state where the concept of self and an experience are at one.

Western ideas about "self' and "self regulation" have not gone any further. It is not easy to come this far. There are a number of programs on psychotherapy and behaviour therapy with "self regulation" set as a goal and a lot of effort has been put into these programs. However, the theory on "self' based on Zen thought has further ramifications. Picture 7 depicts nothing but "I." Having returned home, a place for peaceful living and my destination, I feel completely secure. There is no longer any need for the "bull" and he may be forgotten. However, this condition may be dangerous. Where is the "bull"? It may have gone back to the wilderness and may be turning into a wild animal and it may again be necessary to start looking for the "bull." This is called "relapse" by psychotherapists and it is a common occurrence among people or men and women.

Why does anything like this happen? Picture 6 seems to show that "I" and the "bull" are in harmony and at one. However, there are "I" and the "bull." "Self' is separated into a subjective self and an objective self. As long as this idea prevails, the two will necessarily be separated again and the process will be repeated. It is likely that "I" (subjective self) in Picture 7, although satisfied with the acquired state of harmony, may not be able to forget the "bull" (objective serf completely. It is because "subjective self' alone would be inadequate and the existence of an objective self is necessary.

Picture 8 seems to aim at resolving this issue. There is no sight of "I" which has been in the pictures described above. Neither "I" nor the "bull" can be seen in this picture. The picture depicts Non-self. The picture is based on Zen thought. Zen assumes no "concrete" self, and teaches that it is wrong to assume a subjective self which could be considered to comprise the core of self. As long as there is an attempt to separate "self' into a subjective self and an objective se1f there would necessarily be a relapse from Picture 7 to

Picture 1. To resolve this issue, the practice of separating them must be discontinued. This requires the disappearance of "I" (subjective self as depicted in Picture 8.)

Picture 9 depicts a scene in which there is no trace of "I." "Flowers are red and willows are green." The mind which has become completely free from bias can see them as they are. This scene of nature should be understood to mean that it is all right the way we are, instead of the subjective self trying to control the objective self of its own accord. This is because the English term "nature" means "as it is" even in Japanese. Picture 6 also depicts this state but it is still fraught with the problem that the two are separated. It is Picture 10 that depicts the situation described in Picture 9 in the form of a human being. When the subjective self and the objective self melt into one, I return to the market-place (the world of human beings) relaxed with both hands dangling down. It should be noted that the person in Picture 10 looks totally different from the person ("I") in Picture 7. Jung might describe this as self-realization. In Japan we refer to the person in this picture as "Hotei-san" who is believed to bring happiness. Hotei-san is always smiling.

REFERENCES

Akizuki, R. (1989). *Ten Bulls Pictures and the Way of Zazen*. Tokyo: Shunjusha (in Japanese).

James, W. (1980). *Principles of Psychology*. NY: Holt, originally published 1902.

Mead, G.H. (1934). *Mind, Self and Society: From the Standpoint of a Social Behaviorist*. The University of Chicago.

Rogers, C.R. (1951). *Client-centered Therapy*. Houghton Muffin Co.

Skinner, B.F. (1953). *Science and Human Behaviour*. NY: Macmillan.

1. *Jingyu* (Searching for the lost bull)

2. *Kenseki* (Finding the Traces)

3. *Kengyu* (Finding the bull)

4. *Tokugyu* (Catching the bull)

5. *Bokugyu* (Gentling the bull)

6. *Kigyukike* (Returning home on the back of the bull)

7. *Bogyuzonjin* (Bull forgotten – man remains)

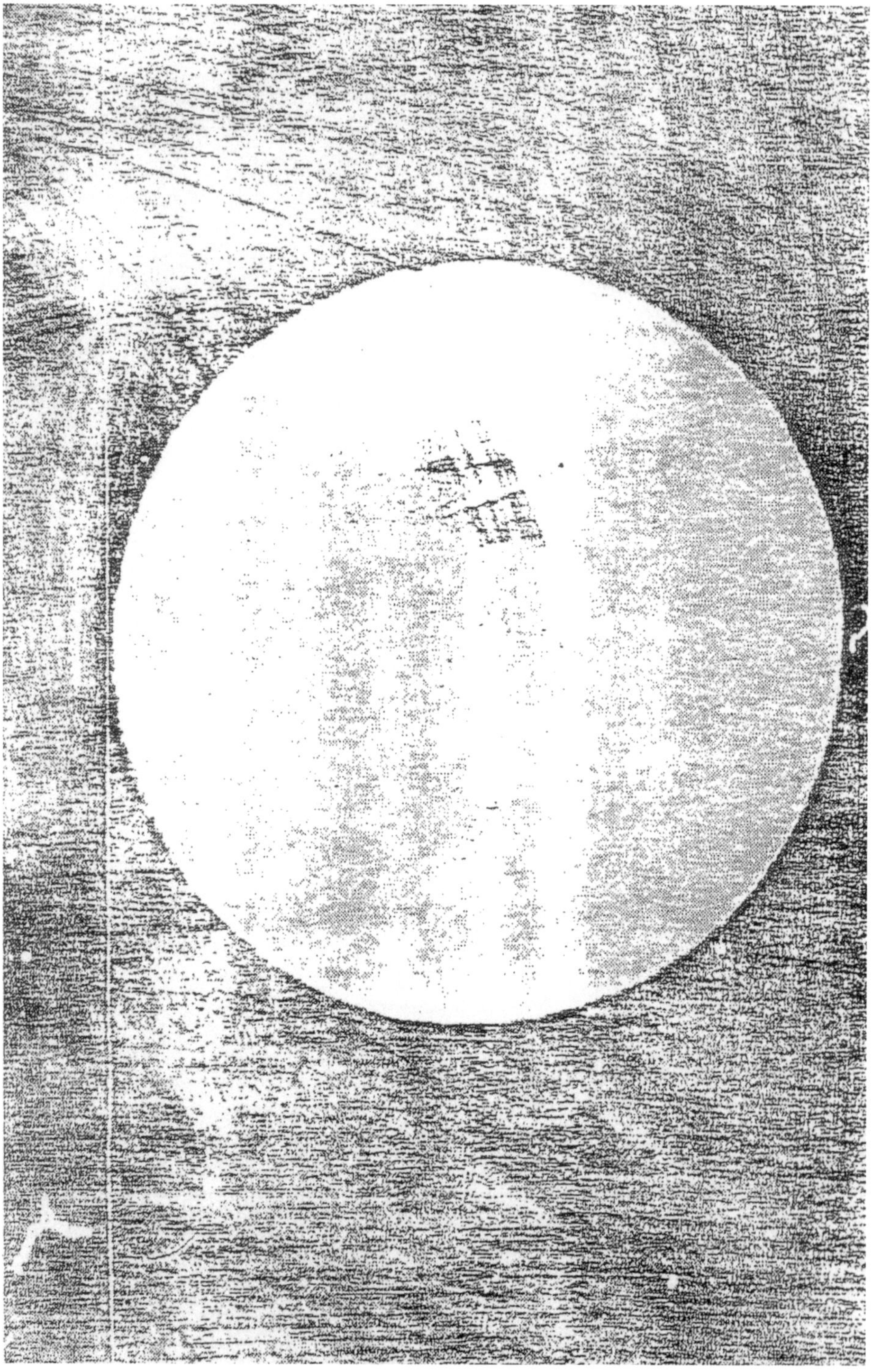

8. *Jingyugubo* (Both bull and man forgotten)

9: *Henponkangen* (Return to the origin, back to the source)

10. *Nittensuishu* (Entering the market place with bliss-bestowing hands)

Exploring the science of spirituality: a hybrid's view

Saroja Srinivasan
Clinical Psychologist, Sydney Australia

Introduction

Most practitioners of psychology would agree that any attempt to alleviate the distress of those they seek to help has involved some acknowledgement of their spiritual belief systems. However, academic psychology's attempts to understand these belief systems within existing theory and frameworks have often reduced them to simplistic and inappropriate variables.

Most of the time therapists and those they try to help are chasing a rather elusive thing called "happiness" and ways of acquiring it and keeping it forever. Many ways of "acquiring" happiness are offered in the consumer world, yet they are found to be unsatisfying in the long run. The large numbers of "everyday problems" seemingly attest to this presence of "unhappiness". In contemporary literature the term "well being" is used. It is now widely acknowledged that well being is closely related to how we see ourselves, whether we call it a sense of self-efficacy or how we make sense of our experiences on a day to day level. It is acknowledged that all people desire "happiness'' (Krishna Mohan, 2001).

Well being or level of happiness is also the term people use when they evaluate their life and existence in its entirety – physical, psychological and spiritual. It is a relative term; it depends on the situation, the place and time and also the values of the culture. An often used phrase is "feeling good", whatever that may mean to each individual at any one time.

Many psychologists and other health professionals consider spirituality to be an important part of their clients' life and also their own personal and professional lives. A sustained level of happiness is also seen as being related to meaningful religious faith which forms part of the spiritual experience.

The World Health Organisation included 'spiritual well being' as part of its definition of optimum health many years ago and so it seems appropriate that as professionals we explore the role of spirituality and the methods by which we examine it. The wisdom traditions are a result of the curiosity of man to understand his relationship to the universe. Happiness encompasses making sense of the world and our existence, and spirituality is a salient part of that endeavour. This does not fit easily into existing scientific methods. So, let us explore what we mean by science and spirituality. Then we can see if accommodation between the two is feasible.

The science debate

The Oxford English dictionary defines science as "a branch of knowledge that requires systematic observation and collection of data to explain phenomena that follow natural laws". Statistical modelling is invoked to reduce the observed data.

While the developed nations accept that other cultures may have sophisticated systems of philosophy and religion, science is still seen as unique to the west. As Harman puts it simply, "Science in its present form is the product of a particular stage of European society, a stage that placed high value on such attributes as the ability to predict, control and manipulate the total environment; a different society would have created a different science. Society shapes sciences by the kinds of scientific activities it supports and the kinds it does not support, the places it bestows honour and those it does not. Science is as much a product of culture as culture is a product of science" (Harman 1991 p25).

The politics of knowledge is extremely powerful and dictates what will and will not be valid topics of exploration yet it appears that modern science is unable to fully deal with the diversity of human experiences. We acknowledge now that physical and mental health are interrelated and taken further there is an overall cosmic reality of mind and all matter. This brings into play the two dichotomies of 19th century physics that still dictate present day scientific views to a large extent, that of Descartes' mind-matter dichotomy/dualism and Newton's tangible versus intangible. Over time, some concession to the second dimension has been made by accepting the intangibles if their effects were real and measurable.

The intangibles thus become a source of inconvenience in science. All the same, most of us will agree that these inconvenient facts cannot be ignored or explained away as irrelevant if they don't fit existing theory. After all at each stage of the world's history thinkers have followed the path of seeking to investigate such 'inconvenient' facts and by doing so helped move along the so called "scientific progress".

Modern physicists from Einstein to Hawking, while acknowledging that there may be order in the universe despite its overt apparent chaos, still begin from the premise that theories that we have are the only relevant starting point in making sense of this universe. Hawking however acknowledges that there may not be one theory but many possible theories that describe universes that exist. In the physicist's mind we are still talking about physical universes. The study of the human mind and its functioning requires an acknowledgement of the quintessentially unique reality within which each of us functions. Often this uniqueness may also include some commonalities with other individuals. Accepting this dual presence of uniqueness and commonality requires a major shift in mind set. Here we are moving away from the physical to the supra physical.

Present day society reflects a clear ambivalence towards science. This stems from the lack of answers provided by science for many of the more fundamental questions of existence that have been raised in recent debates. Advances in science have led to new discoveries and new methods of solving problems, but with a focus on the objective world. There is now a yearning to fill the void that still exists in the realm of the subjective world, the world that rests wholly within each individual. When the subject and object of study are the same, scientific methods, as we know them, or as accepted by the establishment, become inadequate for the exploration. If we choose to reduce them to observable, measurable and quantifiable data alone, a vast ocean of intuitive knowledge remains untapped.

If we continue to place spirituality in the realm of mythology as we do, we find inevitably that the process of understanding becomes one of deconstruction. If we however place it in the realm of experience and intuitive knowledge, it takes on the mantle of synthesis which is the true essence of this experience. Experiencing the sense of completeness, a whole that we are each capable of experiencing, but may not necessarily be able to verbalise, is the ultimate goal of this exploration into the science of spirituality.

History of modern western science

To avoid the pitfalls of a tunnel vision view of science, let us briefly consider the beginnings of modern western science as we know it. It is generally agreed that it had its beginnings in the Medici court in the 15th and 16th centuries. Scholars debated and professed on themes drawn from philosophers from the past. Combining astral and medical sciences, the proponents synthesised common components from the three dominant cultures of 13th century Iberia, the Muslim, Jewish and Christian. They explored the complex levels of being and organisation through the symbols and the various contemplative methods. However by the 16th century, the rise of the Roman Catholic power saw the beginnings of a different path both intellectually and politically. The astral linking with universal harmony was now disregarded. Descartes followed with the dualistic position, the mind-matter split, that the two were totally dissimilar and hence could never interact. Many other changes in the economic, social, political and the state-institutional area began asserting their influence on what was to be the "right" explanation. "Scientific explanations won the day and Descartes' mind-body dualism became common sense and mechanistic explanations were assumed as adequate for scientific purposes" (Harman p41).

There is an interesting comparison drawn by Harman (1991) of what he terms Separateness science and Wholeness science which seems relevant here (Harman op cit). The latter approach clearly illustrates a moving away from Aristotelian logic of "either-or" "tertium non datur" to the relativity assertion of Einstein's theory of "this as well as that".

The spirituality dimension

The definition of spirituality varies considerably depending on the source. Many words and phrases occur in varying combinations. Spirituality, in most definitions, includes experiences that are transcendent to ordinary sensory reality and is not necessarily related to theology or religion. It also presupposes several identifiable values as being an essential part of the behaviour of a spiritual person. These may include belief in a supreme being, sacredness of life, a belief that while material things may give pleasure, the ultimate basis for happiness lies in their spiritual value, a sense of wanting to attend to the needs of others by virtue of the connectedness that is experienced, betterment of society at large both through individual meditation and/or prayer and concrete action and in general being seen as a source of empowerment of others.

There is a great difficulty when one looks for concrete evidence for the strength that is derived from spirituality. According to the earlier mentioned prerequisite for being accepted as 'scientific', the intangibles have to be shown to have measurable effects. However what one gets more often is a personal affirmation of an experience that defies words.

While the west was debating about matter-mind dualism, the perennial philosophy of India had accepted the non-dualistic nature of existence for over 4000 years, the Vedic texts dating back to that time. So around the time of Descartes, in the Indian subcontinent, the nature of mind had already been explored. The physical manifestations of matter and their relationship with the mind-body complex were being debated and these debates were based on long commentaries already written for well over 4000 years. Ontological questions had been debated extensively after sustained contemplation and several treatises presented by 'seer-scientists'. Buddha and his teachings had already made major inroads into people's thinking as far back as the reign of King Asoka, based mainly on the Buddhist philosophy dating back to 260 BC. While all of this was occurring other scholars had been studying and writing on subjects such as mathematics, astronomy, as well as the practical applications in health care as in the Yoga treatises.

In the Indian system of thinking, the universe is holistic, with an underlying unity of microcosm and macrocosm. Hence the study of spirituality, defined as presented earlier, appears to present no conflict for an investigator steeped in this tradition.

The major difficulty in exploring spirituality in a 'scientific' way starts with the experimental methodology. Here we cannot pre-emptively have a hypothesis that will be supported or negated. Studying and understanding spirituality demands that we start with experiencing it. Before allowing oneself to gain this experience, we need a mind-set that allows for such an experience; a mind-set that entertains the possibility of universal presence and connectedness of all things material and non-material. Having such a belief is not much different from many implicit beliefs we already carry around. For example, it is no more bizarre than a mind-set that allows one to accept that a bird-like machine called the aeroplane will take off into the sky and land where one needs to go. Many of the people who fly in aeroplanes do not know the principles of aerodynamics. There is an implicit trust placed on the minds of the aeronautical engineers who designed the plane who in turn trusted the physicists who formulated such theories that would result in an aeroplane. We do not always understand or have evidence for everything before we do or accept things. We cannot all understand everything, some of us have to work on the basis of trust while some are able to critically evaluate material already presented.

For centuries many wise men in their wisdom and from their experience have conceived of some truths and described methods by which others may also gain such an experience. The main prerequisite would be to develop a systematic, trained mind. To this end many of the wisdom traditions have described hundreds of practices starting with the simplest to the most demanding and complicated. There is room for individual variations in the skills thus allowing a wide range of appropriate applications. As with all skills, the path to the attainment of spiritual knowledge demands persistence, fortitude and a willingness to participate until the goal is reached.

The role of language

The main method of communicating is language. Semantic and linguistic problems constantly arise when we try to communicate an experience that defies words. As Dennet (1993) aptly says "You are the program that runs on your computer". How does one get one's mind to devise a way of communicating without using verbalisations? While such may be possible we may have to accept it is not probable. Yet in languages such as Sanskrit and Pali, there appears to be an ease in using such descriptions as they were originally conceived specifically to communicate intuitive experiences of the wise men. These were developed from their inner experiences of sounds which were seen as playing an extremely important role in explanations of cosmic processes. "Sound is (seen as) a form of radiation in which energy is transferred by means of pressure waves in matter" (Mishra 2000 P416). Such explanations often form the basis of chanting and repetitive prayer. Meaning also is presented as occurring in several layers. Each word and its meaning can be seen as a synthesis of matter, space and time (Ibid P412).

David Bohm, the well known 20th century physicist, in his later years carried his exploration into mind and matter well beyond the boundaries of science. He discusses the powerful role of language in influencing the way we see reality. He further elaborates on how verbal language sets fragmented and static parameters within which we see reality, which in turn does not allow for the experience of its true dynamic nature (Keepin 1994).

Language and narrative are now seen increasingly in the social sciences as being important vehicles to elucidate the experience that is being communicated. It could not be more pertinent when the study of spirituality is undertaken. Rowe (1996) discusses the role of language in presenting experience and the incongruence it creates when one is describing experience for "the meaning comes only from our experience" (Ibid p10). Vico, as quoted in Rowe (1996; p11), two centuries ago aptly commented "the language we speak creates the reality we live in".

A recent example of the limitations of language was illustrated by Laurence Freeman (2002). Writing on "the nature and meaning of time" he stated: "If it is measurable it is *chronos*, one of the Greek words for time. If it is real but cannot be measured, it is *kairos*, the other Greek word. It helps to have more than one word to describe things that are subtle ... *Kairos* refers to an event whose significance is more than we can describe at the physical or psychological levels but that seems to open a direct access into the spiritual dimension where time and space are no longer limitations on our experience of reality. This is the sort of time that is meant when one says "It took time. I'm getting over it but it will take some time yet' while describing a significant loss or life event. When we meditate ... reality appears more spacious and more friendly than it did before when stress blinkered our perception of everything and even made it seem that we just didn't have time to meditate".

Hybrids

The Oxford English dictionary defines hybrid as "something made by combining two different elements". This term is used here specifically to draw attention to the fact that studying the science of spirituality places one in the role of a hybrid. In the context of studying the science of spirituality, it seems there are many hybrids. There are cultural hybrids, where one is born, where and how one is educated to where one chooses to live; acquired hybrids, becoming someone different to who they were before yet remaining also different from those around whom they live (Krygier 2000) and add to this vocational hybrids who live within one world view while having come from another totally different one. Moments of awkwardness, of not knowing where one belongs punctuate the life of hybrids. They don't feel completely 'in' nor totally 'out'. The value of being a hybrid is that one can become a major resource bank of a range of experiences that continue to influence oneself and others. Having experienced at first hand both sides of the coin as it were, hybrids can offer insights not easily available to those who do not possess that experience. A major asset that hybrids possess is the capacity to embrace differences that allow for a comparison not purely at an academic level but at the level of personal experience.

A tradition that allows cultivated awareness to observe in an unbiased fashion changes taking place within oneself requires that we take on board a completely different methodology from that with which we are familiar as scientists. One cannot deny that humans have the facility, the capacity of mind to study themselves from their experience. And yet often one is faced with the conflict of being a "scientist" and yet wanting to explore subjects such as spirituality that do not easily conform to the rules of gathering the evidence that are required of a 'scientist'. Perhaps as an "acquired hybrid", it is somewhat easier to minimise what is problematical and "try to enjoy the variety of experience and make out of it a rich and coherent whole" (Krygier 2000 P8). In this context, what comes to mind is the term "*sangam*", a Sanskrit word which loosely defined would translate as a place of confluence, as in a confluence of rivers, a concept that captures the vitality, the living vibrations of movement that happens for a fleeting moment before they merge and become one, not a static heavy dark coming together but a joyous, light vibrant union. Perhaps as "acquired hybrids" we may capture the essence of being truly a place of confluence where the scientist and the spiritual seeker meet!

So what are the prerequisites of the subjects of this endeavour, the ones who are going to embark on the exploration into the science of spirituality? In "normal scientific experimentation" we set the parameters, quite clearly. Yet in this unchartered journey who decides these parameters and why should one be any more "right" or valid than another? If we all have a history to our being of where we are and who we are that has already been established, how do we "control" for this variable? Can the experience of spirituality be transformed into alpha values for a large group that would statistically remove the anomalies and thus satisfy the seekers of evidence? Would N=1 be the way to research this subject matter? Yet again how does one control for the prerequisites already demanded such as lifestyle, nutrition and moral discipline that are held as salient in a holistic model?

Combining the different concepts of science, spirituality, language and the role of 'hybrids', brings to mind a very illustrious example from my country of origin. I come from a country, India, that is host to a plethora of religious beliefs, each jostling to find a place and space and does so, for in the minds of a billion people there is room for everyone. Particularly in Hinduism, every task is reframed in an attempt to link the profane to the sacred. Each task is a keyhole into the divine. This is true to a large extent even in contemporary India.

Many 20th century Indian philosophers and thinkers have opened the gates for millions of prospective students of the Indian system by writing in languages that are easily comprehensible and presented strategies that are culled from the essence of many previous paths to this knowledge. One such is Sri Aurobindo with his Integral Yoga. He was indeed a true "hybrid", an Indian brought up in the UK in the early 1900s with all of his formative schooling from the age of seven to twenty one in the UK. However he returned to India, when twenty one and, after forays into the political arena for some years, decided to enter a spiritual life, experiencing, reflecting and writing, in English, his synthesis of the ancient wisdom which he termed Integral Yoga. This treatise is a true synthesis for it delves not only into spiritual truths at the theoretical level but also presents methods and strategies to develop skill and experience at a very personal level. It requires the aspirant to start with a self surrender to a higher being, or a conscious power or a delight in the Divine. It combines the goal of enjoyment of the spiritual power and the light and joy of human existence. Humanistic values such as seeing the divine in all and an active participation in all work and knowledge-seeking that empowers and leads to self perfection are a vital part of this psychology.

In summary, the questions that form the hypothesis in the realm of spirituality exploration are those relating to existence and the purpose of existence. They focus on the nature of reality, ontology, and how we acquire knowledge of reality, epistemology. As soon as we use this scientific jargon, we exclude vast numbers of people who believe it will be beyond them intellectually. It may be intellectually challenging to many, but not experientially. Everyone is capable of this experience at their own level. For truly in ontology and epistemology, each individual has to make the journey, as they already are, every microsecond of their existence. What one may offer as a scientist or professional, is some help in developing the abiliy to reflect and make sense. Surely this is the goal of a psychology that has the utmost relevance in contemporary society. This scientific exploration of spirituality illustrates at a very personal fundamental level the unity between nature and gnosis, the knowledge which though hidden is accessible to imaginative thought and feeling, a knowledge that transforms both self and other leading to greater harmony (Harman 1996).

References

Cornelissen, M. (ed.) (2001), Consciousness and its transformation. Paper presented at the *Second International Conference on Integral Psychology,* Pondicherry, India: Sri Aurobindo International Centre of Education.

Dennet, D.C. (1993), *Consciousness Explained.* London: Penguin.

Freeman, Fr. Laurence (2002), Editorial. *Christian Meditation Newsletter, March.* London: St. Mark's Myddelton Square.

Harman, W.W. (1991), *A re-examination of the Metaphysical foundations of Modern Science.* Sausalito, California USA: Research Report, Institute of Noetic Sciences.

Keepin, W. (1994), David Bohm: A life of Dialogue between Science and Spirit. *Noetic Sciences Review.* Sausalito, California USA: Inst of Noetic Sciences.

Krippner, S. & Wech, P. (1992), *Spiritual Dimensions of Healing.* New York: Irvington.

Krishna, Mohan, K. (2001), *Spirituality and wellbeing: an overview.* In M. Cornelissen. (2001). op cit.

Krygier, M. (1997), *Between Fear and Hope – hybrid thoughts on public values.* Sydney: ABC Books.

Mishra, R.K. (2000), *Before the Beginning and After the End – Rediscovering Ancient Insights.* New Delhi: Rupa &Co.

Rowe, D. (1996), The importance of personal construct psychology. In Walker BM *et al.* (Eds.): *Personal Construct Theory – A psychology for the future. Melbourne*: Australian Psychological Society.

Taimini, L.K. (1961), *The Science of Yoga.* Madras, India: The Theosophical Publishing House.

Indigenous healing practices: traditional forms from the Core of Being

Christopher Rybak
Department of Educational Leadership, Bradley University

Abstract

This paper offers a basic view of the ways in which traditional indigenous healing practices such as those from American Indian traditions emanate from a psycho-spiritual place referred to as the Core of Being. Jung provided a model by which these indigenous practices might be understood. American Indian worldviews, traditions, and healing practices are described along with examples of ways in which counsellors and psychotherapists might work within such a healing context. Gaining knowledge of indigenous healing practices adds depth to our understanding of the human condition across cultural conditions and provides insight into important aspects of psychological and emotional development frequently missed in modern, non-indigenous cultures.

Throughout the cultures of the earth, all peoples have known severe hardships and suffering. Each culture has provided its people with a spiritual and psychological context for dealing with suffering and offered pathways toward healing processes. A powerful context for healing occurs at the symbolic level since symbols can carry with them the deepest intertwined connections to sacred, mythic, and transformational experience, which reach well beyond the common everyday consciousness levels of rational understanding.

Sandner (1991:11) reflected upon the existential givens of human life:

> Suffering is an integral part of human life. The process of growth from infancy to childhood, from childhood to adolescence, and on to adulthood, old age, and death, involves inescapable suffering. If the process is blocked at any level, the suffering increases to the point of acute and painful symptoms. To a doctor or medicine man that works with people in distress, this has an immediate daily reality. He learns that man can accept a tremendous amount of legitimate suffering; what he cannot accept is suffering that has no purpose. To be endured and accepted, suffering must be given a meaning.

Indigenous healing practices are the psycho-cultural-spiritual traditions, rituals, and ceremonies that provide meaning in life and relief from suffering though connection with sacred symbols. Traditional indigenous healing practices, such as those from American Indian traditions, emanate from a common psycho-spiritual place referred to as the Core of Being. J. T. Garrett (2001:xii) observed: "Spirit memory is written in our DNA, and in every cell of our body". For all cultures, the Core of Being refers to that substrate of common human experience that underlies the conscious expression of the deepest and most profound connections that human beings experience with the cosmos. Joseph Campbell (1949:384-386) referred to the Core of Being in the following way:

> The asceticism of the medieval saints and the yogis of India, the Hellenistic mystery initiations, the ancient philosophies of the East and the West, are techniques for the shifting of the emphasis of individual consciousness away from the garments. The preliminary meditations of the aspirant detach his mind and sentiments from the accidents of life and drive him to the core. "I am not that, not that," he meditates: "not my mother or son who has just died; my body, which is ill and aging; my arm, my eye, my head; not the summation of all these things. I am not my feeling; not my mind; not my power of intuition." By such meditations he is driven to his own profundity and breaks through, at last, the unfathomable realizations.

The garments to which Campbell refers are the superficial trappings of appearances, which can easily obscure the inner Core of Being.

American Indian ceremonial leader Ed McGaa (1992:4) expressed his view of the way in which indigenous healing practices flow from the Core of Being in the following way:

> Natural people throughout the planet are exploring revelation from created nature, exploring that extension made directly by the Creator, the Higher Power, the Prime Mover, the Ultimate Force, or the Great Mystery. They are learning from what is directly revealed and from what they can taste, touch, feel, observe, and study. Now, modern seekers ...are beginning to recognize the visible powers of the universe. They are addressing, cultivating, and nourishing the heart of the spirituality that has been with their unbroken gene link, their beginning, down through the circles of time. Like the native tribal ones of old, they too are sensing that we, and all the life forces that surround us, are extensions of that Great Mystery force itself and have a great purpose for being here--especially at this time.

JUNG

Jung (De Laszlo, 1993) provided a model by which indigenous healing practices might be understood which included distinguishing the personal unconscious from the universal or collective unconscious. The personal unconscious is made up of all that we have experienced but may have forgotten or repressed. The collective unconscious represents the common foundation of psychic life that all humans experience and contains what are referred to as the archetypes. Archetypes are often brought to the conscious level through mythological fables, sacred tribal lore and ritual, as well as the common and uncommon religious practices of today. These all represent efforts to reveal that which was formerly well hidden. *Psychically and spiritually speaking, these legends and tribal stories are the fingers pointing at the moon rather than the moon itself.*

For Jung, the individuation process represented a lifelong effort at meaning making. Individuation is a continuous dialectical process of making meaning as individuals negotiate the differences between who they believe themselves to be and who they discover they actually are (or are not). This integration process can take place on many levels, including the psychological, spiritual, emotional, ceremonial, and social. Jung identified the employment of various kinds of tribal restorative practices that serve a healing and psychotherapeutic function (De Laszlo, 1993). The Jungian view is that the Self connects the individual to the very "structures of Being" (Stein, 1998: 152). Thus, the Self is transcendent of the personal experiences in which the ego is embedded.

The psychological transformation that occurs as one's state of consciousness moves from the ego to the Self does not lend itself well to any type of verbal description, but instead is better expressed on a symbolic level. Moreover, symbols can transform psychic energy into a healing force to reduce suffering in the following manner:

> Therefore the heart of all cultural-psychological methods of healing, whether they occur in literate or preliterate societies, is a symbolic structure that explains, or at least provides a context for, the sufferings of its members. There is much to be endured: the dreary monotony of everyday life, the apocalyptic appearance of illness and misfortune, and the painful result of man's own ignorance and malice. Within the symbolic structure of his culture, man attempts to create a satisfying meaning for these afflictions and a method for curing them (Sander, 1991: 11-12).

Symbolic forms such as the mandala can provide a gateway to the transcendent aspects of healing experiences. "Mandala" was a Sanskrit word chosen by Jung to describe the sacred circles he and his clients drew to depict the deep interconnections that people experienced at a fundamental level (Fincher, 1991). Many times mandalas are circles divided into quadrants that depict different, often polar opposite, aspects of life. Drawing these divergent aspects of life offers one a highly symbolic way of consciously acknowledging and integrating these experiences. Jung felt that the act of creating mandalas was in itself deeply healing (De Laszlo, 1993). Sacred circles have been found to be of great spiritual importance to many indigenous peoples, including American Indians. Symbols such as mandalas can offer suffering individuals a sense of safety, comfort, and familiarity (Sandner, 1991) that engenders hope.

THE MEDICINE WHEEL

The American Indian Medicine Wheel itself can be compared to a mandala. Jung believed that mandalas could in themselves provide some psychic relief from chaotic states of mind (De Laszlo, 1993). Held sacred in American Indian spirituality, the circle represents a key aspect that is highly symbolic in American Indian philosophy. As life, death, and rebirth succeed one another, the circle symbolizes this never-ending cycle (Garrett, 1998). Circles are used as sacred spaces in many ways in American Indian ceremonies, not only including the Medicine Wheel, but also including the round shape of the sweat lodge, the circular arrangement of stones around a spirit fire, and the dance arena at powwows (Rybak & Lakota Eastin, in press).

The Medicine Wheel is a conceptual method of orienting to the four compass directions and the different dimensions in life represented by the four directions, and it includes the spiritual as well as the physical dimensions. The Medicine Wheel is a symbolic means of describing a holistic view and balance that fits with many American Indians' understanding of life and worldview (McCormick, 1996). Particular associations may differ when comparing one American Indian nation to another. Many times, in meditating on the significance of the directions, adherents will stand and face the different directions in a reverential manner. One commonly used interpretation starts with the East that is associated with the spiritual dimension and the color red, the color of the rising sun at the start of a new day. Turning toward the South, the participant connects this direction with the environment and nature as well as the color yellow. Turning toward the West, one recalls the physical aspects of the body and the color black, as it is associated with the darkness that comes after sunset. As one turns finally to the North, an association is made with the mind and the color white, the color of snow that visits from the North (Coggins, 1990; Garrett, 1998; Rybak & Lakota Eastin, in press).

Jung (De Laszlo, 1993; Duran & Duran, 1995) described basic functions of the psyche as involving the opposing pairs of thinking vs. feeling, sensation vs. intuition, and introversion vs. extraversion. Taking place within any individual, but also heavily culturally influenced, individuation involves the process of learning to achieve a balance among these functions. To the degree that certain functions are overemphasized, this creates a significant imbalance and contributes to neuroses. This idea of a balance or a sacred centre within all things fits closely with the American Indian perspective of the Medicine Wheel (Duran & Duran, 1995).

Jung and the archetypes: aspects of the core of being

Jung felt that there were commonalities among humans in the way in which they tend to face the universal aspects of existence. These are the archetypes. However, the specific manifestations differed from one culture to another in response to a group's particular history and the influence of the environment. Jung observed examples in which particular wisdom traditions demonstrated the flow of energy in the psyche to produce some startling parallels among otherwise diverse cultures. For example, consider the sacred and symbolic use of sand paintings developed both by Navaho culture and Tibetan culture. These diverse cultures had no obvious means of communication across the distances that separated them, yet they both developed sacred rituals around the use of sand to depict deeply meaningful aspects of existence. For both Navaho and Tibetan cultures, strikingly beautiful sand paintings were produced but were only kept intact for the special sacred purposes, and then they were destroyed, symbolizing the transitory nature of the material world.

Particular archetypes that Jung distinguished included the Self. The Self can be tapped to inform one's personal development in conscious and unconscious ways. The deeply intuitive and non-rational wisdom of the Self can be accessed in many ways including the use of the active imagination; dreams, sacred symbols and rituals, as well as other meditative and consciousness-expanding techniques developed within the wisdom traditions of particular cultures. The Self is representative of the Core of Being into which indigenous cultures tuned in order to understand their ultimate and universal experiences. These intuitive experiences were shared and developed into the uniquely manifested wisdom traditions practised by each indigenous culture and represented by symbols appropriate to the particular culture.

An important common mythological symbol is that of death and rebirth. A person 'dies' to his old self and is 'reborn', transformed in some ways (Sandner, 1991). While undergoing such a transformation, people often experience a profound sense of loss of conscious control of their lives. As they fight against this process they may become emotionally and physically ill. As they begin to die to their old sense of self, they open themselves to a flood of symbols from their unconscious core of being which presents rejuvenating energy that drives the healing and maturational processes. Initiation practices relevant to the particular developmental change can be helpful in absorbing the special energy of the self-renewal process associated with these symbols. Indigenous healing practices offer guidance in tapping into these rejuvenating forces.

American Indian worldviews

Since there are over 500 American Indian tribes (Helms & Cook, 1999), there is certainly a great diversity of perspective among these various cultures. As a result, it is clear that whatever descriptions can be offered are not going to apply to every single case. However, these general statements can be of help in the beginning, especially for those for whom this perspective may be wholly new and in strong contrast with the views from one's own culture. At the same time, many of these perspectives may also resonate for a number of other indigenous cultures from continents other than America.

Compared to Western thinking, the meaning of and emphasis on lineal time is likely to be quite different among American Indians. Much more emphasis is given to *where* events took place as compared to *when* (Duran & Duran, 1995). The focus is on the context of the situation, rather than some isolated facts (Gallant, 1999). The focus is also much more on life as process than as the content of object relationships (Duran & Duran, 1995).

From an American Indian perspective, life is more of a whole experience and cannot be easily compartmentalized into mind vs. body vs. spirit. Instead these are all part of a larger enveloping and developing relationship with the entire cosmos (Duran & Duran, 1995). A central issue is whether individuals live in harmony with nature. Disharmony is equivalent to illness. *Being in* harmony makes much more sense than some attempt to *become in* harmony.

Duran and Duran (1995) suggest that for those wanting to understand the culture of American Indians, it is necessary to consider the historical context of cultural imperialism that has inflicted what he calls deep "soul wounds" (p.24) on American Indians. In order for therapists to understand the individual's soul wound and assist in the healing process, they will need to become deeply familiar with other Jungian concepts including "*psyche, myth, dreams, and culture*" (p.24). A true understanding of the individual soul wound with which a therapist might work and any potential healing process will include becoming deeply aware of how aspects of these other terms are thoroughly intertwined with the psychic injury suffered by the individual.

Using a Jungian orientation, the psychotherapy process works to restore balance for human beings, which can be seen as consistent with the American Indian notion of harmony (Duran & Duran, 1995). The bridge to harmony can be built upon culturally appropriate symbols to reconnect and resynchronize those aspects of life, which have moved into a state of disharmonious conflict. Symbols can be particularly powerful in working with the psyche to transform and liberate energy.

American Indian wisdom traditions

American Indian healing practices are examples of wisdom traditions of indigenous cultures. Such practices generally offer a circular and holistic model that connects multiple dimensions of life experience. From an American Indian perspective, the restoration of health involves the re-establishment of harmony with nature. The American Indian Medicine Wheel is a powerful symbol of harmony with nature. The circular aspect of the Wheel is a strong representation of the interconnection of the entire cosmic experience.

A variety of healing practices based on the wholeness of the circle have been employed to restore harmony, including the pipe ceremony and sweat lodge. *These practices can be contrasted with more narrowly drawn psychotherapeutic views, which tend to consider humans in relative isolation not only from one another but without reference to their inner and outer connections with nature as well.*

The pipe ceremony

Lakota legend describes how the holy person White Buffalo Cow Woman appeared to their people to bring them the pipe and other sacred rites (Brown, 1953; Rybak and Lakota Eastin, in press). The pipe consisted of a stem made of wood, a bowl carved from red stone, and feathers from an eagle. The pipe is used to smoke tobacco and sacred herbs as a potent symbolic method of connecting people to the heavens through the prayer of the smoke. Often, the pipe is smoked and prayers are offered in acknowledgement of the special gifts of the four directions. Participants in the pipe ceremony form a circle and pass the pipe from one person to another, each person in turn smoking the pipe, or just holding the pipe to recognize how it honors the sacredness of the Deep Mystery.

The sweat lodge

The sweat lodge acts as a purification ceremony for participants (Brown, 1953; Rybak & Lakota Eastin, in press). The lodge is generally a low, rounded structure with the only door facing the East to invite in enlightenment. The lodge is said to represent the womb of Mother Earth, and participants are reborn through the purification ritual. The lodge is often constructed of a frame of willow tree branches that are covered by a tarpaulin. A flap covers the door so that the hot steam is trapped inside during the ritual. Stones are heated in a sacred fireplace just outside the entrance to the lodge. The stones symbolize the caring nurturance of Mother Earth, and the fire is the life-giving energy of the sun. During the sweat lodge ceremony, participants sit inside on the ground. Hot rocks are brought inside, and water poured over them to release steam. It becomes very hot inside. The sweat lodge leaders guide the ceremony with prayers and sacred songs while occasionally sprinkling sage or sweet grass onto the warm rocks to release the special aroma (Brown, 1953; Rybak and Lakota Eastin, in press).

American Indian healing practices

Indigenous healing practices can offer psychological, emotional, and symbolic expressways to the Core of Being to tap the essence of self-renewal. The traditional healing practices of American Indians have gained a heightened level of importance for counsellors, psychologists, and educators who strive to increase their understanding of systems of healing from diverse cultures (Wyrostok & Paulson, 2000). American Indians often view healing as part of a holistic experience involving many aspects of being including the spiritual, emotional, and physical.

From a Navaho American Indian tribal perspective as described by Hammerschlag (1988:45), mental health is:

> ...having your head, mouth, and heart in a straight alignment. Mental health happens when what you believe in your heart is the same as what you say with your mouth. You are mentally healthy when what you feel is something you also believe. When the alignment isn't straight, when the mouth doesn't say what the heart feels or when the head knows something the heart doesn't choose to acknowledge, then sooner or later you will get sick".

In his work with American Indians, the psychiatrist Dr. Hammerschlag met a holy man who articulated the simple acknowledgement that the mind is something "mysterious," a direct appreciation of a complexity that years of higher education can sometimes obscure more than illuminate.

Some tribes such as the Pueblo Indians have no special word for "religion". Instead, the knowledge and practice of spiritual life and sacred responsibilities are a part of the fabric of every hour of living (Sando, 1997) that fits within the great circle of life. The connection with life through the sacred pathways brings one into wholeness and harmony. Through circular sand paintings, Navaho people expressed their views of the circle as a place of spiritual emergence (Cornell, 1994). Through masked dancers, prayers, and painted sand figures, symbols of great inner powers are manifested as human participants are afforded an opportunity to deeply identify with the healing potential within these powers (Sandner, 1991). Chants may be a part of healing rituals in which the repetition continues for long periods of time during which the participants may enter an altered state of consciousness with increased receptivity to the song images.

Hammerschlag (1988) gave a description of a Navaho healing ceremony in which a medicine man created a sand painting on the ground. A client by the name of Mary was returning to her family and tribe as an adult after having been removed as a young child and spending many difficult years during the intervening time. The sand painting depicted a Navaho legend about a lost child returning to the tribe in another form. To aid in the process of making Mary whole again, she was invited to sit in the center of the painting to more deeply encounter the heroism of the figures and take in their strength. The medicine man tied sacred objects to Mary and twirled a wooden noisemaker that made a breeze blow over her to blow away her old anger and confusion.

Deep mystery

The American Indian perspective on their sacred relationship to the world is frequently expressed through symbolism within rituals and ceremonies, since words are often insufficient to describe the concept of deep mystery embedded within these views (Beck, Walters, & Francisco, 1977). Symbolism within the context of cultural tradition serves to describe what words cannot, through sacred ceremonies.

McGaa (1992:8) commented on the power of ceremony in the following way:

> To do ceremony, natural ceremony that calls upon the Great Mystery, you must begin to understand the essence of truth; the essence of thinking and doing without ulterior motive and flowing in unison with the stream you are becoming. Without truth your endeavor will have no power. Conversely, when you comprehend and live your truth, it can be far more powerful than you would ever imagine. It is not a big mystery why some holy persons have discernible, "mystical" power, especially when in beseeching ceremony. They have lived their truth!"

Working with American Indian healing practices

McCormick (1995) conducted an exploratory study of ways in which the healing of American Indians could be facilitated. He approached this project in a qualitative way, interviewing American Indians and having them describe the process that they went through in their healing. A list of approaches that contributed to healing included:

- participation in ceremony,
- expression of emotion,
- learning from a role model,

- establishing a connection with nature,
- exercise,
- involvement in challenging activities,
- establishing a social connection,
- gaining an understanding of the problem,
- establishing spiritual connection,
- obtaining help/support from others,
- self-care,
- setting goals,
- anchoring self in tradition,
- and helping others (p.317).

These approaches helped the individuals in various ways to leave behind unhealthy lifestyles, gain social support, and learn to live a healthy lifestyle. It is clear that these approaches were successful for a number of reasons: the availability of varied and multilevel healing resources, the provision of counselling services which were effectively based on a true understanding of American Indian culture and worldviews, clear communication to American Indian people that the goal of the healing approaches were to assist them in regaining and in maintaining balance, and the empowerment of American Indian individuals to self-transcend both through their own efforts and through their strong interpersonal connections with others.

Through years of work with American Indian populations, Hammerschlag (1988) learned the deep significance of the cultural and spiritual contexts of American Indians. In his description of the process of healing, Hammerschlag (1988: 137) wrote:

> Patients don't want to be cases – they want to be healed. They want to participate in their own wellness or their own death. Patients are the principal agents in their lives, and as much as they want to be well, they want peace and understanding. To find such a healing peace they need to feel that a connection exists between themselves and the healer and between themselves and something larger than self or science.

Healing circle

The healing circle from American Indian culture can be used with a counseling group. It is preferable if an American Indian is leading or co-leading such a group as a sign of respect to the culture (Heilbron & Guttman, 2000; Rybak & Lakota Eastin, in press). Heilbron and Guttman (2000) described one such approach. A group session can open with a purification ritual in which traditional medicines such as sweet grass, sage, or tobacco are burned in a shell. Each group member wishing to participate can "smudge" by cupping the smoke and drawing it over themselves, especially their head.

Once the purification process has been completed, while group members are holding hands an American Indian prayer may follow in a native language, if a group leader or member has some fluency. The prayer sets a tone of thanksgiving for the opportunity for the group members to come together and it serves to remind group members to speak truthfully and from the heart in respect for the sacredness of the occasion. The prayer also serves to invite the Creator to lend support and wise guidance to the group members.

Group members can use a talking stick (Rybak & Lakota Eastin, in press) or eagle feather (Heilbron & Guttman, 2000) to serve notice to others that this one person is the designated speaker. As each person completes his or her statement the talking stick or eagle feather is passed from member to member. At the end of the group, a concluding prayer is spoken while everyone stands and hold hands. After the session is concluded, each member goes around the circle and hugs other members as a sign of their caring and supportive relationship.

Feeling a connection to the whole of the circle or social network is an important healing element. On a larger scale, culture-based initiation practices can provide that culture's developing members with a social, emotional, psychological, and spiritual place within the circle of the cultural group. This crucial link tends to be bypassed in Western style societies.

Implications of the loss of initiation

American Indian traditions included significant rituals for the initiation of adolescents into adulthood. Prechtel (1999) offers an eloquent description of this process in respect of the village of Santiago Atitlan, a Mayan village in Guatemala. The initiation process in this village extended for over one year, and a large portion of the village were involved in some manner. Through rituals and ceremonies expressing the deep support offered by the villagers to the budding adults and challenges to aid the adolescents in expanding their self-awareness, the elaborate initiation process resulted in the adolescents having learned who they were in relation to all other aspects of village life, as well as their role and position within the great cycle of life. It also prepared them well for the role of parenting the next generation.

To a great extent the initiation rituals have been lost for American Indians as well as other modern day societies, with little of significance to replace them. As a result, adolescents are left to search for these intricate and ultimate meanings largely on their own with not a great deal of success. Thus, the traditional indigenous worldview of balance and harmony with the forces of nature and the physical, spiritual, intellectual, social, and psychological aspects of life has been terribly fragmented (Duran & Duran, 1995). This disintegration of the traditional cultural connections has contributed heavily to the incidence, among American Indians, of domestic and other violence, drug and alcohol abuse, mental illness, debilitating physical illness, suicide, and hopelessness. These same afflictions trouble the youth of most modern cultures on an epidemic scale.

Dreams & visions

For many American Indian tribal traditions, dreams and visions are highly valued. For example, Black Elk's report of his visions continues to have deep significance for many American Indians (Brown, 1953). In the view of Duran and Duran (1995), the "soul wound" from the severe cultural disruption that has occurred for American Indians is at the core of their being, that area of great mystery which arises from the collective unconscious. Healing for these soul wounds can also arise from the collective unconscious through the form of dreams or other visions. For the counsellor, healer, or therapist, it will be important to be aware of a client's particular tribal beliefs about dreams, how they should be handled, and under which circumstances they can even be reported. If the dreams are held in sacred regard, they might only be related provided certain rituals are followed or other conditions met.

Alcoholism and using active imaginations

When dealing with alcoholism, Duran and Duran (1995) described a particular use of the active imagination process in a way that meshes with American Indian worldviews. Active Imagination is a process in which a person consciously invites and opens him/herself to the imagery of their own unconscious. The approach used by E. Duran included a client suffering with alcoholism imagining the spirit of alcohol as a spiritual entity, making appeasement offerings to this alcohol entity, and even engaging in dialogue with that spirit. This approach helped the client become more aware of the unconscious power which had been given to the alcohol entity and it was a way to regain some of that power through a courageous encounter with the powerful entity.

The limitations of western psychological world views

Traditional Western perspectives on human development and counselling have tended to be linear and reductionistic, sometimes quite removed from nature, often overlooking holistic perspectives. Many assumptions that form the foundation of Western psychological therapies are at odds with the basic beliefs of American Indians (Duran & Duran, 1995) and many other indigenous peoples across the globe. Such assumptions include the notion that the

Western view and perspective is ultimately superior and should subsume any indigenous psychology that may be termed "primitive" and therefore somehow lacking in validity. As a result the indigenous psychologies and cultural healing practices are demeaned, overlooked, or even assumed to be completely nonexistent. Add to this the devastating colonial experiences that so many indigenous peoples have experienced at the hands of Westerners, inflicting a vast and severe physical, social, emotional, and spiritual trauma on a culture-wide basis. The net result is that the context as well as the delivery of Western psychological services is often anything but therapeutic for American Indians.

This situation creates an ethical mandate for Western trained counsellors and psychotherapists not only to learn about the culture of American Indians, but moreover to learn which therapeutic approaches are appropriate (McCormick, 1998). To this end, researchers such as Eduardo Duran have developed approaches that attempt to integrate the higher potentials of Western psychotherapy such as some of the concepts and techniques developed by Carl Jung with the already existing strengths inherent in American Indian cultural healing practices.

Conclusion

Jung has provided a framework by which to understand the power and potential of indigenous healing practices from various cultural traditions. Such healing practices, while their form is very specific to particular cultures such as the American Indians, play a transcendental and transformational role which addresses a basic human need to make meaning out of life's difficult experiences.

Knowledge of indigenous healing practices adds depth to our understanding of the human condition across cultural conditions and provides insight into important aspects of psychological and emotional development frequently missed in Western, high-tech cultures. From this perspective, indigenous healing practices may offer approaches which fill in the gaps left by traditional Western psychological models, whether they are applied to indigenous cultures or not.

References

Beck, P.V., Walters, A.L., & Francisco, N. (1977), *The sacred: Ways of knowledge, sources of life*. Tsaile, AZ: Navaho Community College Press.

Brown, J.E. (Ed.) (1953), *The sacred pipe: Black elk's account of the seven rites of the Oglala Sioux*. Norman, OK: University of Oklahoma Press.

Campbell, J. (1949), *The hero with a thousand faces*. Princeton, NJ: Princeton University Press.

Coggins, K. (1990), *Alternative pathways to healing: The recovery medicine wheel*. FL: Health Communications.

Cornell, J. (1994), *Mandala: Luminous symbols for healing*. Wheaton, IL: Quest Books.

De Laszlo, V.S. (1993), *The basic writings of C.G. Jung*. New York: The Modern Library.

Duran, E., & Duran, B. (1995), *Native American postcolonial psychology*. Albany, NY: State University of New York Press.

Fincher, S.F. (1991), *Creating mandalas for insight, healing,and self-expression*. Boston: Shambhala.

Gallant, S.M. (1999), Cultural assumptions in cross-cultural relations. In A. L. Cook, M. Brazzel, A.S. Craig, B. Greig, (Eds.), *Reading book for human relations training(8thed.)*, (pp.103-110), Alexandria, VA: NTL Institute for Applied Behavioral Science.

Garrett, J.T. (2001), *Meditations with the Cherokee: Prayers, songs, and stories of healing and harmony*. Rochester, VT: Bear and Co.

Garrett, M. (1998), *Walking on the wind: Cherokee teachings for harmony and balance*. Santa Fe, NM: Bear & Co.

Hammerschlag, C. (1988), *The dancing healers: A doctor's journey of healing with Native Americans*. San Francisco: Harper & Row.

Helms, J.E., & Cook, D.A. (1999), *Using race and culture in counseling and psychotherapy: Theory and process*. Boston, MA: Allyn & Bacon.

Heilbron, C.L., & Guttman, M.A.J. (2000), Traditional healing methods with first nations women in group counselling. *Canadian Journal of Counselling*, **34(1)**:3-13.

McCormick, R.M. (1995), The facilitation of healing for the First Nations People of British Columbia. *Canadian Journal of Native Education*, **21(2)**:251-322.

McCormick, R.M. (1996), Culturally appropriate means and ends of counselling as described by the First Nations people of British Columbia. *International Journal for the Advancement of Counselling*, **18**:163-172.

McCormick, R.M. (1998), Ethical considerations in first nations counselling and research. *Canadian Journal of Counselling*, **32(4)**:284-297.

McGaa, E.(1992), *Rainbow tribe: Ordinary people journeying on the red road*. San Francisco: Harper.

Prechtel, M. (1999), *Long life, honey in the heart: A story of initiation and eloquence from the shores of a Mayan lake*. New York: Tarcher/Putnam.

Rybak, C., & Lakota Eastin, C. (in press), Native American Healing Practices and Counseling. *The Journal of Humanistic Education and Development.*

Sandner, D. F. (1991), *Navaho symbols of healing: A Jungian exploration of ritual, image, and medicine*. Rochester, VT: Healing Arts Press.

Sando, J. S. (1997), Pueblo Indian religions. In N. Wood (Ed.), *The serpent's tongue: Prose, poetry, and art of the New Mexico pueblos*. New York: Dutton Books.

Stein, M. (1998), *Jung's map of the soul*. Peru, IL: Open Court.

Wyrostok, N.C., & Paulson, B.L. (2000), Traditional healing practices among first nations students. *Canadian Journal of Counselling*, **34**:14-24.

Wisdom from the Bhagwad Gita for modern life

Usha Ram
Reader in Psychology, University of Poona

Modern living is a search for ever increasing comfort (sukh) and a desire for this to be a permanent state (anand). Man's suffering and pain has initiated this search in his lifetime. In fact, a large part of our life in this world is spent in pain than pleasure, hence this search for the latter.

Philosophers down history the world over have been to date spending time and thought for the solution to human suffering. Psychology for over a century has been studying human behavior with the purpose to understanding why we behave the way we do and to find out ways and means of changing such behavior that causes distress and pain to oneself. In this, psychologists aimed earlier on at explaining abnormality more than discovering ways to achieve the human goal of healthy peaceful living. The Freudian depth approach traced the cause of distress to the unconscious, the behaviorists and learning theorists like Watson and Skinner emphasized the reinforcement and punishments as determining our behavior and experiences, but it was the humanistic approach of Rogers and Maslow that turned our attention to the higher, constructive understanding of the goal of human living.

Psychotherapists all along have been more individualistic than collectivistic in their approaches to treatment of clients. Though very useful to improve oneself and then relate with the others effectively, by and large psychology has not moved very much in the direction proposed by the existentialists. The latter philosophy brought into existential psychology drew our attention to three types of relationships – with the world (i.e. others), with self, and with the creator of this world – and the freedom to choose. Most of modern psychology emphasizes self-development, to function effectively for oneself, with little attention to our fellow-beings.

Modern life had provided us with technological developments, which render us with all physical comforts, and we believe that ever – increasing comfort at the physical level is the solution to our pain and suffering. This search and the resultant inventions have only helped maintain this delusion.

The ancient Indian book of wisdom, *Bhagwad Gita*, tells us differently. This wisdom is eternal and offers solutions to our entire search for the permanent joy. *Bhagwad Gita* provides us with solutions that would appeal to modern psychologists. Lord Krishna, in this book of wisdom counsels a distressed representative of human beings in the form of in the form of

Arjuna, his dearest friend, regarding human beings' relationships with the world, and the role to be performed while on the earth.

The World: all of creation has emerged from one source or energy and

> – My self is the very source of creation'.....
> IX-5 (tr. Easwaran,1997, vol.II)

Therefore, in essence we are all connected even though we seem different. All creation consists of the five elements (*panca tatva*) namely, earth, water, fire, air and space, all of which have three qualities or characteristics (*triguna*), namely, *satva, rajas,* and *tamas.* (goodness, activity, inertia)

> Earth, water, fire, air, ether, mind, intellect, egoism, these are
> My eight- fold *prakriti*.....
> VII – 4 (tr. Chinmayanada, 1984)

The human beings thus consist of the five elements in varying combination with the *trigunas.* We human beings, thus, in effect, are made of the same material just as all crockery is made from the same material, only appearing to be different because of their shapes, sizes and utility.

The human being has the five senses of taste, smell, touch, sight, and hearing, and their five sense organs. These organs receive stimulation and thus we perceive pleasure and pain, comfort and discomfort. This only means that physical experiences are neither intransient nor continuous, they are fleeting ones:

> The contact of senses with objects which cause heat and cold,
> pleasure and pain have a beginning and end, they are
> impermanent, endure them bravely.....
> II – 14 (tr. Easwaran,1997,vol.I)

Now the dweller of the body gets attached to the body and develops an identity restricted to the body and the experiences it provides. The body undergoes changes because it is a transient form, though the dweller does not:

> The body is mortal, but he who dwells in the body is said to
> Immortal and immeasurable.........
> II-18 (tr. Easwaran,1997,vol.I)

We are, therefore, not the body we live in. The body is perishable but we the

> occupants of the body are intangible and infinite.
> The Self ... is everlasting and infinite
> II – 25 (tr. Easwaran,1997, vol.I)

> The self is unmanifested, beyond all thought and beyond all change ...
> II – 25 (tr. Easwaran, 1997, vol.I)

We are driven to eliminate the pains and discomfort because of physical "beingness" being so important to us. The body's importance is not determined, as it is the means through which we experience the world. In fact, the bodily needs, which Maslow mentions in his description of the hierarchy of motivation, are necessary to be met to rise toward higher goals in our lifetime. But modern man attends to these needs in overwhelming quantities, verging on obsessions, all his abilities being directed towards body gratifications and comforts beyond the needs.

In ignorance and inadequate knowledge we believe that each person is different and that our goals are different when there is only one goal for all humans, that we are really not at all different from each other in our true nature. The goal common to all is the perennial joy (*anand*) which is our true nature. But the modern person's goal succinctly stated by Easwaran (1997, vol. p. 11) is that the world has been thinking and working on the physical level: more prosperity, comforts, leisure time, better health, more variety of things to do and enjoy.

Modern man is driven to seek comforts through the three "p's": profit, prestige, and power. All these nourish the ego, inflating it, making man more and more egoistic in his thinking, values, and behaviour.

Roots of pain and suffering

Our problems of suffering pain in this world in whatever degree or duration, stem from our desires which cause us to think repeatedly of the object of desire.

> When a man thinks of objects 'attachments' for them arises;
> From attachment 'desire' is born; from desire arises 'anger'...
> I – 62

> From anger comes 'delusion'; from delusion 'loss of memory;
> From loss of memory the 'destruction of discrimination'; from
> Destruction of discrimination he 'perishes'....
> II – 63 (tr. Easwaran, 1997, vol. I)

Desires in themselves may not be the culprit of our suffering as much as our strong beliefs that the desires which attach us to the objects of the desire must be fulfilled just as and when we want them to be so. Those of us who are driven to have the transient pleasures of the world remain in ignorance of the permanent joy, the supreme human goal...

> Those whose minds are swept away by the pursuit of pleasure
> And power are incapable of following the supreme goal and will not attain samadhi....
> II-44 (tr. Easwaran, 1997, vol.I)

Remedy for the pain

Bhagwadgita has counseled us to handle, reduce and eliminate pain and suffering in various ways. These may be called cognitive (knowledge), affective (devotion, love, compassion) and behavioural (action/deeds/karma) ways.

Knowledge refers to the distinct information regarding the Creator, the world, and the self knowing that the source is one and therefore, all of life in its various forms is one and this is Reality will enable us to understand all the occupants of this world, and feel and behave compassionately than selfishly.

Devotion/love finds a home in the human heart once the true knowledge establishes itself with profundity and conviction that all of us human beings and all living creatures are essentially one and of the same origin, therefore, in essence not different at all. Therefore, gratifying the others' basic needs is as good as doing so to oneself. The true knowledge about the source, about the self leads to devotion for the self and hence for all creation, and therefore, for all the people alike.

Renouncing

Many thinkers have often prescribed renouncing. Renouncing one's attachment and lust for the worldly pleasures and comforts which are experienced through the body, and not doing anything is not the prescription. In fact, as one becomes steadfast in devotion which makes one live, serve the world as equal to serving the Creator/Lord, one's attachments and cravings for the world shed on their own account, for these latter seem petty and insignificant vis-à-vis the higher goal of service and devotion to the Lord. Thus, one does not have to make a conscious effort to renounce the world, for one's devotion takes care of all the obstacles in the form of worldly desires, thus rendering one with peace and freedom from pain and distress to one.

Deeds/*Karma* are carried out by us all the time, more so to fulfill our desires. Most human beings perform deeds/acts with a purpose which is mostly self-oriented. We look for the consequential profit, prestige, recognition or power when we undertake to do something: 'What is there in this for me?'

What are the costs and benefits for me if I do this? are the questions we raise. To this Lord Krishna's counsel is:

> Let not the fruit of action be thy motive, nor let thy attachment be to inaction....
> II – 47 (tr. Chinmayananda, 1984)

"You have the right to work, but never to the fruits of work" (Easwaran, 1997, vol. I). Far too often have we lost the opportunity to gain rewards of high order only because we dwelled on the returns from the work to be done and not performed adequately or appropriately. At the same time man must not sit back settled into inaction for that is the character of one dominated by inertia or *tamas*. Each one is advised to do his / her best at the task at hand but not looking for the rewards from doing the task. Preoccupied with the rewards than the task has as many would recall, ruined the work at hand, bringing pain. Nor is it advisable to be attached to refraining from or avoiding doing any work, even if only to avoid the anticipated pain. We are counselled to do our work, duties, service, and so on

> ...as a man established within himself – without selfish attachments, and alike in success and defeat.
> For yoga is perfect evenness of mind.
> II-48 (tr. Easwaran, 1997, vol.i)

This is possible if we can be steady in ourselves, knowing that we are united with the Creator, and do our duties toward our family, community,country and the world as a whole with all of whom we are related (tr.Easwaran, 1997,vol.1,p.99).

Modern psychologists have repeatedly talked of fear of failure and of success among people. These fears and anxieties prevent us from participating in several activities, thus living an increasingly meaningless, lonely miserable life. These fears will cease to be if the task is focused on rather than being preoccupied with the possible failure or success. Cognitive therapists have also emphasized self-defeating thoughts, beliefs and self-verbalizations as causing fears and anxieties(e.g. Hauck, 1974).
The *Bhagwad Gita* emphasizes that

> The world is imprisoned in selfish action; act selflessly, without any thought of personal profit...
> III – 9 (tr. Easwaran, 1997, vol I)

All of us are part of this world and related with everyone. Working and serving the world selflessly with no aims of personal profits, placing the others before oneself will help gratify our desires:

> Through selfless service you will always be fruitful and find fulfillment of all your desires...
> III – 10 (tr. Easwaran,1997,vol.1)

In serving selflessly in this world we can attain intransient/permanent joy, the supreme goal of all human beings.

> Strive constantly to serve the welfare of the world; by devotion to
> Selfless work man attains the supreme goal of life...
> III-19 (tr. Easwaran, 1997, vol.I)

Conclusion

In this busy modern life, people would find it difficult to spare time for the much advised meditation, which has been researched in recent times by psychologists. This requires about a couple of hours daily. Meditation is an effective way to reduce distress, to gain peace, to gain wisdom regarding this world and creation and about how one is connected strongly with every living creature and with the creator. Finally, anchored in this wisdom one can live for all uniformly and selflessly. In serving others we are really serving the world, which means ourselves too! However, selflessly serving our family and community is no less significant in the search for reducing and eliminating pain and suffering. Pain and suffering cannot be avoided when we strive for selfish goals – such as those based on individualistic achievement. Realizing who we are paves the way to realizing that we are one with of all other living beings, respecting, loving and serving all alike, thus removing pain, fulfilling our goal of permanent joy (*anand*).

References

Chinmayananda, Sw. (1976), *The Holy Geeta*. Bombay: Central Chinmaya Mission Trust.

Easwaran, E. (1997), *The Bhagavad Gita: For daily living*. Vols. 1-3, Delhi: Jaico.

Hauck, P. (1974), *Overcoming Worry and Fear*. Philadelphia: Westminister Press.

Animal images:

A critique of the ways of conceptualizing animals in the western and in the eastern literature

Barbara Noske
Research Institute for Humanities and Social Sciences, University of Sydney

Western scientific ways of conceptualizing animals

The mainstream western image of animals has largely been shaped by the natural sciences which tend to be reductionist and objectifying in their approaches. The so-called Scientific Revolution created a specific image of the natural world: nature as a semi-divine life force was replaced by nature as a useful, technical object with no purpose or value of its own. In the eyes of modern scientists nature became mechanical, measurable and quantifiable matter. This process, known as *the disenchantment of nature* (Berman, 1981) was subsequently strengthened by the advocation of *the parsimony principle*, a principle which required scientists to reduce natural phenomena to their lowest possible, that is, most material and measurable level. According to this principle scientists should try to stick to material levels of explanation such as neurophysiological or genetic ones, instead of opting for explanations of a mental, let alone socio-cultural nature (Dijksterhuis, 1985). This has led to a neglect of the complexity of animals and animal life, since cognitive priority was given to those aspects of animals which can be measured and controlled. The other aspects of animals, those which can hardly be measured in terms of mainstream biological methodology, are therefore dismissed as secondary or, worse, rationalized out of existence. Thus, the part of animals under scrutiny in the laboratory and under control of the average natural scientist comes to represent *the whole animal*.

On top of all this came the Cartesian notion of animal-machine, a view which denied animals all subjectivity, agency, feeling, suffering, needs, fear or knowledge (Dibon, 1954). Animals end up as passive and law-bound products of the laws of living matter. In the eyes of scientists they appear like objects, to be broken down into their constituent parts and measurable properties, as though they are some kind of construct which one can get to know by examining its building-stones (Easlea, 1980). This approach boils down to the registering of the animal's measurable properties by way of exterior cognitive contact, that is, *from without*.

Whether inorganic nature can be understood that way is itself doubtful, but as soon as one starts treating living beings in this manner one is bound to run into difficulties. The only equipment mainstream science seems to have available is concepts and methods pertaining to machine-like phenomena. Indeed, a machine's totality is a juxtaposition of bits and pieces with different functions and properties. But animals are not machines. They are more than the sum of their measurable parts: they are unities which are hard to subdivide without losing their character. For example, if one dissects them they may die, and building them up again will not bring them back to life. The very processes of living and dying, so crucial in living beings and so unlike machines, seem almost to be embarrassments to the measuring scientist who, not knowing how to handle these things, chooses to ignore them. Rather he endeavours to transform what is alive into something lifeless: an object with properties. Erich Fromm has called this the necrophilous tendency in modern science (Fromm, 1973).

Animals are unlike machines in that they move and react to their environment. They grow, develop, and have capacities for self-building and self-repair. Machines on the other hand, have been put into motion from without, their movement being basically repetitive. Contrary to machines animals possess an inner-directedness as well as a capacity for self-direction. Most of all, animals distinguish themselves from machines by what Adolf Portmann has named 'inwardness' (Portmann, 1973). Besides exterior properties, notable from without, animals have a mysterious inner side, a self if you like, which is bound to evade a science which contents itself with registering from without.

Even within the paradigm of that science which concerns itself specifically with animals i.e. Darwin's nineteenth century theory of evolution and its twenty century extensions such as sociobiology, animals tend to be portrayed as outcomes of the blind-working mechanism of natural selection. Darwin himself still left some room for purposeful action, judgement and choice on the part of the animal as well as for tentative animal cultures as *causal* factors in evolution. But, on the whole, Darwinians consider social and cultural behaviour as a result rather than as a cause of evolution. From the perspective of mainstream biologists animals are primarily passive vehicles for genes. According to this view animals will inadvertently exhibit that behaviour which will promote their genes into the next generation. Note that in this view all crucial animal properties are conceived of as hereditary, that is, they are taken to reside 'in the genes'. This is inevitable if one sees the natural selection of genes as the engine behind all animal life (Wilson, 1975). After all, genes are present in individual organisms, not in cultures. And it is by means of the individual's reproductive organs that genes are transmitted.

Generally speaking, mainstream scientists do not possess the methodological equipment to conceptualize the non-material aspects of the animal condition such as subjecthood and agency, let alone sociality, culture and meanings as adhered to by animals in groups (Noske 1989). Needless to say that people in the mainstream life sciences are running the risk of giving biological deterministic explanations of animal behaviour. Many researchers of animal behaviour do indeed impart a very mechanistic sort of animal image. Judging from their comments (at least when they speak professionally) animals do not prefer, want or love, let alone create culture, but instead are endowed with a certain behaviour caused by some mechanism and triggered by some stimulus (Caplan, 1978).

Underlying this failure to acknowledge animal-human continuity in its mental and cultural capacity is yet another factor: the fear among biologists of being accused of *anthropomorphism,* of attributing exclusively human characteristics to animals. Characteristics which usually come under this heading would typically be the ungraspable and unmeasurable aspects of animals, such as personhood, sentience, inwardness and agency, precisely those which cannot be tackled within the framework of animal science. However, only if an animal scientist goes as far as saying that all animal traits which cannot be measured in the laboratory therefore do not exist, can he or she safely brand any comparison of non-physical animal features as misplaced anthropomorphism (Noske 1997).

Presently there are some courageous animal scientists who do say that animals are more human-like and less machine-like than their own sciences will have us believe. Often they will say such things off the record and rather apologetically, aware that they are committing something close to sacrilege from the point of view of the sciences. As a result, such people often reveal a curious tension between the accepted scientific codes and their own experiences with animal personhood. Basically they face a dilemma in that there seems to be no option to imposing upon animals either object status or *human* subject status. However animals are neither machines nor human. As yet there exists in mainstream scientific thinking little room for the notion of a non-human Subject.

Little attention has so far been paid to the possibility that it is not just human subjects who socially and collectively construct their world but that animal subjects may do so too. These animal constructions are likely to be markedly different from ours but none the less real. We may even note that animal world-views are in many respects much more refined than ours (Roberts 1996, Parelli 2002).

Not many people have seriously tried to imagine what it must be like to perceive and conceive the world in terms of olfactory images (such as dogs must do) or tactile images (as horses do). These examples make it abundantly clear we, humans, are heavily biased towards the visual. For us, seeing is believing; our truths are in terms of visual clues. If we were suddenly confronted with a world constructed in terms of scent, we would be at a complete loss and a dog might easily come to doubt our consciousness, the way some of us worry about the existence of consciousness in animals.

Compared with dogs we are absolutely scent-blind (Hearne 1987). The horse's world is also different from ours. In addition to being eye-oriented horses speak and listen with their skins to an extent which has caused horse expert Vicki Hearne to use the term 'skin mode of thought'. According to her, every muscle of the human rider will be a loud symphony to the horse underneath, but the horse has no way of knowing whether the rider is talking to him intentionally. The rider's skin talk may just be 'tactile noise', inadvertently created by the rider. The horse in turn will send out messages which, however, will often be misinterpreted or even go unnoticed by the rider. To a horse, feeling is believing, many horse truths are tactile.

Animals are social and cultural Others with their own agency and we should acknowledge them as such. They see, smell, feel, taste or hear the world against the background of their own frames of reference. They, like us, distinguish and select among sense impressions, distinctions which we do not even know are there (Griffin, 1982). There is a way things look, taste, smell, feel or sound to an animal, a way of which we will have no idea as long as we go on believing that we humans are the only ones with Subjecthood in the world; as long as we insist that the only things worth knowing about are our own constructions, scientific or not.

Eastern ways of conceptualizing animals

What about Eastern wisdom traditions? How do they conceive of animals? Although I cannot claim to be an expert on Eastern approaches, I can offer several comments. In Buddhism there is a sense of kinship of all life. Theoretically this would open the way for an appreciation of animal-human continuity. It is acknowledged that animals are sentient beings who suffer like we do (Kunzang Lama'I Shelung, 1994, 202-204). There are numerous texts which admonish people against killing, hurting and torturing animals, especially in Tibetan Buddhism (Kunzang Lama'I Shelung, 1994, 77-78, 102-104.), and also against forcing – domestic animals (sic) – to work too hard for us (Kunzang Lama'I Shelung, 1994, 199).

Eating meat is a dilemma for Buddhists. Early Buddhist texts in the Pali language permit monks to eat meat with certain exceptions. Many texts do contain prohibitions against eating meat though in some monks are allowed to eat meat in specific circumstances. The Buddha does allow monks to cook and eat the remains of animals killed by lions, tigers, hyenas and wolves (Vinaya Pitakam, I, 98). In modern terms, the monks are obviously permitted to 'scavenge' and perhaps even to steal (?) from animals.

In some Buddhist texts animals are anthropomorphised. Over half of the Jataka stories show animals as chief characters such as The Goat That Laughed and Wept (Kawasaki 1995) and similarly dog, snake, tiger, lion, hyena, rabbit, hare, fox, crow, cat, bull, elephant, bear and others figure in these stories. Just like humans all these animals are shown to be talking, plotting, winning, as well as losing and blundering.

In these Jataka stories and related texts it is argued that animals may not be ethical but could be called virtuous. Animals, according to this view, have a latent capacity for affection, devotion to their offspring, and even heroism and self-sacrifice. The possibility of the animal mind 'having ideas' and self-consciousness has also been put forward (Sugatananda 1961, pers. comm. Sarao, 2004). So it appears that the Buddhist tradition does grant animals 'inwardness'.

There is also a strand of Buddhism however – less popular but certainly present – which puts forward a much less favourable view of animals. In this context animals are said to suffer continually, on the one hand from being exploited by humans, but on the other from their own stupidity (cf. Kunzang Lama'I Shelung, 1994, 76, and Schmithausen, 1997). Not only are animals intellectually inferior and lacking insight, but since they cannot understand the Buddhist doctrine, they therefore cannot attain liberation. They would achieve this only if, in a later existence, they were reborn as humans, which is regarded as possible but very rare (Schmithausen, 1997). The same author lists a number of other reasons why, according to Buddhism, animalkind suffers more than humankind. The animals' existence is considered to be extremely unhappy, not only because of certain aspects of nature itself, such as predator-prey relationships, but also because many animals live on 'disgusting food' or in uncomfortable places. In contrast to the Jataka stories, where animals are endowed with human-like inwardness and virtues, here they are considered to be morally inferior to humans and even wicked, because of their promiscuity sometimes even including incest (Schmithausen, ibid). In contrast to rebirth as a human, rebirth as an animal is hence regarded as an evil rebirth (Schmithausen, ibid.). Those humans who lead a bad life are punished by being reincarnated as an animal (Vibhanga, 1969, 444).

Questions arise from consideration of the Buddhist literature. How can Buddhists be so confident about animals being morally inferior and living a lower and unhappier life than humans? Have these Buddhist teachers really thought through what it is like to be an animal? What does this tell us about their underlying image of animals? One is almost tempted to conclude that Buddhist teachings are equally biased against animals and their behaviour, and that they too are measuring animals with a human yardstick like the Western scientists.

Animals clearly reside at the bottom of the Buddhist hierarchy which, it has been argued, makes it indeed not all that different to the western idea of the Great Chain of Being (Preece, 1999). The Great Chain of Being, originally an Aristotelian notion, was characterised by both continuity and hierarchy (Noske 1989 and 1997). In Buddhism there is mention of a similar chain: *The Chain of Becoming.*

So, what hope do Eastern traditions, at least as shown in the Buddhist literature, hold for animals? They undoubtedly view animals as sentient subjects with inwardness, and neither as just objects for human use nor as parsimonious vehicles for genes. But does it go any further than that? Are these Eastern philosophies any less anthropocentric in content than their Western counterparts? Are they willing to pay attention, not just to animals as victims of human practices but to animals in their own right, as Other but not necessarily Lesser beings? Is there room for non-human Subjects, endowed with a different kind of subjecthood, yet perfectly capable of experiencing and constructing their own worlds? These will be interesting questions to pursue.

In his book on the treatment of animals in the various cultures of the world Rod Preece is asking yet another important question: If Buddhism and other oriental traditions claim such a respect for their non-human fellow beings, why is that respect not generally realised in those areas where these thought systems predominate (Preece, 1999)? The answer according to Preece is 'disengagement': the non-assertion, non-forcing, an attitude of withdrawal into the self in many Eastern religions. There is not a cohesive and strenuous effort for the general welfare of humankind, let alone for the welfare of animalkind. In practice, animals often go unprotected in these regions. There is perhaps one clear exception to this rule: the religion of Jainism, one with a relatively small number of followers who nevertheless are the most radical in their reverence for life. Their philosophy is an activist one which indeed has made some difference in the region (Preece ibid.).

Acknowledgement

With many thanks to Professor K.T.S Sarao, Head of the Department of Buddhist Studies, University of Delhi, India, for clarifying Buddhist concepts and providing references to Buddhist works, in personal communication.

References

Berman, M. (1981), *The Re-enchantment of the World*. Ithaca: Cornell University Press.

Caplan, A. L. editor (1978), *The Sociobiology Debate, Readings on Ethical and Scientific Issues*. New York: Harper & Row.

Dibon, P. (1954), Le problème de l'âme des bêtes chez Descartes et ses premiers disciples néerlandais. *Mens en Dier. Opstellen in een gedenkboek voor Prof. Mgr. Dr. F.L.K. Sassen*. Amsterdam: NV Standaard Boekhandel.

Dijksterhuis, E.J. (1985), *De Mechanisering van het Wereldbeeld*. Amsterdam: Meulenhoff,

Easlea, B. (1980), *Witch Hunting, Magic and the New Philosophy, An Introduction to Debates of the Scientific Revolution 1450 - 1750*. Brighton: Harvester Press.

Fromm, E. (1973), *The anatomy of human destructiveness*. New York: Holt, Rinehart and Winston.

Griffin D. editor (1982), *Animal Mind – Human Mind,* Dahlem Konferenzen. Berlin: Springer Verlag.

Hearne, V. (1987), *Adam's Task, Calling Animals by Name.* London: Heinemann

Kawasaki K & V. (retold by) (1995), *Jataka Tales of the Buddha,* Part 1. Kandy (Sri Lanka): Buddhist Publication Society.

Kunzang Lama'I Shelung. (1994), *The Words of my Perfect Teacher,* translated by the Padmakara Translation Group, edited by Kerry Brown and Sima Sharma. San Francisco: HarperCollins.

Noske, B. (1989), *Humans and Other Animals.* London: Pluto Press.

Noske, B. (1997) *Beyond Boundaries: Humans and Animals.* Montreal: Black Rose Books.

Parelli, P. (2002), *Natural Horse-man-ship.* Colorado Springs: Western Horseman Magazine.

Portmann, A. (1973), *Biologie und Geist.* Suhrkamp, Frankfurt am Main.

Preece, R. (1999), *Animals and Nature, Cultural Myths, Cultural Realities:* Vancouver: UBC Press.

Roberts, M. (1996), *The Man who Listens to Horses.* New York: Random House.

Schmithausen, L. (1997), The Early Buddhist Tradition and Ecological Ethics. VI The Status of Animals. *Journal of Buddhist Ethics,* **4**, 1-74.

Sugatananda, A. P. (1961), *The Place of Animals in Buddhism (Francis Story),* Vol. **VIII**, 3.

Vibhanga. (1969), *The Book of Analysis,* translated from Pali by Pathamakyaw Ashin Thittila (Setthila) Aggamahapandita. London: Pali Text Society/Luzac.

Vinaya Pitakam (1938-1966), *The Book of Discipline,* 6 Vols. translated by I.B.Horner. London: Pali Text Society.

Wilson, E.O. (1975), *Sociobiology, the New Synthesis.* Cambridge Mass: Bellknap Press.

Clinical meditation: fundamentals and principles

Maurits Kwee
President of the Transcultural Society for Clinical Meditation

Dr Kwee chose to give a PowerPoint display at the Seventh International Conference of the Transnational Network for the Study of Physical, Psychological and Spiritual Wellbeing. It was not possible to reproduce that here, in this book.

His work for the Transcultural Society for Clinical Meditation (TSCM) may be followed up by contacting Dr. Kwee <dr.k.t.kaku@planet.nl>

Website http://www.constructivism123.com/Links/TSCM.htm [Google, Teoma].

An article, "NeoZEN", published in *Constructivism in the Human Sciences,* **8(2):** 181-202, by Dr Kwee is recommended for students interested in the thrust of his approach.

On the substance and structure of the 'soul': comparing, contrasting and complementing methods of eastern and western approaches to holistic health

Otto Reichard
Fellow of the Australian & New Zealand
College of Psychiatrists

Evolutionary background common to east and west

Consciousness and self-consciousness are the substance of the 'soul'. These are emergent processes in the brain and, in my opinion, constitute *mind*, which is essentially a response by representation as distinct from direct reflex action. In its efficiency and intricacy it is exponential and creative. It is not an epiphenomenon. Our Western language structures our experience with phenomenological dualities such as body and mind, nature and reason, behaviour and experience which help create an illusion of a disconnected mind.

The Darwinian principle of natural selection, useful though it is in accounting for the progression to increasingly complex organisms, is insufficient. It is necessary to postulate a process of *integrative selection* to understand sufficient complexity organized in a hierarchical, morphogenetic fashion; that is in tiers; energy, information and meaning. That is, a selection process with energy at its base, carried piggy back on it but creating a new tier of cybernetic selection is information, and finally, meaning carried on the back of information – ecce home.

Differences between us or complementary principles?

Rather than just fit in with immediate necessity, human beings have constructed different traditions and different styles of coping. And these acquired *cultures* transform the individual. The physical and social environment is actively changed under the influence of cultural values. In Western societies we have created environments, both physical and social, that risk being very artificial and unsustainable. We have, as human beings, the creative resources, at least potentially, to solve the problems that we have made for ourselves.

Rather than weigh in on the side of one or other cultural pattern, or religious doctrine, East or West, it may be more useful to see the differences as complementary. Then we could expand our resources for corrective action. And we need to learn from each other to build a more cohesive world.

A few general points

As therapists, working with individuals, we should not, in my opinion, work only with symptoms, the self or the situation alone but see their interaction. Neither should we work only with what is pathological but with the whole person, including his/her intrinsic healing power, hopes, happiness and affirmation of their humanity.

Therapy is an art, and should remain so, albeit based on science, to be practiced in an ethical framework, understanding one's own ethics and the ethics of the patient. In practice, disorders and faulty ethics are not as separate as doctors sometimes seem to think. The Wisdom traditions, rather than Western medicine, point to that interconnection.

In assessing questions of health, a holistic approach should be used, the total *gestalt* of whole human beings and ecology.

Structure and function are the dialectics of natural science, but facts and values are the dialectics of human science.

With these preliminary thoughts, I offer some illustrative diagrams dealing with the principles of:

1. Phenomenological duality

2. Anthropological structure

3. Eastern versus Western Philosophy

4. Holistic Health and Healing

5. Positive Skepticism and Post modem plurality

The principles of phenomenological duality

Human experience rests on phenomenological dualities such as:

The body and the mind,
Nature and consciousness,
Behavior and Experience.

Each of these pairs of terms

i. Are experienced as two separate (nay sometimes disparate) entities, but constantly inter:acting.

ii. Even though ontologically there need to be no duality (Descartes error!)

iii. But only an increasingly 'complex evolution" of morphogenetic structures has the potential to explain it!

Yet I am still in awe of Awareness: the magic, mystery and miracle of Consciousness!

THE PRINCIPLE OF ANTHROPOLOGICAL STRUCTURE

It is based on the complexity of 'Integrative Selection' that operates (in nature, society and therapy) on the evolutionary structures:

i. Hierarchically
ii. Morphogenetically
iii. Selectively

The anthropological principles

The toolmaker
(who transforms
him/herself and
the environment
in adjusting)

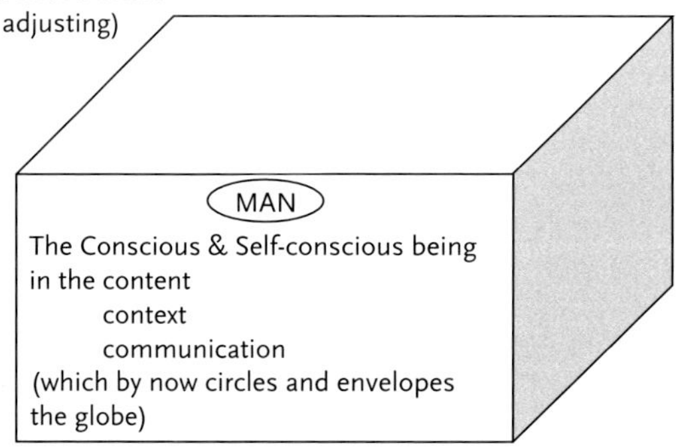

(With the limitless potential
of abstract thought and symbols
the linguistic animal

The Social being
(his/her second nature):

The Cultural Creature the creator
of it and the one created
The synthetic confluence by-Selective
Integration -of technology
language
society
(created a 'spiritual' being who
eventually grasped the infinite and
the eternal)

1. His (her) problems are a paradox: imbued by the love of Power (his evolutionary heritage) and the potential gift of the power of Love.
2. Structure and Function: are the dialectics of natural science but
3. Facts and Values: are the dialectics of social (human) science, therefore ethics as well as utility should be a central selector in health and healing

The philosophical principles of east and west

A philosophical analysis (critical evaluation) of the conflicting and contrasting approaches of the East and West leads us to a complementary resolution in a great synthesis.

The West arguing from matter to mind (the bottom up approach) the East from the spiritual qualities of Consciousness to the manifestations of the body (the top down approach)

	West	**East**
Self	Essential Psychological Reality	Superficial, even harmful A projection of our experience An illusion
Human Ecology	Passion dominated individualistic	Compassion dominated Collectivistic
Consciousness	From below: 'emerges' Reductionistic	From above 'descending' Holistic
Methods	Experimental 'objective' manipulative	Experiential 'subjective' cognitive (mindful)

THE PRINCIPLES OF HOLISTIC HEALTH & HEALING IN THERAPY

My central point is that one always has to consider the 'gestalt' of the whole human ecology in therapy and not the symptoms, the self or the situation alone.

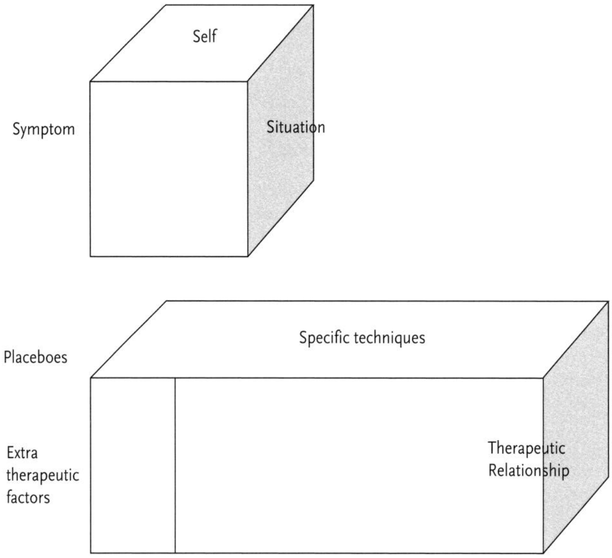

Equally: only in their interaction do they make full sense.

See Postulates

The principles of holistic health & healing in therapy II

The *different cultural approaches* with their different models, methods and masters may appear very different, but precisely because of that: complementary nevertheless

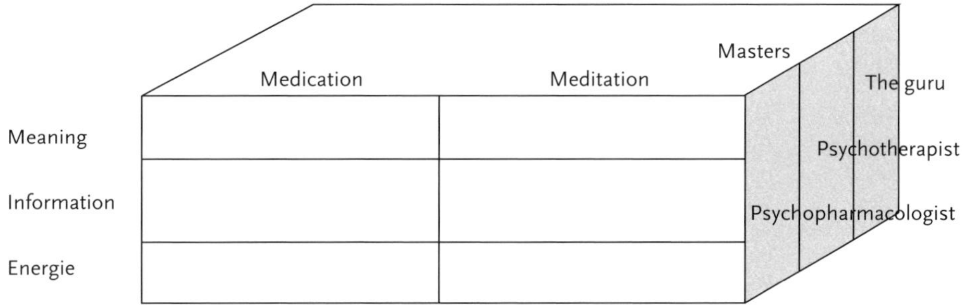

Medication
Meditation
Etc.

Have their selection mechanisms at different levels of this Energy Information & Meaning "chain of change"; one working from below-up, the other from top down yet operating on the same ends by different means

In the spirit of positive skepticism and using pluralistic approaches we would like to throw open the debate to the problems and paradoxes of Consciousness, Self, the Human ecology toward Holistic Health and Healing in bridging the Gaps

Interdependent themes and theories of reality associated with postmoderism

Constructive	Pluralist	Contextualist	Relativist	Perspectivism
Individuals are Constantly and actively constructing their realities a. **Radical:** no reality beyond personal experience b. **Critical:** accept existence of real world but it can never be directly known c. **Social:** self not a personal but social construction	There is no single theory but rather a plurality with claims Michael Faucault: do not ask me who I am and do not expect me to remain the same".	All knowledge or truth are intelligible only within their specific context	Challenges science's causal explanation suggests instead a 'descriptive model' of infinitely complex interwoven relationships; emphasis on how things are related or interact	Is the process of decentering the Self and seeing all views as perspectival, interpretive or constructive. **Deconstruction** Recognition of how construction relies both on 'presence' and 'absence'

Mindfulness and cognitive therapy in the management of chronic pain

Lynne Bousfield
Clinical psychologist, Sydney

The following paper is derived from a workshop that aimed to provide some understanding of Buddhist mindfulness (Vipassana) meditation and explore its application alongside cognitive therapy in the treatment of chronic pain and its consequences, such as depression. While the paper notes more recent research, the workshop was first presented in 2000 at a Buddhism and Psychotherapy Conference and emphasised a practical experience of mindfulness rather than a theoretical discussion. While practical exercises have not been included in the paper, without the understanding that comes from training in and personal experience of a technique that develops mindfulness, such as Vipassana, attempting to apply it in a therapeutic context either alone or in conjunction with a psychological therapy is likely to be unskilful and unsuccessful.

Cognitive therapy

Underlying rationale

Cognitive therapy is an approach to the treatment of psychological problems that teaches us about how we have structured our everyday experiences. The cognitive model is based upon the rationale that "an individual's affect and behaviour are largely determined by the way in which he structures the world" (Beck, 1967, 1976; cited in Beck, Rush, Shaw and Emery, 1979, p. 3). This means that as we experience daily events the way we think about them results in the development of attitudes and beliefs. In time, certain beliefs may become dominant and dictate our thought processes and as a consequence the way we feel and behave (Beck *et al.*, 1979). That is, we build a belief structure through which we filter our experience and determine our reactions to the events in our lives. Should that structure become lopsided or be built upon shaky foundations it can mean that the way in which we react becomes maladaptive. We may notice certain unhelpful patterns in our lives, or difficulties in particular areas of behaviour, or at worst we develop a mental disorder. In that case cognitive therapy can teach us how to identify our psychological structures (our dysfunctional beliefs) and how to rebuild or restructure them.

In cognitive therapy, cognitions or thoughts are the focus of treatment, for the individual and for the therapist. However, treatment techniques are usually an integration of cognitive and behavioural approaches. This combination is generally referred to as cognitive behaviour therapy and both dysfunctional behaviours and thoughts are modified through its systematic approach.

Cognitive therapy relies upon a supportive partnership between the client and the therapist, the aim being the mental health of the client in line with the client's goals. In this partnership the therapist is responsive to the client's present moment experience in therapy as well as to the prior experiences the client recounts during therapy. Cognitive therapy requires clients to pay attention to the here and now. Earlier life experiences are understood as influencing current experience but recollections of them are not the stuff of therapy (Beck *et al.*, 1979).

STRATEGIES

Primary to cognitive therapy is the teaching of the connection between thoughts, feelings and behaviour. Cognitive therapy posits that the client's core problems or beliefs are accessible and modifiable through investigation of dysfunctional cognitions (Beck *et al.*, 1979). The aim is not simply symptom reduction but changing the belief systems that have underpinned them (Beck *et al.*, 1979). Clients learn to monitor the thoughts they have, especially in situations when they feel disturbed or distressed and to become aware of the connection between those thoughts and how they feel and act. They are taught to test their thoughts, to evaluate them and not to simply assume that because they have a thought it must correspond to reality. They learn to test unhelpful patterns of thinking, like "double standards", "all or nothing thinking" and "unrealistic expectations". On the basis of this testing they learn that it is possible to re-think their reaction to identified situations – that is, they learn that there may be many other ways they can think about a particular situation and that these other ways of thinking may also be more valid or reasonable reflections of the situation. Through this process clients begin to develop an awareness of patterns of thought processes that point to underlying beliefs and the possibility of changing those beliefs (Beck *et al.*, 1979).

Cognitive therapy is an educational process – strategies are taught, learnt and applied. It has been used in the treatment of all manner of clinical disorders. As a psychological therapy it aims to relieve psychological distress and is therefore aimed at a clinical population.

Mindfulness

Underlying rationale

According to Lazarus, "the bulk of psychotherapeutic endeavours may be said to centre around the correction of misconceptions" (1972:165). The Buddha also said something along these lines, not about therapy, but about the alleviation of the suffering associated with the human condition. As far as the Buddha was concerned we are all in need of the therapy that achieved this result.

Therefore the basic issue in the teachings of the Buddha and the practice of mindfulness is seeing the misconceptions or errors of perception inherent in our everyday experience – and through seeing them, overcoming mental suffering.

The Buddha spoke about the kind of suffering that our clients' report, that is the emotional pain associated with mental conditions and physical illness. He also spoke about the suffering or unsatisfactoriness that we experience as a result of change. We do not normally think about conditions like persistent pain or depression in this way, that is, as a change from a more pleasant state. However, the practices the Buddha taught lead to seeing change at a microscopic level and he taught that the understanding borne of this perception reduces the suffering associated with all conditioned phenomena, that is anything that arises from causes.

So, this is one of the first things we need to understand about mindfulness – it involves attention to change.

The Buddha taught about suffering, the cause of suffering and the cessation of suffering. He taught that meditation practice was not only for the benefit of people we as therapists may consider psychologically disturbed. Psychological disturbance is considered to exist for anyone who lacks the understanding of the impermanence, the intrinsic unsatisfactoriness and the lack of controllability or personal identity associated with all experience. Any understanding other than this is considered a misconception – and all of what Buddha taught was directed at overcoming such misconceptions. Mindfulness is a central component but there is also an ethical component that is based upon the understanding that ethical or moral actions will produce skilful results, while unethical actions lead to unpleasant results (Guneratana, 1993).

So another thing to understand about meditation practices that develop mindfulness is that they are embedded within a theory, just as the strategies we use within cognitive therapy for example, are also embedded within a theory.

Like cognitive therapy meditation practice requires being here, now. The educational process involved in learning mindfulness is primarily experiential, not intellectual. Similar to the role of a therapist in cognitive therapy it is also important to have a guiding teacher when learning mindfulness meditation.

Perhaps most importantly, we must also be clear that mindfulness as taught by the Buddha is part of the path to enlightenment. This path is based upon the teaching that suffering is the result of desire, which has arisen due to our misunderstanding of what makes us happy. In terms of cognitive therapy enlightenment could perhaps be likened to the removal of all negative or maladaptive cognitive and behavioural patterns. This is something that cognitive therapists would not generally formulate as a goal even if it were considered possible. So the end goal of mindfulness is not the same as a time-limited therapeutic intervention such as cognitive therapy, although the pursuit of some kind of happiness is surely a reason why people attend therapy. The development of mindfulness was not aimed at a clinical population in the same sense as is cognitive therapy.

With this preliminary information about mindfulness, can we now say what mindfulness is and how we develop it?

What mindfulness is

On reading about mindfulness in books on meditation we will see it described along the lines of "being in the present moment, seeing the true nature of experience" or "seeing things just as they are". What does this mean? The practise of mindfulness is experiential, not intellectual. Without being told what to see, meditation techniques are practised that will evidently allow the practitioner to "see things as they are". Understanding comes from direct experience rather than trying to think it through and put it into a psychological or scientific frame of reference.

How, then, can we make sense of it from a scientific psychological perspective?

The first step in "seeing things as they are" is paying attention. This basic attention is the kind of superficial mindfulness we already have and apply in our day-to-day lives.

Therefore, mindfulness has something to do with attention and its development.

Mindfulness requires effort to remember to pay attention to our present moment physical or mental experience. We do not usually notice making this effort in our daily lives or with our clients because we have usually moved on to *thinking about* our experience. Quite often when people begin to learn meditation they report they are "thinking about" their experience rather than simply noticing it. Observation of experience and thinking about experience are not the same. In the practise of meditation the effort we make to develop mindfulness is to repeatedly observe all experience, mental or physical. In cognitive therapy the effort we make is primarily to repeatedly challenge or evaluate thoughts. This means mindfulness involves applying our attention and maintaining or sustaining attention. When we make the effort to pay attention to our experience we will notice how that experience behaves, meaning we will be able to "see it as it is".

Mindfulness is not a passive state of mind or a trance-like state. It is not passive attention. Mindfulness is an active, penetrative observation, free of thoughts or judgements about what is observed (U Pandita, 1992). Attention is not forced but it is regulated and directed. So mindfulness entails some control of attention.

However, while mindfulness and attention control may be used interchangeably in the psychological literature, equating mindfulness with attention control does not allow a complete understanding of mindfulness. In the Buddhist literature the Pali word translated as mindfulness is *sati* and there are several other Pali terms for different kinds of attention, including *manisekara* (the initial turning of the mind towards the object) and *vittaka* (taking attention to the object) to name two (U Silananda, 1994). Concentration (*samadhi* in Pali) can also be considered a form of attention control. While concentration and mindfulness are developed and balanced in practices that train the mind in mindfulness, they are considered to be separate mental factors.

The psychological literature has also described mindfulness as a meta process, as meta cognition and meta awareness (Teasdale, Moore, Hayhurst, Pope, Williams & Segal, 2002). Meta cognition is described as the awareness of thoughts as thoughts without the usual personal identification with the thoughts involving a conscious shift called "decentering or disidentification" (Teasdale *et al.*, 2002). In practice, mindfulness entails observation of the emergence, development, elaboration and disappearance of conditioned phenomena, not just thoughts. Mindfulness engages the object of attention directly, while not identifying with it. Perhaps non-identification conveys this sense better than disidentification, which could imply negation or separation.

Seeing it as it is according to the Buddha

The Buddha taught that by paying attention to body sensations, thoughts and emotions, indeed whatever experience arises and passes, then we shall "see the true nature" of experience. What we begin to see and understand is that each sensation, thought or emotion is simply that, a sensation, a thought or an emotion, that has no power over us other than the power we invest through self-identification ("its happening to me"). Ultimately, what is seen is that entanglement or self-identification is unnecessary because these experiences are intrinsically impermanent and unsatisfactory.

In Buddhist *abhidhamma* (psychology/metaphysics) the process of experience commences with contact or awareness of an object of experience at a sense door (eg, a person is seen by the eye and the conscious mind) (U Silananda, 1994). At this moment of contact there is a passive recognition of the presentation of that object (the person) at the sense door (the eye), without fully understanding the nature of the object, the nature of what is seen (U Silananda, 1994). What is understood is whether what is seen is pleasant or unpleasant, in varying degrees. What follows is a clearer perception of the person, recognising, investigating and naming the person, making decisions about them and thinking about acting upon these thoughts. It is here that we make discriminations about the person, such as whether we like them or not. This process happens very quickly yet should we be able to observe our experience with some degree of refinement. It is at this point that we are in the position to *choose* what follows, whether misconceptions are conditioned and identification and entanglement arise, whether our thoughts, emotions and action will be helpful or harmful.

Not seeing it as it is

Our clients often present to therapy because they feel they no longer have any choices. In our everyday lives, our train of thoughts and emotions can become a well-worn way of reacting to what we find is difficult or uncertain or threatening. Often no real threat may be involved but we may continue to react as if there is one. Chronic pain is a typical case. We normally think of pain as a signal – a signal that something is wrong. This signal is sent by specialised nerve endings from parts of the body along the spinal cord to the brain. This is the moment of contact. Without fully understanding the nature of the signal we experience it as unpleasant. Based upon our past experiences the unpleasantness leads to a perception of threat and that leads to an array of physiological responses to enable us to avoid or overcome the threat. Unfortunately with chronic or persistent pain, the signal is no longer a signal of threat. If we continue to understand it in that way we magnify the suffering associated with it, because the perception of threat enhances the perception of pain. It turns into a self-defeating spiral. The reactions to the pain become habitual and in this sense we mistake them for some kind of enduring reality – we no longer see the connections – the connection between pain and reaction to pain – so we no longer see that we have a choice about how we make some of those connections.

Mindfulness can cut through this well-worn way of reacting and bring back the possibility of choice. This occurs through observing experience, through observing the reactions in the present moment. While we could equate this to a kind of self-monitoring in the language of cognitive therapy, in meditation practice the interest is not in the content of thoughts, only that thinking has occurred *and dissolved and is not me, not my pain*. There is no attempt to change the thought or underlying belief as in cognitive therapy. (Although the Buddha did teach techniques of thought challenging – see Appendix). There is also no interest in the history that conditioned the arising of the thought. The connection between thought and emotion in the present moment is observed. When emotion arises, the interest is in the observation of the emotion, as far as that is possible depending upon the intensity of the emotion and the strength of mindfulness. With mindfulness the aim is clear seeing – learning how to observe the experience rather than only see it fleetingly before our habitual conceptual interpretation of it kicks in and we just start thinking about it. Training in this way reduces the tendency to become entangled with thoughts, with pain. It increases our ability to redirect attention away from engagement with them and allows us to be more dispassionate and tolerant of them.

The various practices of developing mindfulness taught by the Buddha had the specific aim of bringing about psychological change. Mindfulness is non judgemental and does not aim to rid the mind of certain experiences or thoughts and get other ones in their place. However, through the careful practice of mindfulness we will notice that the mind does become conditioned such that unskilful thoughts will arise less and more skilful ones will take their place. It may be a little hard to understand how observation alone can bring about change – it doesn't – the reality is that the observation is *of the change*. The more we clearly see change the more we reduce our normal tendency of getting caught up in our reactions of trying to resist change. The more we accept change the more we see we have choice.

Experiencing mindfulness

The essential teaching of the Buddha that most explicitly discusses mindfulness and the development of mindfulness is the Satipatthana Sutta or The Four Foundations of Mindfulness (see Soma Thera, 1975). U Silananda (1990) presents the text of the Sutta accompanied by explanations that clarify both the understanding and practices that develop mindfulness. It is not possible to offer detail on the Sutta in the brief account below, nevertheless, it is important it be included for completeness since the Sutta is a resource for any proper understanding of mindfulness, or of any practice that claims to develop mindfulness.

The four foundations of mindfulness

These four foundations cover all our phenomenal experience. They direct us to look at our experience in a way that is a little different from what we are accustomed in our everyday lives. They are as follows:

(i) *Mindfulness of the Body*: Mindfulness of the body includes the repeated observation of body movements of bending, stretching etc. as well as the movement of the abdomen as we breathe, and body postures of sitting, standing, walking and lying.

(ii) *Mindfulness of Feelings*: Here feeling does not mean emotion. Rather it includes the observation of both physical and mental impressions in terms of whether they are pleasant, unpleasant or neutral. For example, it may be observation of the unpleasant quality associated with a particular physical experience. When we experience painful physical sensations our normal tendency is to react to the pain, with dislike, annoyance and wishing for the pain to disappear. If we can apply effort to develop mindfulness to observe the sensations, the arising of this reaction is guarded against or limited. This will reduce the suffering associated with the reaction and with the physical pain. Of course until mindfulness is strong enough it requires some courage and patience to be able to observe the more unpleasant sensations and to begin to see that negative affect is only one possible construction in response to nociceptive input or the signal of pain.

(iii) *Mindfulness of Consciousness*: This is knowing the overall condition of the mind, for example, whether the mind is concentrated, distracted, stressed, calm, sleepy, speedy, jumbled, clear, quiet, angry, bored etc. The mind is considered to consist of both consciousness (or bare awareness) and the mental factors that colour consciousness (U Silananda, 1990). It is not possible to separate consciousness from what colours it, but in mindfulness of consciousness emphasis is given to bare awareness (U Silananda, 1990).

(iv) *Mindfulness of Mental and Material Objects*: This area includes the contemplation of the array of those things that colour consciousness. That is, the emphasis is mindfulness of those things rather than of the consciousness that arises with them. It includes thoughts, ideas, sense perceptions and even mindfulness itself.

Labelling and mindfulness of pain

Labelling is a technique used in the practice of meditation described in my workshop (Vipassana meditation in the tradition of the late Ven. Mahasi Sayadaw). Some people think labelling the object of observation does not fit with the cultivation of mindfulness because it could encourage thinking about it instead. This is a misunderstanding of the use of labelling. If when using labelling attention is placed on the words rather than what is being observed then labelling is not being used appropriately. Some benefits of labelling are described below and are in accordance with the Satipatthana Sutta (U Silananda audiotapes). In the following outline the usefulness of the labelling technique when developing mindfulness in relation to pain and the reaction to pain is described.

As we pay attention to each mental or physical experience that arises (the objects of our attention) we name or label them. This arouses concentration because the label reminds us to sustain attention on the object being observed, for example, pain or an emotional reaction to the pain. We need concentration to keep the mind steady on the object. We cannot examine an object with mindfulness unless we can focus and sustain attention on it.

By labelling, we also identify the object. For example, we know it as one kind of mental or physical state or another. When pain arises, we can label it according to its quality that is, as a sensation according to its elemental nature. For example, "heavy, heavy", or "hard, hard" or "hot, hot" etc. Similarly when fear arises, we can label it "fear, fear" and we know fear is in the mind. Labelling can help us to stay with the experience of the pain or emotion and begin to know its characteristics. Applying the label is not a message to start having thoughts about the object, like, "hmm, this is interesting, why am I feeling fearful about this?" This is not labelling and it is not mindfulness, it is thinking. Practice with labelling can be extremely helpful in reducing discursive thinking because it reduces identification with what is observed. The label is not "I am heavy" but simply "heavy", not "I am frightened", simply "fear".

By naming the pain or fear being experienced we are acknowledging it for what it is and not trying to camouflage it or suppress it – it is right out in the open – and this is invaluable for us to understand it. The experience of having chronic pain can be scary – there are persistent symptoms that clients might think mean they are dying or going crazy and then someone gives it a name, "chronic pain". Naming it has not really done much to increase their understanding of it, but somehow they do not feel like they are dying or going crazy anymore. The label has reduced the self-identification and opened up the possibility of choice – choosing craziness or something different. Labelling can have this result when arousing mindfulness as well. Mostly clients with pain are not encouraged to look at the pain and one consequence can be they believe they have no choice about their aversive reactions – they respond to what is difficult by trying to avoid pain or by feeling a failure. However, by learning to be mindful of the sensations of pain, and by coming face to face with them again and again, this exposure weakens the aversion. Labelling helps maintain this exposure to the experience. Mindfully observing the nature and behaviour of pain leads to meeting it better prepared. And then when pain arises it is identified for what it is with less reaction.

This will only happen if mindfulness is practised correctly. Simply passively paying attention is not enough. Mindfulness requires effort. Labelling assists with the arousal of effort as labelling encourages concentration, which activates energy. Mindfulness has to keep the object in view and is meant to be deep and penetrating not superficial, in order to observe experience clearly (U Pandita, 1992). Mindfulness does not stand off from experience – it comes face to face with it. Guneratana (2001) has called it participatory observation. When mindfulness is practised with some skill we begin to see how pain for example is not some solid endless mass. Instead it varies in intensity, it comes and goes, it arises out of various causes, it is associated with various thoughts, it manifests in different parts of the body, it creates a certain quality in the mind and body whether it be rigidity, contraction, tension or wanting the unpleasantness to go away. When these details of the experience become clear a relationship to pain develops that is quite different from getting caught up in the usual reactionary story about the pain (Guneratana, 2001). The reduction in personalisation means that instead of me being in pain, angry, depressed, whatever, there is just pain, anger, depression, and an understanding of how these things behave – that they will pass without the need to avoid or suppress them.

Doing cognitive therapy mindfully

Benefits of training clients in mindfulness

The training in the cultivation of mindfulness found within the teachings of the Buddha was not developed to overcome psychiatric illness. So for our clients what is the therapeutic value of mindfulness?

Put simply, using thoughts as the example, there is:

- everyday mindfulness – a superficial untrained level of attention that mostly misses how we automatically identify with thought;

- mindfulness as a skill – a strengthened mindfulness that increases exposure to the experience and that begins to notice the changing nature of thoughts, emotions and body sensations as they are, without judgement and with less self-reference; and

- mindfulness as a factor of enlightenment. Ultimately the purpose of cultivating mindfulness as taught by the Buddha is to see thoughts as they really are, as impermanent, dissatisfying and without any sense of ownership or self-identification.

If we are not offering clients training in mindfulness as a factor of enlightenment what we can offer is training in the skill of mindfulness. Teaching strategies to cultivate skilful mindfulness goes beyond simply paying attention to or knowing that there are thoughts or pain for example. Chronic pain patients already know they have pain, just like my cat knows the sound of the lid coming off the tuna can. Both the pain patient and the cat are paying attention (everyday mindfulness) but that does not mean they are sufficiently mindful to understand or effect any change in their relationship to their experience. Patients need to learn another way of relating to or paying attention to the experience of pain that results in less suffering. Unfortunately my cat is never likely to develop any other relationship to tuna.

Where's the (research) evidence?

In the psychological literature there is still only preliminary evidence of the efficacy of mindfulness but it is beginning to be taken more seriously. Bishop's (2002) literature review of studies using mindfulness included the following:

Randomised controlled studies (clinical samples):
A 65% reduction in total mood disturbance and a 35% reduction in stress were reported in a randomised wait-list controlled trial of the effects of a mindfulness meditation-based stress reduction program on mood and symptoms of stress in cancer outpatients (Speca, Carlson, Goodey & Angen, 2000; cited in Bishop, 2002).

Teasdale, Segal, Williams, Ridgeway, Soulsby and Lau (2000; cited in Bishop 2002) reported that a program of mindfulness-based cognitive therapy halved the rate of depression relapse.

Non-controlled studies (clinical samples):
Kabat-Zinn, Lipworth and Burney (1985; cited in Bishop 2002) applied mindfulness meditation to the self-regulation of chronic pain, following up outcomes and compliance four years after program participation (Kabat-Zinn, Lipworth, Burney & Sellers, 1987; cited in Bishop 2002). They report reduction in self-reported measures of emotional distress, psychiatric symptoms and functional disability.

Other studies, that are less methodologically robust than these according to Bishop, have examined the use of mindfulness meditation with fibromyalgia, generalized anxiety and panic disorder.

WHY USE MINDFULNESS WITH CHRONIC PAIN PATIENTS?

Teasdale *et al.* (2000) argued that the reason mindfulness contributed to reduced relapse in depression is that it modified a characteristic of depression called overgeneral memory. This is the tendency that depressed patients have to encode and recall their experiences in broad ("overgeneral") patterns rather than in more specific detail. They state that through cognitive therapy the frequent repetition of a different interpretation of experience leads to this alternative being stored in memory and therefore being more likely to be accessed. In order to circumvent future episodes of depression it is necessary that many repetitions of the adaptive pattern are stored in memory if it is to be accessed over the depressogenic pattern (Teasdale *et al.*, 2000). They go on to state that mindfulness allows this to occur as well, but without changing the thoughts themselves. How does this occur?

Mindfulness of thought involves the repeated observation of thoughts (depressive or otherwise). For this reason Teasdale *et al.* (2000) suggest mindfulness encourages more specific encoding and retrieval of information in memory, thereby also changing the overgeneral style. Importantly, mindfulness is not simply confined to the period of time that has been set aside to practise it as a formal exercise – mindfulness is applicable anytime, anywhere, from noticing a flush of embarrassment to observing the enjoyment of a sunset. Within a day there are many opportunities to strengthen our mindfulness of thoughts. This repeated mindfulness means the thought patterns that are typically associated with depression are noticed more quickly and are less likely to become overwhelming and habitual. This same reasoning obviously applies to mindfulness of painful sensations and the thoughts often associated with pain.

Treatment programs for chronic pain generally involve training in relaxation. The practice of mindfulness meditation will produce the same results as a relaxation technique, in terms of relaxation of physical and mental tension (that is, a "relaxation response") but has additional benefits, such as:

- The development of mindfulness leads to the emergence of greater awareness and we really need an awareness of what disturbs us before we can do something about it. Therefore mindfulness can lead to improvement in the ability to identify thoughts, emotions and physical sensations allowing increased discrimination between them and enhancing cognitive therapy.

- Mindfulness, like cognitive therapy, enhances our sense of responsibility and self efficacy – that there is the possibility that we can help ourselves with our problems.

- Through mindfulness painful sensations can be seen as distinct from the reactions to them. Mindful observation of painful sensations allows a controlled exposure to the sensations resulting in less fear, avoidance and self-pity.
- Mindfulness enhances concentration by reducing interference by pain in the performance of routine activities
- Practising mindfulness reduces the risk of depression relapse (depression being common among patients with chronic pain)

These improvements are the result of the change in relationship to our experience that occurs through practising the skill of mindfulness. It is evident from the cited research that even beginners in meditation, doing the amount of practice requested in a therapeutic intervention, can acquire these changes. That is, you don not have to be an advanced practitioner to experience results.

Concluding thoughts

Mindfulness is not a technique – although the psychological literature tends to portray it in that light. There are meditation techniques or methods we can follow to practise or develop mindfulness. Certainly, for many clients it is as much of a struggle to learn to meditate as it is to learn to evaluate or challenge their thoughts and beliefs. Yet some can establish an experience of tranquillity fairly quickly, others can learn to relate to their pain without fear and every now and then someone notices that their relationship to what was distressing has *dramatically* changed.

With an understanding of the psychotherapeutic application of mindfulness and the goals of meditation alongside an understanding of the theory and strategies of cognitive therapy, I hope it is clear that one is not a replacement for the other. Nor is there a need to assimilate mindfulness meditation into cognitive therapy or vice versa. The goal of cognitive therapy is to loosen the grip of certain types of dysfunctional thoughts, emotions and assumptions. As I have said, ultimately, the practice of mindfulness is not simply the replacement of negative mental states with positive ones or the replacement of dysfunctional thoughts or core beliefs with more rational ones, although this does happen. Ultimately it is the recognition that happiness or freedom from suffering is not dependent upon any thought, emotion or belief.

Appendix

The Buddha's techniques of thought challenging

The Buddha taught not only how to observe the thinking process but also how to think more rationally using techniques of thought challenging not unlike cognitive therapy. One of the aims of cognitive therapy is to make rational thinking more automatic than irrational thinking. The Buddha also taught how to cultivate thoughts that were more skilful, more likely to result in less suffering. This teaching is outlined in one of the suttas (Vitakkasanthana Sutta – Majjhima Nikaya #20)(cited in Muesse, 2001). Of course, just like in cognitive therapy, in order to challenge our unskilful thoughts we need some awareness of their unskilfulness in the first place. With mindfulness we begin to recognise unskilful thoughts just as with cognitive therapy we begin to recognise irrational ones. Muesse (2001) outlined the Buddha's techniques for dealing with unhelpful thoughts. They are listed below accompanied by a suggested comparison with a cognitive therapy technique:

- Replacement – substituting a skilful thought for an unskilful one (compare with cognitive therapy's, "what is an alternative way of thinking about this?")

- Reflection on consequences – thinking about the likely results of continuing a certain line of thinking (compare with cognitive therapy's, "what is the worst thing that will happen?")

- Redirecting – use of distraction, especially if the thought or associated emotion feels too intense to challenge we can distract ourselves until it weakens (compare with use of distraction in cognitive therapy)

- Deconstructing – use of intellectual or experiential understanding of cause and effect to understand how unskilful thoughts depend upon mistaken beliefs (compare with identifying underlying beliefs and belief rating)

- Resistance – the recognition of the debilitating effects of unskilful thinking and that these thoughts must still be strongly resisted when all other approaches fail to modify the thoughts (some similarities with thought stopping).

References

Beck, A.T., Rush, A.J., Shaw, B.F. & Emery, G. (1979), *Cognitive Therapy of Depression.* New York: The Guilford Press,

Bishop, S.R. (2002), What do we really know about mindfulness-based stress reduction? *Psychosom. Med., 64(1)*, 71-83.

Guneratana, H. (1993), *Mindfulness in Plain English.* Boston: Wisdom Publications.

Guneratana, (2001), H. *Eight Mindful Steps to Happiness.*Boston: Wisdom Publications.

Lazarus, A. (1972), *Behaviour Therapy and Beyond.* New York: McGraw-Hill.

Muesse, M.(2001), Taking responsibility for our thoughts: Reflections on the Vitakkasanthana Sutta. *Insight (2)* 31-33.

Soma Thera. (1975), *The Way of Mindfulness: The Satipatthana Sutta and Commentary.* Kandy: BPS.

Teasdale J.D., Segal Z.V. Williams J.M.G., Ridgeway V.A., Soulsby J.M., Lau M.A. (2000), Prevention of relapse/ recurrence in major depression by mindfulness-based cognitive therapy. *J Consult Clin Psycho, 68*: 615-23.

Teasdale J.D., Moore R.G., Hayhurst H., Pope M., Williams S. & Segal Z.V. (2002), Metacognitive awareness and prevention of relapse in depression: Empirical Evidence. *J Consult Clin Psychol. 70:* 275-87.

U Pandita, A. (1992), *In This Very Life.* Boston: Wisdom Publications.

U Silananda (1909), A. *The Four Foundations of Mindfulness.* Boston: Wisdom Publications.

U Silananda, A. (1994-1996), *The Four Foundations of Mindfulness* – a series of ten audiotapes. U Silananda, A. Abhidhamma Course audio tapes. Tathagata Meditation Centre, San Jose.

The client,the therapist and the dance floor of therapy

Meditation: Training for the Counselling Therapist

Michael Anderson
National Convener for the Australian Psychological Society's Buddhism and Psychology Interest Group

Psychology has developed a rigorous approach to the science and theory of psychological Therapy. However, the profession has historically struggled with the actual art of therapy and is still doing so. After training, the therapist is left to struggle with their experiences of incompetence and competence, effectiveness and ineffectiveness, their liking and disliking of a client, their fears of their client and for their client. The therapist may not even be aware of the influences of this dance with the client and the space on the dance floor of therapy. The role of supervision may be instrumental in developing this aspect of the therapist's skill repertoire. However, the increasing emphasis on theory and science expands academic training but not supervision (and may even reduce its importance).

I am suggesting in the dance floor metaphor that there is a third element that exists beyond the therapist's therapeutic approach and the client. At a physical level this is easily accepted. There are chairs, a room, a desk, etc. At an experiencial level this is less accepted. The art of therapy or the wisdom of therapy occurs beyond theory and even beyond the therapist but actually in this element that can co-exist with the therapist and client. What we do as therapists in opening our minds may in some way create a space in which healing and movement can more effectively occur. It is beyond the knowledge of the therapist and beyond the issue presented by the client. The possibility of this third element of therapy ... the dance floor, may be discussed infrequently, but it is not new. Freud (1912) and Bion (1970) were strong proponents of this optimal state in which therapy should occur.

Freud (1912) proposes that the therapist should maintain a particular attentional frame.

> It consists simply in not directing one's notice to anything in particular and in maintaining the same 'evenly suspended attention' (as I have called it) in the face of all that one hears.... Or, to put it purely in terms of technique: He should simply listen, and not to bother about whether he is keeping anything in mind (Freud, 1912: 111-112).

Freud suggests this element is the optimal state of mind in which therapy should occur. It contains a number of characteristics. These include the uncritical observer, absence of reason and equal and impartial attention to what occurs in awareness. Epstein (1984, 1995) discusses the apparent disappearance of "evenly suspended attention" a key element of Freud's therapeutic approach. This disappearance can be attributed to the difficulty of achieving this optimal mental frame. It is far easier to hold to a theoretical framework, which provides the process for therapy.

> Many listen with their theoretical and diagnostic preoccupations or with their "plan of treatment" in mind and overlook what may differ from these. Or they listen with their countertransferential notions about what the patient ought to be like to suit their ideas of the most desirable adaptation to society or their idea of what man should be like. They may feel exasperation if the patient is not at all like that, or impatience if he does not seem to want to be like that, or not be in a hurry to change... All of this is apt to get in the way of open attention, of evenly suspended attention that wants to see the other person as he really is. (Schachtel, 1969: 75-76).

Bion (1970) is one of a few, who have attempted to expand on Freuds earlier work. He describes an optimal state which can be achieved through the practice of discarding mental activity and desires as "worthless but inevitable" (Bion: 35)

> Anyone who considers it possible to achieve a suitable frame of mind in a few minutes of psychological tidying up before starting work cannot have grasped the nature of the discipline necessary to be an analyst ... (Bion: 67).

Epstein (1982) states "Despite the exhortations of Freud and Bion, the general trend in Anaylitical literature is away from acknowledging the importance or even the existance, of such states of mind in the analyst". Epstein (1995) commented that "..... no specific training in the cultivation or maintenance of this attentional attitude ever developed". He believes the profession has been deprived of one of its most important tools.

To date the discussion has had psychoanalytic support. It is difficult to find support for this "optimal state of awareness" as described by Bion and Freud in other theoretical arenas. This is not surprising considering that other theoretical propositions are merely attempting to support and solidify their own constructs. The discipline required to achieve this "optimal" therapeutic state is also a factor in its absence in other traditions. Speeth (1984) states that, "All therapists, regardless of their theoretical orientation, must draw upon essentially the same raw sensory data". He concludes that all therapists, regardless of their theoretical orientation will benefit from the development of their attentional "instrument".

It should be noted that I am not saying that a therapist should throw out their theoretical orientation. I am of the view that in having this more open approach, we will achieve a more transparent process through which we use our particular methods. You can dance to different music on the dance floor, but understanding what drives your selection is useful. Historically the therapy my clients received has had more to do with where I am at at a particular time rather than their particular circumstance. Reducing my anxiety does not seem the ideal motive for using a particular approach with a client.

It would appear that Western pychology has no inherent process for developing this "optimal" therapeutic stance. When examining the Eastern spiritual traditions it is evident that there is a rich array of tools and techniques that may assist this development. Both Epstein (1984, 1995) and Speeth (1982) suggest that meditation has a valuable role to play in assisting the practitioner of psychology and counselling to become more skilful and effective. Meditation is an important practice for spritual development in most of the spiritual traditions. In the Buddhist traditions, it is through meditation that the practitioner can purify their mind, develop mental stability and move beyond the dualistic mind to the spaciousness and wisdom of the natural mind – Buddha nature.

It is not suggested that a counselling therapist needs to attain enlightenment before they can be a successful therapist. It is more about developing a particular way of dealing with one's attention. It is about being more skilful in the way a therapist manages their mind in therapy. It is in the similarities expressed in Buddhist meditation practice and those discussed by Freud and Bion that the possibilities for meditaion for the therapist emerge. Interviews involving 20 psychologists and counsellors from the United States of America who use Buddhist principles in their therapeutic work, identified the benefits of meditation for the therapist (Anderson, unpublished). This research identified that although therapists were divided over the therapeutic use of meditation for the client, they were all in agreement that their own effectiveness as a therapist was strongly related to their own meditation practice. For many of these therapists, meditation was an essential part of their training as therapists. However, for 95% of the participants in this study, their academic training as therapists did not include meditation.

Meditation was used by these therapists as a practice that enabled them to be more effective for their clients rather than meditation being used as a tool for their clients. It was also used by the therapists as a way of self sustaining their work, and for many of these therapists, it enabled them to avoid the "burnout", so often described in the helping professions.

A framework and some practices may be desribed that may assist therapists to become more skilled on the dance floor. I present a simple structure for the therapist to develop the skill of "evenly suspended attention". It breaks down the concept of "evenly suspended attention" into discrete micro skills and so in a practical way illustrates how these skills relate to the therapist.

Clearly, the following distinctions and discussion are arbitrary. They are constructions that I am presenting merely to help others to appreciate the value of meditation. As one practises more, these arbitrary boundaries of skill become more transparent and less relevant. The process of meditation practice is then experienced as more fluid and dynamic. I would like to think that these "skills" as presented here could be researched and found to be reliable and valid predictors of effective therapy. To my knowledge, they have not achieved this status yet. I am also cognizant that the arbitrary boundaries and concepts fail to be scientifically supported for many reasons, including inadequate measuring instruments, poor definitions, and other flaws inherent in assessing what is both an art and a science.

WHAT IS MEDITATION?

The objective of meditation is not to achieve relaxation in the sense of torpidity. Tranquillity is a different matter. It can be seen as a way of developing our mental skills. It is in some ways a form of mental gymnastics. Meditation is the practice field for developing mental skills that can be applied in therapy as well as in day to day living. Meditation is about creating a controlled environment that enables you to practise these complex skills.

We train the mind to be more skilful in the way it functions in therapy. However it is a simple, yet difficult task. Like any skill, mastery is achieved over long periods of practice and with much persistence and effort. However, noticable changes can be experienced in a relatively short period of time.

MENTAL SKILLS

There are four core skills.

1. Stability of Mind

The ability to keep your mind stable. This differs only mildly from totally focused concentration. Total focus on one object without shifting your attention is extremely difficult. Our minds have a tendency to wander. It is also rare for people to be trained in concentration. Due to this normal tendency and lack of training, we find concentrating difficult and sometimes frustrating. Stability of mind is a milder form of concentration, in that it accepts the normal tendency of the mind to wander; what we are attempting to achieve is a reduction in this wandering.

2. Flexibility of Awareness

Look at an object about 5 metres in front of you. Now switch your awareness to an object about 2 metres to the right of the first object. Switch your awareness between these two objects at about 5 – 10 second intervals for a period of two minutes.

The question I typically ask after this exercise is: How difficult did you find switching between these two objects? The answer is typically, "not difficult at all" and ocassionally "I found that to be relaxing". In about five percent of cases someone will find it difficult. (This can be worked through individually after the training session). This ease or effortlessness is what one is trying to develop in relation to distractions in meditation. You stabilise your mind on an object. When it wanders from this object, you effortlessly return it to the object that you are focusing on, with the same effortlessness that you found with the earlier exercise. Achieving this effortless is a significant skill outcome. Its relevance to therapy is that upon noticing your mind has wandered it is then important to bring it back and not for example get into some self admonishment/abuse about how incompetent you are as a therapist when you cannot even maintain your attention on the client. Immediate return means that you minimise the disruption to your attention to the client.

3. Observer

Being able to observe your mind without attachment enables you to better understand yourself and the patterns that interfere with your therapeutic work. We are typically unskillful in the management of our mind. We can get caught up in conversations with ourselves regarding, our incompetence, our dislike for the client, our fear of not knowing what to do, what approach should I take, etc. More problematic may be the total absence of awareness of any such mental activity. This skill can be developed so that you can be more effective at witnessing the way your mind works, so that you watch the habitual way your mind reacts to help or hinder your therapeutic effectiveness.

4. Non Reactivity (Equanimity)

This skill is the process of not reacting to the habitual patterns that you become aware of as you attempt to keep your mind "evenly suspended". It can be practised with an itch. You get an itch, then attempt to let it go and return your mind to the object of focus. This is not always easy, but an easier starting point than in the midst of the intensity and complexity of therapy. You are learning not to react to your thoughts, emotions, aversions and desires.

How to meditate

The process itself is simple to explain. Actually doing it is the difficult bit. You achieve stability of mind or improved concentration by focusing your attention on one object and practising keeping your attention on this object. Any object will do. In the following activity we will focus on breathing and counting. These two objects of concentration have been chosen because my experience has shown them to be effective for my clients. However it is possible to use any object. The task is to simply stay focused on whatever you choose for a fixed period of time (ie 10 – 20 minutes).

The next task is to notice when your mind wanders. Remember, any shift in attention from the chosen object of attention is a distraction. For example, if you feel uncomfortable and you shift your body position this would be a distraction. The thought that leads you to move was a shift from the object of attention. That does not mean you should or should not move, but rather that you notice that your attention has shifted (you have been distracted) and you deal with this distraction by calmly and gently bringing your attention back to the object of attention.

Controlling your environment can help minimise distractions (or rather the type of distractions). Practise in a quiet room, so that others/sounds will not distract you. Sit upright so that you will not be distracted by drowsiness. Close your eyes (not essential) so that visual images do not distract you. No matter what you do, you will experience distractions. As a beginner, trying to minimise distractions is a good idea, as it makes the task of concentrating less complex. However, the task of stabilising your mind will be difficult in the beginning. Remember it is important that you become skilful in flexibly shifting your awareness. The more distractions, the more practice you are getting in letting go and developing a flexible awareness. Simply notice your mind has wandered and try to effortlessly bring it back. For example when you notice your mind thinking "this is boring, I should be out doing more reading", let this thought simply drift in, then let it drift by, without entertaining it. You entertain the thought by maintaining an internal discussion about it, or experiencing some emotion, or doing something like getting up and picking up a book to read. Let the thought be. Don't follow it, just calmly bring your attention back to the object of attention.

As you practice more, you will become quick to notice your mind wandering off the object of attention. This is developing your skill as an observer. Your powers of observation will become more refined and acute. You will notice thoughts, sensations and distractions that you were previously unaware existed and you will notice them as soon as they arise. Here are some exercises that I use.

EXERCISE ONE: A TECHNIQUE

The task is to keep your attention on your breath. Focus your attention on the one sensation that tells you that you are breathing in and out. Ask yourself "how do I know I'm breathing in and breathing out?" It may be your abdomen rising and falling. It may be the air as it moves past your nostrils or it could be the sensation of air moving down the back of your throat. It doesn't matter what you choose, but once you have decided on what to focus on then stick to it. Any deviation from focusing on breathing in and out should be treated as a distraction.

Once you have selected your object of attention or focus, you can now begin to count. Counting is not critical; however, I have found it a highly successful technique. (Sometimes it is necessary to give further help to inidividual students who have trouble at this point).

The counting begins with counting "one" to yourself on the "in breath" followed by counting "one" on the "out breath". Then count "two" on the next "in breath" and "two" on the next "out breath". You keep counting each breath cycle until you get to "five" on the "out breath". You then begin counting at "one" again. You continue focusing on breathing and counting each breath cycle from "one" to "five" for the time you set at the beginning of the practice session. each time you notice that your mind has wandered off the breathing and counting, just calmly bring your attention back.

The task is simple. It is difficult because we have an unskilful mind. Our mind has learnt from an early age to wander from one object to another. It is as if it has learnt to be continually dissatisfied. It repeatedly unsettles the stillness and openness that is possible with a skilful mind.

In this form of meditation the objective is not to develop total concentration. The objective of meditation is to observe whatever is happening in your mind. Developing concentration is an aspect of mental development but is not the primary skill that we are attempting to achieve. We use the task of concentrating with a purpose. The purpose is to give the mind something to do so that we can observe it and become aware of the habits of mind.

If you notice your mind constantly wandering off the breathing and counting... GOOD. You are increasing your awareness at a more subtle level. That is, your ability to notice your mind wandering, is improving. As this skill becomes more refined you can start to observe the nature of thinking. You also start to notice that many of your common problems are the result of a stimulus-reaction cycle. You have a thought/sensation (stimulus) and you then respond to this thought/sensation (reaction). This reaction is often inappropriate, as it is an habitual response to a certain cue. For example, a person enters therapy. You find yourself taking control and offering this person solutions. On reflection you realise that this is a reaction to a cue emitted by them. They may remind you of your sister. They may present with a pattern of dependency and seek someone to solve their problems.

In meditation, you are attempting to develop skills such that, rather than identifying with these reactions in you, at the moment they arise, you observe the impulse to react and then flexibly shift your awareness back to the client. This then opens the way for a different dance to occur, which may be more open, transparent and helpful.

Your reactions are habits. These reactions will say more about where you are at as a therapist than where the client is at. This is not to say the data initiating this habitual reaction is not useful. It may well be, but the reaction is unlikely to be useful or skiful when acting as a therapist.

Through the process of observing your mind you will notice a number of habits of thinking. Some of these may be peculiar to your specific experience. Other habits of thinking seem to be more universal. One of these mental habits could be referred to as discriminating mind. This is the term I use to label the tendency for our mind to represent our world/our experiences as two distinct poles.

An example of this is our tendency to either like or dislike. To see things as pleasurable or painful. When we experience something as pleasurable we want more of it. If we can not get more we are then frustrated or disappointed. If we experience something as painful we try to avoid it. Often our attempts to avoid something are in vain as there is no way to avoid what is happening right now. The resistance merely perpetuates the experience of pain or displeasure. The resistance is at its very least unskilful/unhelpful. A client might present with a strong urge to kill themselves. The disasters that have befallen them may be quite significant. The intensity of their despair may be great. As a therapist I can find myself feeling incompetent. Unable to help. Not knowing what to offer this person. Clearly I can feel a strong aversion to being with this person at this time. My thoughts, emotions and reactions may not be helpful if I allow them to take off. It is more appropriate for me to sit with this person, acknowledging these feelings to myself (and at times to the client), but modelling, for the client, the ability to sit with this discomfort without running from it or feeding it either.

Becoming more aware of your disriminating mind and its patterns as it pushes and winds you up is a valuable step in the process of freeing your experience from the bondage of your habits. This can allow therapy to follow a more spontaneous and client centred process, rather than be driven by your habits or mental state at the time.

I previously stated that the object of your awareness could be numerous. Breathing is a traditional object for many reasons. However many objects are used in developing these skills and for purifying your mind. For example, you could focus on your thoughts or the words of your client, which would be more appropriate in a therapy session. In developing mental skills for therapy, I have found a number of useful techniques.

Exercise two: TOUCH AND GO

One of the psychologists that I interviewed in America, Dr Karen Kissel Wegala, introduced this technique to me. You can find her complete presentation of it in "How to be a help instead of a nuisance" Kissel Wegela (1996).

> "... when a feeling or thought or sensation arises, we touch it – feel it completely. We can touch quite completely in a moment. It is like tasting an anchovy. We can taste the salty, pungent flavor in just a moment. We can do the same thing with whatever arises during our practice. Instead of skittering away, we touch. We move toward what is happening instead of trying to get away. Rather than rejecting our experience we show an interest in it.
>
> Then, having touched, we let it go. We touch and then we go with our out breath". (Kissel Wegela, 1996)

Sit comfortably. Focus as we did earlier on your breath. When you notice your mind touches something, even your breath, you let it go and be open to whatever arises next. Be sure to let it go and not follow it.

Exercise three: open and closed awareness

I am not able to recollect where I was first introduced to this technique. However, the theoretical support for its use was from Speeth (1982).

Sit comfortably. Open your eyes and focus on an object in front of you. Now loosen your focus on the object and open your awareness to all the objects in your vision, without moving your head or eyes. This is similar to a zoom lens on a camera. You are opening the zoom lens to take in a panoramic view. Seeing all objects without focusing on any one particular object. Each time you notice your awareness narrowing, or that you are focusing on one particular aspect of your visual field, you merely then open your awareness back out again. Do this for 5 minutes.

Now maintain your panoramic visual perspective, while at the same time including all the sounds you can hear. When you notice your awareness narrowing and that you are focusing on one particular object or sound, then let that object or sound go, and open your awareness to hear and see as much of the sounds and sights that are in their respective perceptual fields. Do this for a further 5 minutes.

Then repeat this process by including firstly, your thoughts and then your physical sensations.

This activity is an attempt to assist individuals to develop a more inclusive awareness. One takes in as much data as possible without being selective. When selection occurs, you let that go and then open your awareness.

Exercise four: chaos

This technique evolved out of training that I did with Peter and Penny Fenner. I subsequently followed this training with readings of Peter Fenner's work and *Dzogchen* (a tradition from Tibet similar to *Zen*) and *Zen* teachings. The term Chaos was used for a workshop I ran while working with a number of organizations. I found that people frequently desired time to do nothing. In developing a workshop where people actually had permission to do nothing, it was found that rather than enjoy this experience people found it to be chaotic. This is not an attempt to replicate the work of Peter Fenner and Penny Fenner. To get a taste of their work, you will need to follow that up with them. This exercise is merely another activity that can assist the therapist to develop "evenly suspended attention" and to work in a more transparent and open process, for themselves and their client.

The task is simple. It is done in a group setting. The simple rules are that you are free to do whatever you wish. In doing this the only request is, that you acknowledge why you might do whatever it is that you do, rather than just automatically doing it.

People's experience of this activity varies from stressful to calm. This is both across individuals and in the same individual during the time of the activity. This clearly highlights that experience is less about the environment and more about what we are doing internally within that environment. Insights often include an awareness of how our minds grasp at experience. For example "I like this" or "I don't like this". The need for structure to alleviate our anxiety is another insight people experience. Further to this people often witness the lengths to which our mind goes to construct or fabricate our experience. People often find themselves singing songs to themselves or meditating in order to feel comfortable, or to alleviate anxiety about just observing one's experience. For a full understanding of this method, I refer you to Penny Fenner's workshops or Peter Fenner's workshops or his written work.

I am sure others are doing some great work in this area, however I am not aware of their work. Students may wish to search in the areas of Deconstructive Contemplation, Interactive Wisdom and dualism. I have introduced a few techniques that I have used in order to open up the dance.

REFERENCES

Anderson, M. (1999), *Interview Transcripts and notes.* Unpublished works.

Bion, W.R. (1970), *Attention and interpretation.* London, Tavistock.

Epstein, M.D. (1984), On the neglect of evenly suspended attention. *Journal of Transpersonal Psychology.* **16 (2):** 193 – 205.

Epstein, M.D. (1995), *Thoughts without a thinker.* New York, Basic Books.

Freud, S. (1912), Recommendations to physicians practicing psychoanalysis. Stan. (ed). London, Hogarth Press.

Kissel Wegela, K (1996), *How to be a help instead of a nuisance.* Massachusetts, Shambala Publications.

Schatchel, E.G. (1969), *Cited in Epstein* 1984.

Speeth, K.R. (1982), On psychotherapeutic attention. *The Journal of Transpersonal Psychology.* **14(2):** 141-160.

Working with the clinging mind

William L. Mikulas
University of West Florida

In this paper I describe step-by-step how to work with the clinging behaviour of the mind. The emphasis is on established, practical, and heuristic methods that are applicable to individuals and groups, and are basic to therapy, personal growth, and spiritual practice. Theory and research are discussed in detail elsewhere (Mikulas, 2002). However, we do need to begin with a little theory.

A central construct in my Conjunctive Psychology is "Behaviours of the mind," how the mind acts and responds. A critical distinction is between behaviours of the mind and contents of the mind. Contents of the mind include the various objects that arise in a person's consciousness, such as perceptual experiences, verbal and visual thoughts, reconstructed memories, attributions and beliefs, and cognitive aspects of emotions and attitudes. Behaviours of the mind are those processes of the mind that select and construct the contents and that focus on and provide awareness of the contents. Behaviours of the mind occur prior to, during, and in response to any particular contents. Western psychologists and philosophers often confuse and confound contents of the mind with behaviours of the mind.

There are three fundamental behaviours of the mind: Concentration, Mindfulness, and Clinging. Concentration is the learned control of the focus of one's attention. It is the behaviour of keeping one's awareness, with varying degrees of one-pointedness, on a particular set of contents of the mind. Mindfulness is the active maximizing of the breadth and clarity of awareness, intentionally moving and sharpening the focus of awareness within the field of consciousness. Concentration and mindfulness are discussed elsewhere (Mikulas, 2000, 2002); but it should be kept in mind that all three behaviours of the mind are interrelated, a change in one affects the others. Thus, developing concentration and mindfulness greatly help in working with clinging.

Clinging refers to the tendency of the mind to grasp for and cling to certain contents of the mind, assumptions about self and reality, and personal frames of reference. This includes certain perceptions, rituals, expectations, opinions, images of the self, and models of reality. Following yogic psychology, the result of clinging will be called an "attachment." Clinging always produces problems, as discussed below, including the suffering and unsatisfactoriness emphasized in Buddhist psychology (Rahula, 1974). A critical distinction, that often has to be emphasized and re-emphasized to clients, is the difference between clinging and the object of clinging. What one clings to may be desirable or not for various reasons, including practical, psychological, ethical, and legal reasons. But the clinging is always problematical. For example, a client may believe that being attached to jogging is a good thing, since it improves her health. But there is confusion here. Even if jogging is good for her, being attached to jogging is not. If because of her attachment to jogging she is upset when the weather does not permit jogging, then there is unnecessary suffering.

Clinging results in resistance to change, distorted perception, impaired thinking, and unwanted emotions. Reducing clinging increases freedom, clarity, peace of mind, love, spaciousness, and enlightenment. Another common misunderstanding among clients, that often has to be addressed many times, is that reducing clinging will make them apathetic and/or irresponsible. Clients often believe that reducing attachments will reduce the joy and zest of living, or that without suffering there can be no happiness or creativity. But all this is dramatically not true! Reducing clinging allows one to more fully engage in life's activities and increases one's related joy and energy. There is, of course, a change in what one is motivated by. For example, the enlightened person is primarily motivated by compassion and appropriateness.

Reducing clinging

The first step is educating the client about how clinging works, the results of clinging, and the distinction between clinging and what one clings to. Having many examples and stories is very important here and throughout training. This can't be emphasized enough. For it is often the stories that the client best remembers and uses to identify similar clinging in himself. It is not possible to include stories in this article; and in any case, specific stories are chosen to best suit the particular client(s). There are also significant cultural differences. For example, with Americans I might act out a story of a person becoming very noticeably upset. But in Thailand, such public showing of emotion would be very inappropriate and hence much less likely.

Second, and often overlooked in attachment work, is the attitude of the client toward discovering attachments. If one's attitude is that finding an attachment is unpleasant, as it is for most people, then it is hard to find them. So the attitude to be cultivated is that one is delighted and appreciative at discovering attachments, for it is an opportunity to become more free and happier. In behavioural terms this change in attitude corresponds to a switch from a punishment contingency to a reinforcement contingency.

The third part of the approach is to help the client realize the difference between the essence of who he is and the way he acts and thinks: "You are not your behaviour." To the extent that a person identifies himself with his behaviours (including his thoughts), then it is harder to see these behaviours clearly and harder to change them. A powerful and heuristic analogy regards one's child. When the child misbehaves you don't want to tell the child he is a bad and/or unlovable person. Rather, you want to convey to the child that you will always love him unconditionally. However, some behaviours are unacceptable and will have certain consequences if continued. A similar approach should be applied to oneself, although many people find this much more difficult. That is, one learns to love oneself, while simultaneously recognizing that one needs to change some of one's behaviours that are undesirable and problematic. One learns to gradually dis-identify with behaviours that were previously used to define oneself.

Assessment / awareness

The next step is to help the client gradually become more and more aware of his own clinging. This is intertwined with clinical assessment in which specific examples of attachments are identified for later discussion and perhaps therapy. Logs and diaries can be very useful here. For example, a person might keep a diary in which, as soon as possible after an attachment manifests, he writes down what was the situation, what did he think and feel in the situation, what did he do, and how did this affect others. Such a diary is often very illuminating to client and counsellor. Common themes and dynamics may be discovered. Also, having to write it down often trains the client to be more objective and investigative.

For almost everyone, the first stage in identifying attachments is noticing the results of the attachment, such as misperception, impaired thinking, or resistance to change. The most common and easiest to notice effect is a negative emotion such as anxiety, anger, or jealousy. When one of these emotions occurs, it is usually a result of an attachment and should be a signal to look for the clinging. As one continues to work with the clinging mind, particularly if coupled with mindfulness training, then one's awareness gradually moves from the results of clinging to earlier stages in the chain of events, and eventually to the clinging itself. This, of course, makes it easier to reduce the clinging and have more freedom and control.

It can also be helpful to have some system for classifying attachments. This helps in finding common patterns and encourages further investigation of the exact nature of the attachments. One heuristic system is based on contemporary interpretations of the yogic chakra system. In yogic psychology it is suggested that most attachments are related to security, sensation, and/or power, corresponding to the first three chakras (Rama *et al.*, 1976). Security attachments produce fear, worry, and paranoia related to things such as one's possessions, social roles and self-concept. Sensation attachments relate to the pursuit of pleasure and complexity, and the avoidance of boredom. Power attachments relate to how much power and influence one has over others. It includes issues of will and the cultivation of followers. When keeping a diary, one would note whether each attachment was primarily related to security, sensation, or power. Of course, some attachments would be a combination.

The most heuristic paradigm for learning about clinging is reality vs. expectation/demand. One has an expectation, desire, or demand for reality to be a certain way (e.g., how a social evening should progress, who should win a sporting event, how a relative or friend should live). When reality matches the expectation or demand, one is pleased. When they don't match, one is upset. Now, there is no problem in noticing a discrepancy between reality and how one would prefer reality to be. And there is no problem in this discrepancy being a source of feedback and motivation to alter reality and/or one's expectations and demands. But to be upset by the discrepancy is an unnecessary source of suffering and evidence of clinging. This type of dynamic occurs many times a day for most people. Hence, it is a powerful paradigm for learning about clinging, and a wonderful opportunity for daily work in personal and/or spiritual growth.

Intervention

The nature of the clinging behaviour of the mind is universal; it is basically the same for everyone everywhere. What one clings to is somewhat unique to the individual; but the clinging is the same. Hence, what has been discussed so far has widespread applicability and underlies a wide range of clinical/personal/spiritual issues and dynamics.

However, what to do about the clinging after one becomes aware of it, is much more complex. Here any of a large number of strategies, practices, or therapies may be appropriate. Perhaps the intervention is something that one can do alone, or perhaps it requires the assistance of a professional counsellor or guide.

All this is well beyond the scope of this paper. However, I do have two books that summarize possible interventions, including behavioural self-control approaches (Mikulas, 1983) and psycho-spiritual practices (Mikulas, 1987). Both of these books in their entirety can be accessed for free on my university web page (http://uwf.edu/psych/faculty/Mikulas.html). Sometimes the intervention involves actively changing the world and/or one's self. Sometimes the intervention involves accepting what one can't change.

The self

Many attachments are related to one's sense of self, which is heavily influenced by the culture. For example, for white American and Western European men, the self is an independent self, a unique, bounded autonomous entity that is distinct and separate from other selves. On the other hand, in

East Asia it is more common to find an interdependent self, which includes other people and parts of the world, and is constituted, defined, and influenced by social roles, relationships with significant others, cultural contexts, and group harmony. These different types of selves lead to different forms of attachments and motivation. The independent client may be more motivated by anger, frustration and pride; while the interdependent client may be more motivated by indebtedness, empathy, and shame (Markus & Kitayama, 1991).

A common variation of the reality vs expectation/demand paradigm is the self vs ideal self. Here one compares one's sense of self with some ideal self of how one wants to be or "should" be. This ideal self might be self-generated and/or imposed by parents, friends, or the culture in general. Sometimes the ideal self is undesirable or unrealistic, and needs to be changed or eliminated. Sometimes we need to help the client develop a program of action to lead to the ideal self. But when the client is unnecessarily upset by the discrepancy between the self and the ideal self, then this is the place for attachment work.

As one gradually begins to encounter and work with subtler and subtler forms of clinging, self-related attachments become more evident and often are an increasing percentage of all attachments. At intermediate and advanced levels of personal and spiritual growth one discovers considerable clinging to a specific sense of self and great resistance to change. This personal self is heavily involved in self-perpetuation. For example, perceptions will be distorted and memories will be altered to maintain a specific sense of self. And people will continue to act in ways that aren't working for them and causing problems because they have identified their selves with these behaviours. Again, helping clients to dis-identify with their behaviours is often important.

Many people believe that the path to enlightenment requires killing or sublimating this self. This is wrong and will not work! What usually happens is the self gets involved with the project of transcending the self. This, of course, can not happen and is just another form of self perpetuation. The critical understanding is that there is no problem with the existence or functioning of this personal self, and psychological therapies can often help here. Enlightenment does not involve doing in this self. Enlightenment is getting free from attachments to this self as being the totality of who or what one is. The enlightened person has a functional self but does not cling to it. (For more on this, see Mikulas, 2002).

A simple, but powerful practice for discovering self-related clinging occurs whenever one is upset, such as angry. At such times one asks "Who is it that is angry?" That is, what is my direct experience of some self that is angry? This is an experiential question, not a philosophical question. And it is an advanced form of enquiry.

OVERVIEW

The ideas of clinging and attachments are easy enough for many people to understand and relate to their own lives. Everyone can profit from reducing clinging, and we have powerful somato-psycho-spiritual practices that can help. The prevalence of clinging and attachments make them important parts of all human endeavors, including therapy and personal/spiritual growth. Reducing attachments helps in, and is in turn helped by, developing concentration and mindfulness, and opening the heart (Mikulas, 1987, 2002).

And all of this can be done by itself or embedded in other practices and therapies. Working with the clinging mind can be exciting, fun, and transformative.

REFERENCES

Markus, H.R. & Kitayama, S. (1991), Culture and the self: Implications for cognition, emotion, and motivation. *Psychological Review, 98*, 224-253.

Mikulas, W. L. (1983), *Skills of living.* Lanham, MD: University Press of America.

Mikulas, W. L. (1987), *The way beyond.* Wheaton, IL: Theosophical Publishing House.

Mikulas, W.L. (2000), Behaviours of the mind, meditation, and health. In K. T. Kaku (Ed.), *Meditation as Health Promotion.* Delft, Holland: Eburon..

Mikulas, W. L. (2002), *The integrative helper: Convergence of Eastern and Western Traditions.* Pacific Grove, CA: Brooks/ Cole.

Rahula, W. (1974), *What the Buddha taught.* 2nd ed. New York: Grove Press.

Rama, Swami, Ballentine, R, & Ajaya, Swami (1976), *Yoga and psychotherapy.* Glenview, IL: Himalayan Institute.

MRI scanning during zen meditation: the picture of enlightenment?

Rients Ritskes,[A] *Merel Ritskes-Hoitinga,*[A] *Hans Stødkilde-Jørgensen,*[A]
Klaus Bærentsen,[A,C] *Tue Hartman*[A,C]

Introduction

A group of experienced Zen meditation practitioners were scanned with fMRI during the conscious switch from normal consciousness to a meditative state of mind. This switching has been hypothesized to be realized by a dedicated "neural switch" (Travis *et al.*, 1999). In the literature increased activity is reported to occur in the prefrontal cortex and the basal ganglia during meditation (Hirai, 1989). On the basis of other publications, de-activation in the *gyrus occipitalis* was expected (Newberg *et al.*, 1997). The present study showed a simultaneous occurrence of patterns of brain activation and de-activation in the mentioned structures. It is hypothesized that this combination of events may reveal the neural basis of the experience of Zen meditation practitioners when entering the meditative state.

Subjects

The group consisted of 8 men and 3 women. These subjects had on average 8 (range 1.5 –25) years of daily Zen-meditation experience. They are all right handed, with a mean age of 48 (range 32 – 62).

Method

During fMRI scanning a blocked on-off design was used, in which 3 periods of 45 seconds meditation were alternated by 3 periods of 45 seconds of random thoughts. During the meditation blocks all 11 subjects focussed on counting their breaths (silently counting from one to ten), just as they were used to do during their daily Zen-meditation practice. All scans were made on

A. MRI Research Centre, Aarhus University Hospital, Skejby, Denmark (rients@zentrum.dk)
B. Biomedical Laboratory, University of Southern Denmark
C. Institute of Psychology, University of Aarhus, Denmark

a GE Signa MRI scanner, which is the most updated scaning technique available. Data ware analyzed with SPM99.

RESULTS

The 3 periods of 45 seconds scanning during meditation were compared to the 3 periods of 45 seconds of random thoughts ("on-off"). After the scanning period, all subjects reported that they had been able to meditate well in the lying position during the scan and that it had been relatively easy to enter their normal meditative state of mind. The results confirm that the subjects were able to shift their state of mind in this on/off experiment. The pictures show a significant increase in activity of the prefrontal cortex (gyrus frontalis medius, right side, Brodman area 10) during Zen meditation (ill.1) and confirmed the findings by Hirai, who did EEG studies in Zen priests. Ryding (1996) later compared the effects of counting loudly and silently by PET scanning and also found an increased activity in the prefrontal cortex during silent counting. This area, sometimes called the Attention Association area, is held responsible for more complex human feelings. Increased activity in this area is thought to be associated with enhanced insights and attentiveness, heightened interests, sharper mental focussing, and deepened emotional reso-

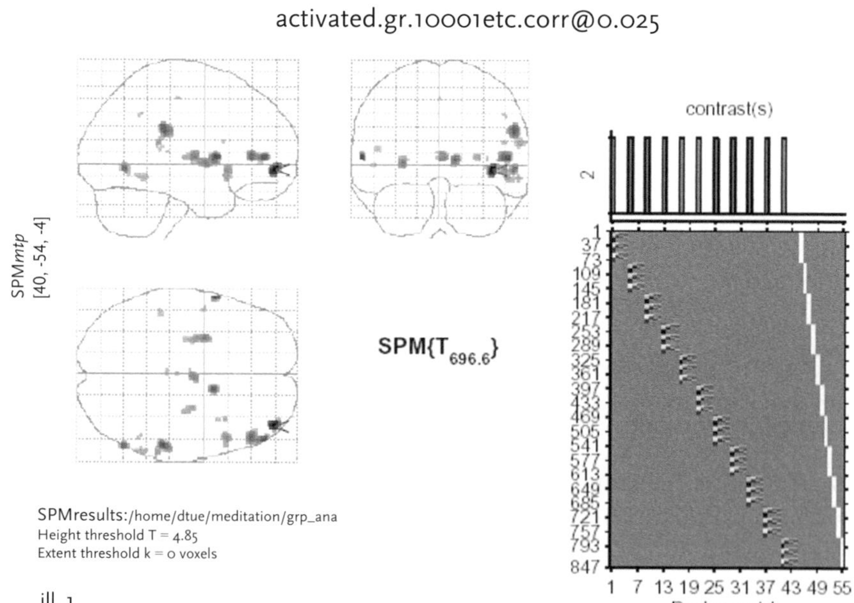

ill. 1

nances (Austin, 1998). That is at least what Austin concludes, based on studies of people with frontal lobe lesions. In the famous case report on Phineas Gage (Damasio *et al.*, 1994), it is reported that the gyrus frontalis medius in the prefrontal cortex was damaged due to an accident. Because of that, he "lost" his personality, developed blunted emotions and lost social interest. This can be summarized as a loss of compassion. Electrical stimulation of the prefrontal cortex was found to be associated with positive feelings (Sem-Jacobsen, 1976). In this study one quarter of the group that got electrical stimulation of this area of the brain reported positive changes in mood. Also the basal ganglia became more active during the meditation periods in our study (ill.1). Current concepts of the role of the basal ganglia consider that their function is to facilitate behaviour and movements which are required and considered appropriate in any particular context and to inhibit unwanted or inappropriate behaviours / movements (Crossman & Neary, 2000).

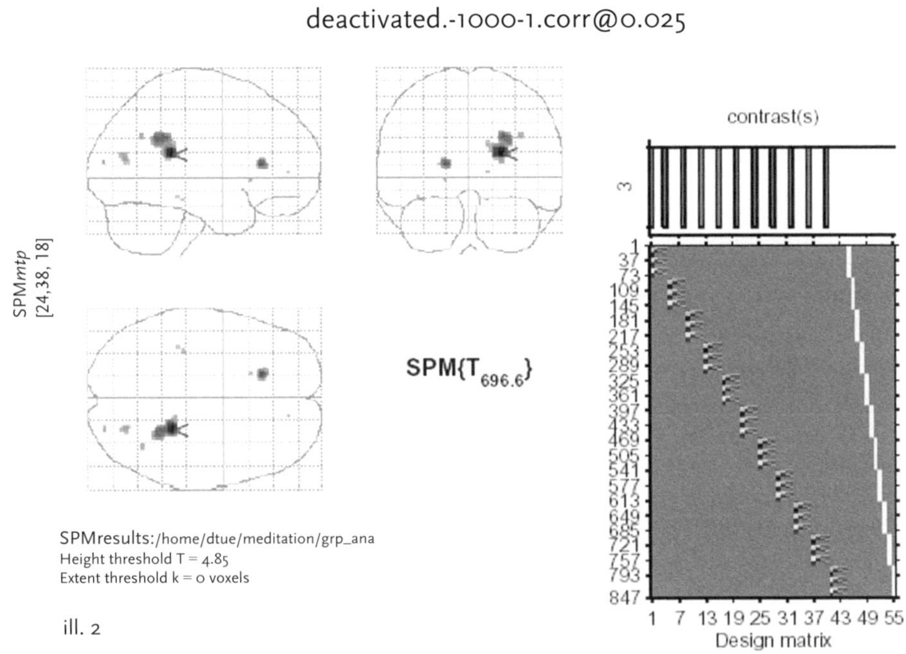

ill. 2

Simultaneously with the activation of the above-mentioned areas, significantly less activity was found in two other areas, namely the gyrus occipitalis superior (ill. 2) and the anterior cingulate (Brodman area 32) (ill. 2). The gyrus occipitalis is related to visual orientation and orientation ability in general, whereas the anterior cingulate, is associated with conscious activities that are directed by the will.

Discussion

Our study shows, like others, that a higher activity in the gyrus frontalis medius arises during the initial phase of Zen meditation. The gyrus frontalis medius is part of the frontal lobe. A PET-study (Raine & Buchsbaum, 1994) demonstrated a decreased frontal-lobe activity in murderers. So there may after all have been a good scientific reason for the New York State prison to have started (1984) a Zen meditation group. This group is still existing within the prison walls. More activity in the basal ganglia during meditation also fits the Zen-image. The tea-ceremony and Zen-archery are just two examples of rituals that need the optimal use of the main functions of the basal ganglia, namely the making of precisely controlled movements. Activation of the basal ganglia could very well be stimulated by counting thereby possibly resulting in the control of movements by the conscious breathing process. Less activity in the gyrus occipitalis superior and the anterior cingulate suggests that during meditation there is less interference of our will and less awareness of where we are. Such a state of mind is possibly related to what is called 'flow' which may have resemblance to the experience of enlightenment.

References

Austin, J.H.(1998), *Zen and the Brain.* London/Massachusettes: The MIT Press.

Crossman, A.R., Neary. D. (2000), *Neuroanatomy,* An Illustrated Colour Text 125.

Damasio, H., Grabowski, T., Frank, R., Galaburda, A.M., Damasio, A.R. (1994), The return of Phineas Gage: Clues about the brain from the skull of a famous patient. *Science* **264**: 1102-1105.

Hirai, T. (1989), *Zen Meditation and Pshychotherapy.* Japan Publications, Inc.

Newberg, A., Alavi, A., Baime, M., Mozley P.D., and d' Aquili E. (1997), The measurement of cerebral blood flow during the complex cognitive task of meditation using HMPAO-SPECT imaging. *Journal of Nuclear Medicine,* **38:** 95.

Raine, A., Buchsbaum, M.S., Stanely, J. (1994), Selective reductions in prefrontal glucose metabolism in murderers. *Biological Psychiatry* **29**:14-25.

Ryding, E., Bradvik, B. and Ingvar, D.H. (1996), Silent speech activates prefrontal cortical regions asymmetrically, as well as speech-related areas in the dominant hemisphere. *Brain and Language* **52**:435-451.

Sem-Jacobsen, D., (1976), Electrical stimulation and self-stimulation in man with chronic implanted electrodes: Interpretation and pitfalls of results. (1976). *Brain-Stimulation Reward,* Amsterdam, North Holland, **6:** 505-520.

Travis, F. and Wallace. R.K. (1999), Autonomic and EEG patterns during eyes-closed rest and Transcendental Meditation (TM) practice: the basis for a neural model of TM practice. *Consciousness and Cognition,* **8**: 302-318.

Development of a scale for measuring cognitive styles modified by meditation

Yosuke Sakairi
University of Tsukuba

The original purpose of meditation was to master the distinctive cognitive style related to "enlightenment", and it was not to increase relaxation. In theoretical studies of meditation, passive attitude, or 'letting it happen' (Benson, 1975), non-analytical, focused-attention (Shapiro 1982) and receptivity, or 'letting be' (Smith, 1987), have been described as the essences of all meditation techniques. Empirical studies of meditation should focus on the effect of meditation on cognitive styles, as much as on physiological relaxation and anxiety reduction. However, there are few studies investigating the effects of meditation on cognitive styles.

The Embedded Figures Test to measure field independency (Linden, 1973; Pelletier, 1974; Dillbeck, et.al.,1986, etc.) and the rotated figure-tracking task to measure perceptual distortion (Martinetti, 1976; Williams & Herbert, 1976), have been utilized for meditation research. However, the modification of cognitive styles resulting from meditation has not been clarified. Moreover, there are no tests of cognitive styles modified by meditation.

Studies using special devices to measure modification of cognitive style related to meditation practice have reported increased flexibility and positive-orientation. Dillbeck (1982) measured cognitive flexibility of Transcendental Meditation practitioners by using an anagram task and a word identify task. Gelderloos, *et al.* (1987), used positive and negative words to measure the positive-orientation of meditators' cognitive style. Sakairi (1996, 1997, 1998, 1999) has developed the Selective Recognition Test to measure the degree of positive-negative orientation and the Figure Matching Card Test to measure the flexibility of cognitive style.

The reason for the paucity of research on cognitive style in meditation may be attributed to the time and effort needed for measuring cognitive styles of meditators by using performance tests. If such a scale were available, then meditation research of cognitive styles would be accelerated.

Here, three studies are presented. In the first study, the characteristics of cognitive styles modified through meditation practice were investigated. In the second study, the Scale of Meditation-related Cognitive Styles was developed through factor analysis. In the third study, its reliability and validity of the scale are confirmed.

STUDY 1: THE COGNITIVE STYLES OF MEDITATION PRACTITIONERS

The purpose of this study was to collect descriptions of different cognitive styles that are modified by the practice of meditation, by using self-reports of Transcendental Meditation practitioners, and to categorize those descriptions to reveal the characteristics of cognitive styles in people who meditate.

METHOD

Participants: Participants were 40 long-term, and 52 Short-term Transcendental Meditation practitioners (53 men and 39 women; mean age 37.1 years), with average practice periods of 33 months and 10 weeks respectively.
Procedure: The participants were asked to complete an answer sheet containing the following request: Please describe your impressions about modifications in your cognitive styles resulting from the practice of meditation. The data were analyzed using the K.J. Method (Kawakita, 1967), which is a category creating and sorting technique.

First, short sentences about the varieties of cognitive styles were transcribed onto individual cards. All cards were arranged based on similarity of content and sorted into 10 groups and others by two experts of meditation (a researcher and an instructor of Transcendental Meditation). A category label was given to each group. The reliability of the classification was confirmed according to the coincidence of sorting by three of the four independent judges.

RESULTS AND DISCUSSION

In the 145 cards, 127 sentences were reliably classified into 10 categories by the four judges. Cards without agreement were discarded (18 cards). The label and a typical sentence for each category, as well as the numbers of participants who reported modification of cognitive styles are shown in Table 1.

Among the 10 categories shown in Table 1, categories (1), positive-orientation, (2) flexibility, (4) receptiveness and (5) objectiveness were strict descriptions about cognitive style. Other categories included descriptions of psychological variables. Category (3), magnanimity, was related to interpersonal relations. Category (6), awareness, was related to perception. Category (7), stability of emotion, category (8), cheerfulness of mood, category (9), activity, and category (10), spontaneity, were related to emotion and behavior.

There were many common characteristics in the cognitive style of long-term meditators and short-term meditators. However, long-term meditators reported descriptions in category 3, magnanimity (χ^2=2.85, p<. 10), 8 cheerfulness (χ^2=6.90, p<. 01) and 10 spontaneity (χ^2=4.14, p<. 05), more often

Table 1 *Varieties of cognitive styles reported by meditation practitioner*

Cognitive Style	Long-term meditator Number (%)	Short-term meditator Number (%)
Positive-orientation "My way of thinking and point of view has become more positive-oriented."	13 /40 (33%)	12 /52 (23%)
Flexibility "I have become less concerned about trifles, and it is easier to shift my mind."	7 /40 (18%)	9 /52 (17%)
Magnanimity "I have become more tolerant of other people"	10 /40 (25%) >	6 /52 (12%)
Receptiveness "I have become more accepting of situations, incidents, my weaknesses and so on."	8 /40 (20%)	5 /52 (10%)
Objectiveness "I have got a wider outlook on things and an unbiased, longer-term view of events."	4 /40 (10%)	3 /52 (6%)
Awareness "My thinking has become so clear that I am aware of various things."	2 /40 (5%)	3 /52 (6%)
Mood and Emotion		
Stability "I have become calmer and less irritable."	7 /40 (18%) <	17 /52 (33%)
Cheerfulness "I am always in a good humor and at ease."	7 /40 (18%) >	1 /52 (2%)
Behavior		
Activity "I have become more active and more positive."	3 /40 (8%)	4 /52 (8%)
Spontaneity "I have become more frank and more genuine."	5 /40 (13%) >	1 /52 (2%)
Others	6	12
Total	72	73

than short-term meditators. Description in category 7, stability, was reported by short-term meditators more often than by long-term meditators (χ^2=2.70, p<. 10).

The major modifications of cognitive styles, reported by meditation practitioners were the followings.

(1) Increased positive-orientation and happy-go-lucky attitude.
(2) Decreased obsessiveness and increased flexibility.
(3) Increased receptiveness of situations, of other people and of self-weaknesses.
(4) Increased objectiveness, such as observing things without reacting.

STUDY 2: THE DEVELOPMENT OF A SCALE OF MEDITATION-RELATED COGNITIVE STYLES

The purpose of this study was to develop a scale of meditation-related cognitive styles.

A number of short sentences were made using the descriptions of cognitive styles that were reported by practitioners of meditation. We selected 24 items from the 60 items based on the results of a factor analysis. A second factor analysis was undertaken using data from meditators, non-meditators, and students.

METHOD

Participants and Procedure

1. Creation of items
   The changes of cognitive styles resulting from the practice of meditation, or relaxation training were investigated in 42 trainees of Autogenic Training (23 men and 19 women) and 92 trainees of Transcendental Meditation (53 men and 39 women). Based on their descriptions, 60 short descriptive items were created.
2. Selection of items
   Undergraduate students (N=268, 106 men and 162 women.) responded to the 60 items by using a 5-point, Likert type scale (1=never to 5=always). The result of factor analysis suggested three main factors and one minor factor. From each of the three main factors, we selected eight items based on the score of the factor loadings. These were used to generate a scale with 24 items.
3. Factor analysis of the Scale of Meditation-related Cognitive Styles
   Normal adults (N=548, 303 men and 245 women) responded to the 24 items by using the 5-point Likert type scale (1=never to 5=always). The participants were 172 meditators of Transcendental Meditation, 164 non-meditators, and 212 undergraduate students. The same factors were identified in these three groups of participants by each factor analysis.

RESULTS AND DISCUSSION

Table 2 shows the results of the factor analysis. The factor loading scores of three items (numbers 23, 9, and 1) were less than 0.50.

Table 2 *Factor analysis of the Scale of Meditation-related Cognitive Style*

		Factor loading		
Factor 1:	**[Obsessiveness (-): Flexibility]**	**Factor 1**	**Factor 2**	**Factor 3**
	5. I worry about the past.	-.77	.16	.16
	20. I am caught up by my worries.	-.77	.16	.12
	6. My faults bother me.	-.75	.15	.14
	7. I am distracted by negative thoughts.	-.75	.25	.19
	19. I am detail-oriented.	-.68	.14	.11
	8. I worry about how others view me.	-.65	.22	.07
	18. Others' behavior irritates me.	-.55	.24	.03
	17. I am overly critical of things.	-.54	.12	.07
Factor 2:	**[Receptiveness] e.g., Objectiveness, Equanimity**			
	24. I see things as they are.	-.23	.70	.17
	12. I accept the past as it is.	-.11	.66	.12
	22. I can think objectively when I am in trouble.	-.19	.63	.18
	10. I see things from various angles.	-.33	.61	.27
	11. I observe things from a distance.	-.14	.58	.11
	13. My attitude is positive.	-.34	.53	.33
	14. My thinking is optimistic.	-.42	.50	.35
	21. I do not push myself.	-.37	.50	.27
	23. My emotions are under control.	-.05	.42	-.09
	9. I enjoy my work without being obsessive.	-.26	.38	.36
Factor 3:	**[Happy–go-lucky attribution] e.g. Luckiness, Thankfulness**			
	15. Good things happen to me.	-.15	.07	.78
	3. Things fall into place for me.	-.08	.14	.73
	4. I feel good fortune smiles on me.	-.19	.12	.73
	2. My small wishes come true.	-.08	.17	.67
	16. There are happy coincidences or synchronicity.	-.03	.06	.64
	1. I see the glass as half-full.	-.22	.30	.37

Proportion of variance (24 items) Total=.48 Factor 1=.19, Factor 2=.15, Factor 3=.14 (21 items: except item 1, 9, 23. Total=.51 Factor 1=.21, Factor 2=.16, Factor 3=.14)

Results of preliminary factor analysis for the selection of items

Factor 1. Flexibility:	Item no. 5, 6, 7, 8, 17, 18, 19, 20
Factor 2. Positive-orientation:	Item no.1, 2, 3, 4, 13, 14, 15, 16
Factor 3. Objectiveness:	Item no.9, 10, 11, 12, 21, 22, 23, 24

The result of the second factor analysis of the Scale of Meditation-related Cognitive Styles

Factor 1. Flexibility:	Item no.5, 6, 7, 8, 17, 18, 19, 20
Factor 2. Receptiveness:	Item no. 9, 10, 11, 12, 21, 22, 23, 24, + 13, + 14
Factor 3. Happy-go-lucky attribution	Item no. 1, 2, 3, 4, 15, 16 (-13, -14)

A preliminary factor analysis isolated three factors: flexibility, positive-orientation, and objectiveness. The result of a second factor analysis with more subjects including meditation practitioners indicated that the factor of positive orientation, divided into two factors; the positive-orientation consisted of item 13 and 14 and the happy-go-lucky attribution included all the rest. In the case of three factors, two items of the positive-orientation and eight items of the objectiveness were integrated into the factor of receptiveness.

STUDY 3: RELIABILITY AND VALIDITY OF THE SCALE OF MEDITATION-RELATED COGNITIVE STYLES

The purpose of this study was to confirm the reliability and validity of the Scale of Meditation-related Cognitive Styles by using the following procedures.

1. Cronbach's α
2. Comparison between meditators and non-meditators
3. Confirmation of the score change before and after practicing meditation

METHOD AND RESULTS

1. Cronbach's α

Cronbach's α were calculated to confirm the reliability of the Scale of Meditation-related Cognitive Styles and its subscales based on the date from 548 normal adults. Item 1 and Item 9, which had low factor loading and Item 23, which had low communality, were excluded. The Cronbach's α of each scale are as follows.

The Scale of Meditation-related Cognitive Styles 21 Items excluding no.1, 9, 23: $\alpha=0.81$

Sub Scale 1. Flexibility:	8 Items, No. 5, 6, 7, 8, 17, 18, 19, 20.: $\alpha=0.89$
Sub Scale 2. Receptiveness:	8 Items, No. 10, 11, 12, 13, 14, 21, 22, 24.: $\alpha=0.87$
Sub Scale 3. Happy-go-lucky attribution:	5 Items No. 2, 3, 4, 15, 16.: $\alpha=0.85$

2. Comparison between meditators and non-meditators

Participants consisted of 3 groups, 172 meditators of Transcendental Meditation, 164 non-meditators, and 212 students-control. The average practice period of meditators was 14.2 months. The non-meditators were normal adults on a waiting list for starting meditation. The students were undergraduate students unrelated to meditation.

The mean scores and standard deviations of each group are shown in Table 3. It is clear that the mean total score ($t=6.52$, $df=334$, $p<.001$ and $t=8.91$, $df=382$, $p<.001$), the flexibility score $t=6.12$, $df=334$, $p<.001$ and $t=8.53$, $df=382$, $p<.001$, the receptiveness score $t=4.55$, $df=334$, $p<.001$ and $t=5.74$, $df=382$, $p<.001$, and the happy-go-lucky attribution score $t=4.93$, $df=334$, $p<.$

001 and t=5.77, df=382, p<.001) of the meditator group was significantly higher than the mean scores of both the non-meditator group and the student-control group. There were no significant difference between the non-meditator group and the student-control group.

There were also no significant differences in the total score, the flexibility score, and the receptiveness score between men and women. However, the happy-go-lucky attribution score in women was higher than in men (t=2.95, df=546, p<. 01).

Table 3 The Mean and SD of the Scale of Meditation-related Cognitive Styles

Participant group (No)	Meditator (172)		Non-meditator (164)		Student (212)	
Flexibility (SD)	31.2	5.1	> 27.3	6.4	26.1	6.4
Receptiveness (SD)	30.9	5.3	> 28.1	5.8	27.9	4.8
Happy-go-lucky attribution (SD)	16.0	3.6	> 13.9	4.3	14.0	3.4
Total Score (SD)	78.1	11.5	> 69.3	13.2	67.9	10.8

Participant group (No)	*Men* (303)		Women (245)		Total (548)	
Flexibility (SD)	28.2	6.0	27.8	6.9	28.0	6.4
Receptiveness (SD)	28.9	5.1	29.0	5.8	28.9	5.4
Happy-go-lucky attribution (SD)	14.2	3.6	< 15.2	4.2	14.6	3.9
Total Score(SD)	71.3	11.4	71.9	13.9	71.5	12.5

3. Confirmation of the score change before and after practicing meditation
The cognitive style of 57 normal adults (24 men and 33 women, mean age was 37.7 years) was measured by using the Scale of Meditation-related Cognitive Styles before and after 10 weeks of Transcendental Meditation practice.

The mean scores and standard deviations of the scale are shown in Table 4. The total score (t=5.58, df=56, p<.001) and the flexibility score (t=8.64, df=56, p<.001) increased remarkably after practicing meditation. The receptiveness score also increased significantly (t=3.02, df=56, p<.01). However, the happy-go-lucky attribution score did not change (t=0.24, df=56, n.s.).

Table 4 The score change before and after practicing meditation

Participant No. (57)	Before meditation	After 10 weeks	Significance
Flexibility (SD)	25.2 (5.6)	31.2 (5.4)	p <. 001
Receptiveness (SD)	27.6 (5.9)	29.8 (5.0)	p <. 01
Happy-go-lucky attribution (SD)	14.0 (4.5)	13.9 (4.5)	n.s.
Total Score (SD)	66.8 (12.3)	74.9 (12.0)	p <. 001

Discussion

The reliability and the validity of the Scale of Meditation-related Cognitive Styles were confirmed on the basis of Cronbach's α and by the difference of score between meditators and non-meditators, as well as by the change of scores before and after practicing meditation.

Only scores of one factor; the happy-go-lucky attribution, remained unchanged after 10 weeks of practicing meditation. The high scores on the happy-go-lucky attribution in long-term meditators suggested that it takes a long time to develop a happy-go-lucky attitude.

CONCLUSIONS

The first study suggests that the following cognitive styles are modified through meditation practice.

(1) Increased positive-orientation and happy-go-lucky attitude.
(2) Decreased obsessiveness and increased flexibility.
(3) Increased receptiveness of situations, of self-weaknesses and of other people
(4) Increased objectiveness, i.e., observing things without reacting.

In the second study, a factor analysis confirmed that the Scale of Meditation-related Cognitive Styles consisted of three factors: flexibility, receptiveness, and happy-go-lucky attribution. In Study 3, the reliability and the validity of the scale were confirmed.

REFERENCES

Benson, H. (1975), *The relaxation response.* New York: William Morrow and Company.

Dillbeck, M. C. (1982), Meditation and flexibility of visual perception and verbal problem solving. *Memory and Cognition,* 10, 207-215.

Dillbeck, M. C., Assimakis, P. D., Panayotis, D., Raimondi, D.,& Orme-Jonson, D.W. (1986), Longitudinal effects on the transcendental meditation and TM-Sidhi program on cognitive ability and cognitive style. *Perceptual and Motor Skills,* 62, 731-738.

Gelderloos, P., Goddard, P. H., Ahlstrom, H. H., & Jacoby, R. (1987) Cognitive orientation toward positive values in advanced participants of the TM and TM-Sidhi program. *Perceptual and Motor Skills,* 64, 1003-1012.

Kawakita, J. (1967), *Hasso-ho: Development of creativity.* Tokyo: Chuokoron-Shinsya.

Linden, W. (1973), Practicing of meditation by school children and their levels of field dependence-independence, test anxiety, and reading achievement. *Journal of Consulting and Clinical Psychology,* 41, 139-143.

Martinetti, R. F. (1976), Influence of transcendental meditation on perceptual illusion: A pilot study. *Perceptual and Motor Skills,* 43, 822.

Pelletier, K. (1974), Influence of transcendental meditation upon autokinetic perception. *Perceptual and Motor Skills,* 39, 1031-1034.

Sakairi, Y. (1996), Anxiety levels and selective recognition of meditators. *Journal of Human Sciences,* 8(2), 64-70.

Sakairi, Y. (1997), Change of cognitive attitudes found through questionnaires: Development of measures for cognitive styles modified by autogenic training.

Japanese Journal of Autogenic Therapy, 16(2), 13-23.

Sakairi, Y. (1998), What does meditation change?: Measurement of cognitive styles. In M. M. Delmonte & Y. Haruki (Eds.) *The embodiment of mind: Eastern and Western perspectives*. pp. 57-66, Netherlands: Eburon Publishers.

Sakairi, Y. (1999), *Health psychological study on effects of meditation in reducing anxiety*. Tokyo: Kazama-shobo Publishing.

Shapiro D. H. (1982), Overview: Clinical and physiological comparison of meditation with other self-control strategies. *American Journal of Psychiatry*, 139, 267-274.

Smith, J.C. (1987), Meditation as psychotherapy: A new look at the evidence. In M. A. West (Ed.) *The psychology of meditation*. Oxford: Clarendon Press, pp. 136-149.

Williams, L. R. & Herbert, P. G. (1976), Transcendental meditation and fine perceptual motor skill. *Perceptual and Motor Skills*, 43, 303-309.s

APPENDIX

The Scale of Meditation-related Cognitive Styles: a 6-point, Likert type scale
Please read following statements and indicate how often you engage in the behaviors described in each statement, by checking a number between:
0, never and 5, always.

		Never	Rarely	Sometimes	Often	Usually	Always
1.	I feel good fortune smiles on me.	0	1	2	3	4	5
2.	I accept the past as it is.	0	1	2	3	4	5
3.	I can think objectively when I am in trouble.	0	1	2	3	4	5
4.	I worry about the past.	0	1	2	3	4	5
5.	I am overly critical of things.	0	1	2	3	4	5
6.	Good things happen to me.	0	1	2	3	4	5
7.	I observe things from a distance.	0	1	2	3	4	5
8.	My thinking is optimistic.	0	1	2	3	4	5
9.	I am distracted by negative thoughts.	0	1	2	3	4	5
10.	I am detail-oriented.	0	1	2	3	4	5
11.	My small wishes come true.	0	1	2	3	4	5
12.	My attitude is positive.	0	1	2	3	4	5
13.	I see things from various angles.	0	1	2	3	4	5
14.	My faults bother me.	0	1	2	3	4	5
15.	I worry about how others view me.	0	1	2	3	4	5
16.	Things fall into place for me.	0	1	2	3	4	5
17.	I do not push myself.	0	1	2	3	4	5
18.	I see things as they are.	0	1	2	3	4	5
19.	I am caught up by my worries.	0	1	2	3	4	5
20.	Others' behavior irritates me.	0	1	2	3	4	5
21.	There are happy coincidences or synchronicity.	0	1	2	3	4	5

The receptiveness scale: 8 Items. No. 2, 3, 7, 8, 12, 13, 17, 18

The flexibility scale (reverse items): 8 Items. No.4, 5, 9, 10, 14, 15, 19, 20

The happy-go-lucky attribution scale: 5 Items. No. 1, 6, 11, 16, 21

Effect of Guolin Qigong on psychological states and the immune functioning of lung cancer patients

Weidong Wang[A], *Yu Wu*[A], *Yang Zhao*[A], *Ishii Yasutomo*[B], *Yutaka Haruki*[B]

Abstract

We aimed to study the effect of Guolin Qigong on the quality of life, depressive and anxiety states and lymphocyte subsets of patients with pulmonary cancer. Forty eight inpatients with pulmonary cancer were randomly assigned to two groups. A control group received conventional medicine. A study group received Guolin Qigong training in addition to conventional medicine. Both groups were tested twice with QLQ-C30, SAS, SDS before treatment and after one month's treatment. The blood samples were collected for assessment of lymphocyte subsets at the above two time-points. There were no significant difference between the two groups in lymphocyte subsets before and after treatment. After treatment, a measure of depressive and anxiety level of study group decreased significantly and their life quality were improved, while the control group experienced no significant change. We concluded that Guolin Qigong can improve the quality of life and decrease the depression and anxiety levels in patients with pulmonary cancer.

Introduction

Cancer is a disease with serious psychosomatic implications. Data published by the WHO and the International Cancer Research Organization document that the speed mortality for lung cancer is among the highest for this type of disease. Some research shows that the morbidity of lung cancer has a positive relation with industrialization. But the effect of conventional treatments, such as surgery, chemotherapy and radiotherapy, are not so satisfactory; so a more effective treatment or a set of therapies should be investigated to meet clinical needs.

A Qigong and Rehabilitation Dept. Guang An Men Hospital China Academy of Traditional Chinese Medicine Beijing, P.R.C 100053

B Center of Human Science Waseda University Tokyo, Japan

For correspondence: wuyu@sohu.com

Although the cause of cancer remains unclear, a lot of factors contribute to its occurrence, such as physical, chemical and biological carcinogens and psychosocial factors. Most carcinogens appear to induce cancer by damaging the DNA in cells, thereby producing mutant cells (Setlow, 1978). The body's defenses include enzymes that destroy chemical carcinogens, processes for identifying and repairing damaged DNA and the destruction of mutant or unrepaired DNA by the immune system (Fox, 1978). The processes for repair or destruction of damaged DNA are critical, since faulty DNA repair is associated with an increased incidence of cancer (Setlow, 1978) The possibility of a linkage between emotional distress and DNA repair was explored in work using blood samples obtained from 28 non-psychotic, non-medicated new psychiatric admissions and 28 age- and gender-matched blood bank controls (Kiecolt-Glaser *et al.*, 1985). Following exposure to X-radiation, the lymphocytes from psychiatric patients demonstrated a reduced ability to repair damaged cellular DNA relative to controls. In addition, within the inpatient group, those patients who were more depressed showed significantly poorer repair of damaged DNA than their less depressed counterparts. Some research shows that psychological factors might have some influence on the development and progression of cancer. Thus a new field of study emerged: Psycho-Oncology. The psychosocial factors believed to be related to the initiation and development of cancer are: life events, especially negative ones, coping style, locus of control, social support and features of personality (Forsen, 1991, Maunsell *et al.*, 1995, Fawzy *et al.*, 1993).

Since psychosocial factors can influence the development of cancer, psychological interventions may affect its progression. Some clinical trials have shown that psychological intervention can prolong the survival time and improve the life quality of cancer patients. Most commonly used psychological interventions are: group psychotherapy, progressive relaxation techniques, guided imaginary and meditation, etc. Some of these techniques are similar to some forms of Chinese Qigong. For instance, the progressive relaxation technique is identical to relaxation Qigong, and guided imaginary is very similar to the Cun Xiang technique.

Qigong is a self-training technique, it was developed from a struggle against aging and disease in ancient China. In Qigong practice, people integrate the regulation of body, respiration and mind to achieve a tranquil state. This integration secures its effect. Current studies on Qigong are mostly focused on its physiological effect, few have been done on the psychological effects. To our knowledge, randomized control trial studies have only carried out twice in the last two decades (Wang Guo Fu, 2001). We aim to correct this and other problems in research design.

Subjects and method

1.1 Patient population

The sample population comprised lung cancer inpatients being treated at the Guang An Men Hospital, Beijing, PRC, from May, 2001 to Dec, 2001.

1.1.1 Criteria for inclusion in the study were:

- inpatient being treated in the Oncology Department, Guang An Men Hospital
- lung cancer diagnosed according to international Criteria, stage III or IV, adenocarcinoma or squamous carcinoma
- aged of not less than 30 and not more than 70
- education not less than primary school
- the projected survival time is at least 6 months;
- Karnofsky performance score of not less than 60
- no other mental illnesses or disturbance of consciousness.

1.1.2 Exclusion criteria

- unwilling to participate
- one subject in the intervention was absent for over 20% of his training. He was excluded.

1.2 Instruments

All participants signed an informed consent form and supplied detailed written sociodemographic information. A complete medical record was provided by their treating physician.

Levels of psychological distress were assessed by the use of two self-report questionnaires, the Self-Rating Depression Scale (SDS) and the Self-Rating Anxiety Scale (SAS), both are 20-item assessment tools used extensively to assess the severity of depression and anxiety. The raw scores are converted into a Depression Severity Index (DSI) and an Anxiety Severity Index (ASI), with an accepted cutoff point for psychopathology of 50 on the SDS. Higher scores on the SDS and SAS indicate higher distress. From the DSI, patients can be divided into four groups: Below 50 is regarded as normal; from 50 to 59 mild; from 60 to 69 moderate; above 70 as severe depression.

The third questionnaire we used was the Quality of Life Questionnaire-Core 30 version 3.0 (QLQ-C30). It was issued by the European Organization for Research and Treatment of Cancer (EORTC) and has been used by many research groups. It is composed of both multi-item scales and single item measures. These include five functional scales, three symptom scales, a global health status/QoL scale, and six single items. Each of the multi-item scales includes a different set of items, no item occurs in more than one scale. All of the scales and single-item measures range in score from 0 to 100. A high scale score represents a higher response level. Thus a high score for a functional scale represents *a high/healthy level of functioning*; a high score for the global health status/QoL represents *a high QoL*; but a high score for a symptom scale/item represents *a high level of symptomatology/problems* (QLQ-C30 Score Manual) The subscale categories are shown in Table 1.

Table 1 Subscales of QLQ-C30

Category	Abbreviation	Name of the subscale
Global health status/QoL	QL	Global health status/QoL
Functional scales	PF	Physical functioning
	RF	Role functioning
	EF	Emotional functioning
	CF	Cognitive functioning
	SF	Social functioning
Symptom scales/items	FA	Fatigue
	NV	Nausea and vomiting
	PA	Pain
	DY	Dyspnoea
	SL	Insomnia
	AP	Appetite loss
	CO	Constipation
	DI	Diarrhea
	FI	Financial difficulties

We chose the peripheral blood lymphocyte subsets as the immunological measures, such as: CD3, CD_4, CD_8, CD_4/CD_8, and NK cell. All blood samples were treated by a professional technician on a flow cytometry, following the standard operation procedure of the Kit.

1.3 DESIGN

Participants were randomly assigned to either a control group (N=24) or an experimental group (N=24). Control group members received standard lung cancer care; experimental group members received standard care plus a one-month Guo Lin Qigong practice. All patients completed questionnaires and had blood drawn at two points in time: within 1 week of recruitment (T1), and 1 week following one-month Qigong practice instruction and practice (T2).

1.4 Analytical plan

First, to assure that group randomization was achieved unpaired *t*-tests and/or chi-square tests were used in the preliminary analysis to examine group differences in age, level of education, professions, diagnostic stage. Next, the baseline of the two groups was assessed from all psychological and immunological measures by using unpaired *t*-tests and/or Mann – Whitney U tests, Wilcoxon signed rank test. The data collected at T2 of the two groups were analyzed by using unpaired *t*-tests and/or Mann – Whitney U tests, Wilcoxon signed rank test to find any significant between-group differences. The significance level was set at P <0.05.

1.5 Intervention

We chose Guo Lin Qigong as our intervention, all participants of the intervention group were taught by the same therapist. Every afternoon from 3 pm to 5 pm, participants would practice Guo Lin Qigong under the instruction of the therapist. Guo Lin Qigong can be mainly divided into 7 set of movements, including Natural Walking, middle speed walking, fast speed walking, very fast speed walking etc. It is a kind of manouver which integrates respiration and the walking movements. While walking, each step should be combined with the breathing (for instance: inhaling, exhaling or holding the breath). The mind should be focused on breathing to induce a state of tranquility.

Results

During the study we found a number of patients who met the inclusion Criteria refused to participate in the study (roughly 30%). The reasons they provided were: 1) not interested; 2) not smart enough to learn the manoeuvre; 3) not strong enough to complete the whole session. 48 patients were included in the final sample, 24 were randomly assigned to the intervention group; the other half were assigned to control group. In the intervention group, 3 cases were excluded due to low attendance rate; in the control group, 7 cases, for they refused to complete the questionnaire or attend the blood collection at T2.

2.1 Preliminary analyses

Preliminary analyses indicated that the treatment and control groups (N=38) did not differ significantly in terms of age, sex, level of education, or diagnostic stage. The details are shown in Table 2.

Table 2 Demographic details

	Intervention group (n=21)	Control group (n=17)	*t*	P
Age(SD)	52.52(7.32)	55.65(8.82)	-1.193	0.241
Education(SD)	11.52(2.60)	12.24(3.27)	-0.748	0.46
Sex				
Male	12	10		
Female	9	7	0.011	0.917
Stage				
III	15	10		
IV	6	7	0.663	0.415

The baseline of psychological and immunological conditions of the two group were also assessed. The data are recorded in Table 3. No significant differences were found between the two groups.

Table 3 Psychological and immunological conditions at T1

QLQ	Intervention group Mean(SD)	Control group Mean(SD)	U	P
QL	57.54(11.46)	53.92(13.22)	146.00	0.352
PF	72.86(11.94)	78.43(9.87)	126.500	0.128
RF	58.73(18.72)	61.76(18.41)	162.000	0.642
EF	75.79(14.41)	77.45(13.1)	166.500	0.728
CF	73.81(11.27)	72.55(14.36)	168.500	0.772
SF	54.76(18.37)	47.06(20.61)	130.500	0.161
FA	36.51(17.27)	32.68(22.73)	171.000	0.839
NV	4.76(13.06)	3.92(9.37)	174.500	0.908
PA	15.87(14.41)	10.78(13.1)	143.500	0.308
DY	46.03(22.3)	41.17(14.58)	165.500	0.706
SL	26.98(24.99)	23.53(25.73)	166.000	0.728
AP	23.81(26.13)	23.53(25.73)	178.000	1.000
CO	14.28(19.92)	7.84(14.57)	150.500	0.416
DI	6.35(13.41)	1.96(8.08)	155.000	0.504
FI	41.27(36.37)	49.02(39.3)	159.000	0.581
			T	*P*
SDS	51.9(7.35)	52.24(6.34)	-0.146	0.884
SAS	47.95(8.02)	50.94(8.84)	-1.092	0.282
CD3	69.89(11.02)	66.61(11.92)	0.881	0.384
CD4	39.18(12.24)	37.40(8.45)	0.508	0.614
CD8	28.67(10.37)	29.15(7.08)	-0.162	0.872
CD4/CD8	1.57(0.86)	1.34(0.37)	1.029	0.310
NK	19.20(9.61)	20.26(10.21)	-0.328	0.745

2.2 EFFECTS OF QIGONG ON QLQ-C30

Comparing the result of QLQ-C30 at T2 (Table 4), we observed a significant difference between the groups for 4 subscales: physical function, emotional function, insomnia and appetite loss. The mean rank of PF and EF of the intervention group is higher than the control group, which means the physical function and emotional function of the intervention group are better than the control group. On the other hand, the mean rank of SL and AP of the intervention group is lower than the control group, which indicate the sleep disturbance and appetite loss of the intervention group is milder than the control group.

Table 4 Inter-group Comparison of QLQ-C30 at T2

Subscale	Intervention group(n=21)	Control group(n=17)	U	P
	Mean Rank	Mean Rank		
QL	21.24	17.35	142.00	
PF	23.10	15.06	103.000	0.026*
RF	19.00	20.12	168.000	
EF	23.07	15.09	103.500	0.026*
CF	19.05	20.06	169.000	
SF	22.40	15.91	117.500	
FA	16.74	22.91	120.500	
NV	18.57	20.65	159.000	
PA	19.69	19.26	174.500	
DY	19.43	19.59	177.000	
SL	16.05	23.76	106.000	0.033*
AP	16.00	23.82	105.000	0.031*
CO	18.64	20.56	160.500	
DI	20.31	18.50	161.500	
FI	18.14	21.18	150.000	

We also compared the within group changes from T1 to T2 (Table 5). The results show that in the intervention group, the physical function and emotional function were significantly improved, sleep disorder and appetite loss were relieved, but the role function and social function had deteriorated. In the control group, the physical function, role function and social function were deteriorated, the nausea/vomit symptom was worse.

Table 5 Within Group Changes from T1 to T2

subscale	Intervention group (n=21)	Control group (n=17)	subscale	Intervention group (n=21)
	Z	P	Z	P
QL	-1.625	0.104	-0.837	0.403
PF	-2.763	0.006*[a]	-2.989	0.003*[b]
RF	-2.330	0.020*[b]	-3.236	0.001*[b]
EF	-2.550	0.011*[a]	-1.254	0.210
CF	-0.184	0.854	-1.633	0.102
SF	-2.530	0.011*[b]	-2.913	0.004*[b]
FA	-1.882	0.060	-0.618	0.537
NV	-1.656	0.098	-2.333	0.020*[a]
PA	-0.500	0.617	-0.601	0.548
DY	-1.887	0.059	-0.107	0.915
SL	-1.999	0.046*[b]	-0.037	0.971
AP	-2.271	0.023*[b]	-0.215	0.829
CO	-1.025	0.305	-1.251	0.211
DI	-1.000	0.317	-1.732	0.083
FI	-1.000	0.317	-0.447	0.655

Note: a indicates score at T2 is higher than T1
b indicates score at T2 is lower than T1

2.3 Effects of Qigong on SDS and SAS

At T2 the SDS score dropped significantly in the intervention group, whereas in the control group it increased slightly. Independent sample T tests revealed a significant difference between the two groups (t=-3.557 P=0.001) at T2. (See Figure 1).

Figure 1 SDS scores of two group at T1 and T2

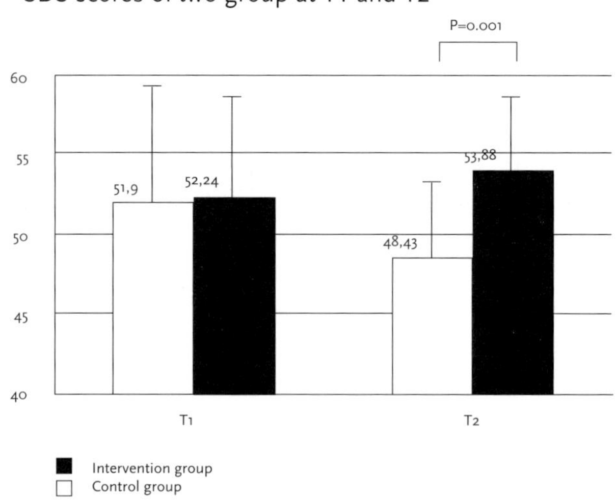

SAS scores of the two groups from T1 to T2 revealed a similar pattern to that of the SDS scores. Details are shown in Figure 2.

Figure 2 SAS scores of two groups at T2

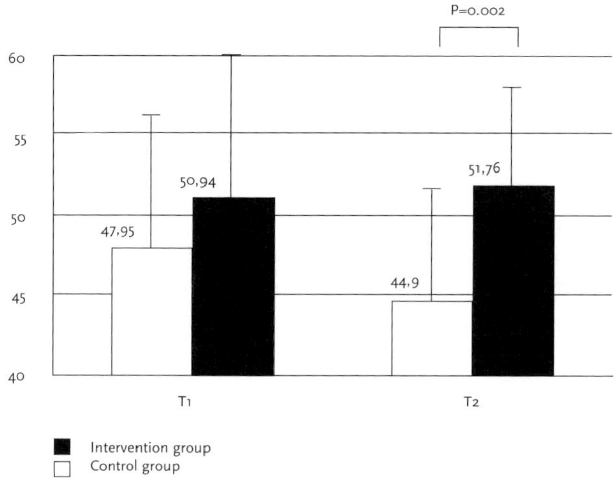

2.4 Effects of Qigong on immune system

All measures of the immune system of the two groups at T1 and T2 are shown in Table 6. Sample t-tests revealed no significant difference between the two groups at T2 (see Table 7). As shown in Table 6, the ratio of CD_4/CD_8 approached significant difference (P=0.064).

Table 6 Immune System Measures of the Two Groups at T1 and T2

	Intervention group(n=21)	Control group(n=17)		Intervention group(n=21)
	T1	T2	T1	T2
CD_3	69.89(11.02)	68.68(12.70)	66.61(11.92)	67.61(12.27)
CD_4	39.18(12.24)	41.53(10.29)	37.40(8.45)	37.16(7.75)
CD_8	28.67(10.37)	26.91(10.04)	29.15(7.08)	28.65(7.21)
CD_4/CD_8	1.57(0.86)	1.73(0.75)	1.34(0.37)	1.37(0.41)
NK	19.20(9.61)	19.59(9.70)	20.26(10.21)	20.22(11.44)

Table 7 Differences between the two groups at T2

	t	P
CD_3	0.262	0.795
CD_4	1.449	0.156
CD_8	-0.600	0.552
CD_4/CD_8	1.917	0.064
NK	-0.183	0.856

DISCUSSION

The present study was designed to evaluate the psychological and immunological benefit of Qigong practice for lung cancer patients. To our knowledge, this is the first time attempt to evaluate the effect of Qigong with QoL. As a result, the present findings are simultaneously both promising and somewhat limited.

3.1 PSYCHOLOGICAL FINDINGS

Beneficial psychological effects were observed in lung cancer patients participating in the one-month Guo Lin Qigong practice. Compared to the control group, four QLQ-C30 subscales (the physical function, emotional function, sleep disorder and appetite loss) of the intervention group showed significant difference at T2. The Qigong practice seemed to have had a positive effect on these aspects. This result is a bit different when compared to another study (Tang, Li Li, 2001), which applied a five-session psychological intervention with 44 cancer patients. They found emotional functioning, cognitive functioning, global health, fatigue, nausea/vomiting and appetite changed for the better in the intervention group. The difference in these results may be related to differences in the intervention method.

Comparing the data at T1, the severity of the score for nausea/vomiting increased at T2 in both groups, but the change in the control group is significant while not so obvious in the intervention group. Should Guo Lin Qigong decrease the side-effect (nausea/vomiting) caused by chemotherapy? We think further investigations should be made before arriving at a conclusion. Other research (Burish & Jenkins, 1992) showed that through biofeedback and relaxation training, the side effects of chemotherapy can be greatly reduced. The reason we did not find this effect may be that the key point of relaxation training is to loosen up all muscles as much as possible, to some extent it is similar to Static Qigong, but Guo Lin Qigong is a Dynamic practice. Although during practice we also asked the patients to get relaxed, the extent of relaxation is obviously different with the relaxation training. To reduce the side effect of the chemotherapy (nausea/vomiting), maybe relaxation training is more effective.

Decreases in both social and role functioning were observed at T2; this may reflect the effects of hospitalization. Patients from both groups had to stay in bed for 6 to 8 hours in the daytime to get transfusions, at night they had to sleep on the same bed. We hypothesize that there would be less negative effect on the QoL if the patients can receive the chemotherapy as outpatients. We were surprised when reviewing the QLQ-C30 that the physical functioning of the control group decreased significantly at T2, but we couldn't make the judgment that conventional treatment would harm the physical functioning, for the sample of our study was very small and there were nearly 30% dropped out in the control group. Any explanation to the changes that took place in the control group should be made more cautiously.

Patients in the intervention group exhibited significant decreases over time in a measure of depression and anxiety whereas scores for control group patients increased slightly for the same measure. We think Guo Lin Qigong can decrease the depression and anxiety levels of cancer patients. But due to the small sample size of our study, insufficient power may have contributed to the large number of negative findings among the psychological measures. It is also possible that one or more of the present "significant" findings is simply due to chance. However, it should be noted that even at the more conservative $p<0.01$, the majority of the present results are still significant.

3.2 Immunological findings

NK cells play an important role in a variety of immune functions, including defence against viral infections (Welsh, 1996), surveillance of tumor cells (Herberman & Ortaldo, 1981) and eliminating metastatic tumor cells (Whiteside & Herberman, 1989, Page *et al.*, 1994). The ratio of CD4/CD8 and NK cell amount are closely related with depression in digestive cancer patients (Zheng, Bo Hua 1999), these immunological measures are significantly lower in the depressed patients than in the non-depressed patients. Some studies, such as that of Gruber *et al.* (1993) also showed that psychological interventions can improve immunological functions. They used relaxation training and biofeedback to treat 10 advanced cancer patients. After a one-year follow up, they found that a lot of immunological measures were improved (e.g. NK cell activity, IgM, IgG, IL-2). In our current research, no significant differences were observed on the immunological measures which were chosen. This is somewhat similar to Mark's study (Mark, *et al.*, 2000). He found psychological intervention did not improve NK cell activity in breast cancer patients, but the IFN-γ levels decreased substantially over time in the control group but not in the intervention group. As IFN-γ can improve immune functioning, they think, compared to the intervention group, the immune function of the control group decreased significantly. In other words, the psychological intervention appeared to be effective on immune functioning in another form. We did not take the IFN-γ as one of our immunological measures. However, future investigations need to examine whether the IFN-γ is more sensitive to psychological intervention than NK cell. The reason for our negative result maybe lies in: 1) too small a sample size to produce a significant statistical result; 2) interference of the treatment: the technician who is in charge of the immunological measures said that, in general, the immunological measures of the patients in our hospital are usually higher than those in western medical hospitals, although we use the same instrument and even the same Kit in the measurement. All patients in the oncology department of our hospital will take herbal medicine as one of their treatments, and most of these medicines can strengthen immune functioning. From the data we collect in our study, the mean of the immunological measures of both groups are within the normal range. 3) The amount of tranquilizers used for the participants. The key element of Qigong practice is regulation of the body, breath and mind. Regulation of the mind is the most difficult and important part. Only when the participant can control the mind, would he be considered proficient as a Qigong practitioner. In the current study, patients had only have one month to learn and practice Qigong, many participants could only integrate movement and breath, and could not achieve the tranquil state, so the result may be somewhat attenuated, as suggested by other research (Wang Guo Fu, 2001): the effectiveness of Qigong practice would be reduced by the tranquilization. The ratio of CD4/CD8 of the intervention group increased at T2, the t test showed the change approached significance ($p=0.064$), but the clinical significance of this kind of fluctuation within the normal range.

Another point we want to mention is that before each practice, the therapist would encourage the patients to communicate with each other about their feelings during their practice. This may have helped them to be more confident in their fight against the cancer. Sometimes he would give the participants some tips to deal with stressful events. The therapist said this is called 'talking therapy'. At the beginning, the participants were not familiar with each other, they seemed to be ashamed to talk. Later they would communicate or even make jokes with others. We think this is somewhat similar to their being in a supportive group. During Qigong practice although there must be some psychological factors, if we could exclude some of them (e.g. the group effect), the effect of Qigong would be more clearly observed.

Conclusion

1. Lung cancer patients (Stage III or IV) who are willing to practice Guo Lin Qigong can improve their Life Quality, reduce the level of depression and anxiety.
2. The influence of Guo Lin Qigong on immunological measures is not significant in our study. We suggest a bigger sample size, better control of treatment and a longer observation period in future studies.
3. If the effect of Qigong practice are investigated, the appropriate procedure would be individual training and practice in Static Qigong, so as to exclude the possible effect of membership in a supportive group.
4. In future studies, we suggest an indicator which can reflect the level of tranquilization should be taken into account, thus the effect of Qigong would be measured more precisely.

Acknowledgement

Special thanks to Mr. Dayuan YU, Ms. Kaifang HE and Mr. Zengjun Shi of the Beijing Anti-cancer Club who provide the instruction in Guo Lin Qigong.

References

Burish, T.G..& Jenkins, R.A. (1992), Effectiveness of Biofeedback and Relaxation Training in Reducing the Side Effects of Cancer Chemotherapy. Health Psychol,11:17-23

Fawzy, F.L, Fawzy, N.W., Hyun, C.S., Elashoff, R., Guthrie, D., Fahey, J.L., Morton, D.L. (1993), Malignant melanoma; Effects of an early structured psychiatric intervention, coping, and affective state on recurrence and survival 6 years later. *Archives of General Psychiatry* **50**, 681-689.

Forsen, A. (1991), Psychosocial stress as a risk for breast cancer. *Psychotherapy and Psychosomatics* **55**:176-185.

Fox, B.H. (1978), Premorbid psychological factors as related to cancer incidence 1. *J Behav. Med.*, **1**:45-33.

Gruber, B.L., Hersch, S.P., Hall, R.N., Waletzky, L.R., *et al.* (1993), Immunological responses of breast cancer patients to behavioral interventions. *Biofeedback and Self-Regulation,* **18(1)**:15-22.

Herberman, R.B. & Ortaldo, J.R. (1981), Natural killer cells: their role in defenses against disease. *Science,* **214**:24-30.

Kiecolt-Glaser, J.K, Stephens, R., Lipitz, P., Speicher, C.E., & Glaser, R. (1985), Distress and DNA repair in human lymphocytes. *J Behav Med,* **8**:311-320.

Mark, R., Larson, Paul R., Duberstein, Nancy L., Talbot, Christopher Caldwell, Moynihan, Jan A. (2000), A presurgical psychosocial intervention for breast cancer patients: psychological distress and the immune response *Journal of Psychosomatic Research* **48**:187-194.

Maunsell, E., Brisson, J., Deschenes, L. (1995), Social support and survival among women with breast cancer. *Cancer* **76**:631-637.

Page, G.G., Ben-Eliyahu S., Liebeskind, J.C. (1994), The role of LGL, NK cells in surgery-induced promotion of metastasis and its attenuation by morphine. *Brain Behav Immun* **8**:241 250.

QLQ-C30 Score Manual

Setlow, R.B. (1978), Repair deficient human disorders and human cancer. *Nature,* **271**:713-717.

Tang Li Li, (2001), The effect of group therapy on cancer patients' emotion and quality of life. *Chinese Behavioral Medicine* **9**:170-172.

Wang Guo Fu (2001), The adjuvant effect of Chinese inner respiration method on advanced cancer patients. *Chinese Behavioral Medicine,***10**, 298-300.

Welsh, R.M. (1996), Regulation of virus infections by natural killer cells. *Natural Immunity Cell Growth Regul.* **5**:169,199.

Whiteside, T.T., Herberman, R.B. (1989), The role of natural killer cells in human disease. *Clin.Immun Immunopathol* **53**:1- 23.

Zheng Bo Hua (1999), Study on the psychological response and immunity of digestive cancer patients. *Chinese Behavioral Medicine* **8**:195-196

Effectiveness of Jikan-ho, a method of self observation, in reducing stress and increasing accessibility of positive memories

Fusako Koshikawa, Yasutomo Ishii, Michiko Sakata, Naoko Akutagawa
(Waseda University)
&
J. Mark G. Williams (University of Oxford)

The purposes of this study are to discuss the mechanism of the effects of Jikan-ho's and to report two corroborative experiments on the effects of the Jikan-ho. First, a brief explanation of Jikan-ho is presented. Second, the mechanism of Jikan-ho's effect is commented upon from the viewpoint of the latest cognitive behavioral models of psychopathology. Then two experiments on the effects of Jikan-ho are reported, the first experiment examining the effect on daily stress and the second experiment examining the effect on accessibility of positive memories. Lastly, the results of the two experiments are reviewed and it is suggested that Jikan-ho may be effective in preventing disorders of depression and anxiety.

1. Explanation of the Jikan-ho technique

Jikan-ho is a technique based on traditional Buddhist meditation, and the term means, literally, "technique to look at oneself." The term 'Jikan-ho' appears in "Psychotherapy" (1904) by Enryo Inoue, a famous scholar of Eastern psychotherapy techniques. Takeo Nimiya (1958) and Reiko Yamaguchi (1991) also discussed Jikan-ho as a technique for stress reduction and improvement of mental health through self-observation (Koshikawa, 2000). Jikan-ho does not require a quiet environment or any specific physical exercise, but rather can be practiced in any place or situation. In other words, Jikan-ho is characterized by its greater practical applicability than Zazen or other types of meditation (Koshikawa, 2000).

As for Jikan-ho's specific procedures, there are several variations. Those used in the following experiments are as follows.

Procedures of Jikan-ho

1. To recall an unpleasant experience, or an incident you cannot leave behind, or any other situation where you were hurt, angered, or helpless.
2. To recall clearly the unpleasant feeling together with the unpleasant situation.
3. To picture in your mind something like a movie screen in front of you when you clearly recall the unpleasant mood, and imagine yourself watching the unpleasant circumstance unfurl on the screen.
4. To think that your "self" watching the screen is not the self ON the screen, that it is simply the self "watching the drama in the screen in front of you" "without thinking anything" or "without making any judgment"
5. To continue to watch the screen with such a non-analytical mind.

Jikan-ho requires that you look at your own past or on-going experience as if from outside of yourself. You are instructed to look at yourself from a detached, neutral position, and when you look at the experience from such perspective, you can more easily look at your own experience without making any evaluation and interpretation. Jikan-ho is a technique that neutralizes the mood attendant on a specific experience through a shift of focus. As a result, it reduces the negative aspect of a stressful experience by helping you recognize the experience with your neutralized mood.

2. The mechanism of Jikan-ho's effects from perspective of models of cognitive behavioural pathology

The latest theories on cognitive behavioural pathology give weight to the effects of secondary depression or secondary anxiety on the onset and course of mental illness. The Differential Activation Hypothesis of Teasdale (1985) and Cognitive Model of Panic Attacks of Clark (1986) are good examples. "Secondary depression" means the depressive state of mind arising due to one's own depression, and "secondary anxiety" means the fearful state of mind over one's own uncontrollable anxiety. Everyone experiences slight moods of depression or anxiety in their daily lives. Negative evaluation of such negative moods would further intensify these moods, and intensified moods would give rise to even further negative evaluations and interpretations. According to the models of Teasdale and Clark, this vicious circle is of central importance to the outbreak of depression and panic attacks. In other words, they hypothesize that intensifying mutual interactions between such negative evaluation and related moods are the main cause of the outbreak of these disorders.

From the perspective of such models, an important element in the prevention of and therapy for depression and anxiety disorders is the prevention of the aggravation of secondary depression and secondary anxiety. What is important is to break the cycle of these mutual interactions between negative evaluations and negative moods at as early a stage as possible. In our view, Jikan-ho is an effective means of breaking such cycles. Jikan-ho requires that one look at one's own stressful experience from a detached viewpoint without being involved in that experience. It might be difficult to change an actually occurring mood and cognitive pattern while going through, or imagining, an unpleasant experience. However, the practice of shifting viewpoint, or getting "another" viewpoint, would make these changes easier. Such shifted viewpoint would enable one to look at oneself and the stressful situation in a unique way that is without any evaluation or interpretation. It is through this process that it is possible to neutralize emotional states.

Why is it possible to neutralize emotional states just by observing an experience without any evaluation or interpretation? When you criticize or evaluate something, you will necessarily end up with an emotion which is either in the positive or in the negative. Whether your emotion is positive or negative naturally depends upon whether the experience coincides or conflicts with your interests, and the intensity of such emotion hinges upon the degree to which you are involved in the experience. To put it differently, what creates your mood is your evaluation of an experience either consciously or unconsciously. Therefore, it will be possible to neutralize a negative mood incurred by a criticism or evaluation by obtaining a cognitive attitude free from any criticism or evaluation. And this attitude will facilitate the process by which you shift a negative cognition induced by the negative mood to an objective and realistic cognition, enabling you to experience the difficulty without adding to it by your reactions.

3. Experiments on Jikan-ho

Now we would like to report on two experimental studies of Jikan-ho. The first experiment concerned Jikan-ho's effect on stress reduction in daily life. It was a study of the long term effects of Jikan-ho. The second experiment concerned the effect of Jikan-ho on memory accessibility. This was a study of the short-term effect of Jikan-ho. In each study, Jikan-ho's effects were compared with those of the technique of breath-regulation.

Experiment 1: Jikan-ho's effect on stress reduction

Method

The participants were 44 undergraduate students, 15 males and 29 females. They were randomly allocated to the Jikan-ho group (22 students, 9 males and 13 females) and breathing technique group (22 students, 6 men and 16 women). The process of Experiment 1 is shown in Figure 1. In the Base 1 period the participants were asked to rate their subjective stress levels every day, before they went to bed, for one week. One week later, a pre-test was administered. The pre-test consisted of 6 sub-scales of the Cornell Medical Index-Health Questionnaire (CMI; Brodman *et al.*, 1955: Japanese version, Kanehisa & Fukamachi, 1976), the Trait Anxiety Inventory, Form X-2 (STAI-T; Spielberger, Gorsuch, and Lushene, 1970: Japanese version, Mizuguchi, Shimonaka, and Nakazato, 1970) and a subjective stress scale using a 7-point rating scale ranging from 0 (felt no stress at all) to 6 (felt very strong stress). Following the pre-test, the students received the training session of their assigned technique. The number of participants in the session ranged from 1 to 7. Each group practised Jikan-ho or the breathing technique for about an hour and a half. For the following two weeks they were asked to practise their respective techniques at least once every day and to rate subjective stress levels every day. Following the end of the two-week period, a post-test that consisted of the same contents as the pre-test was administered and the participants were requested to stop their practise. In the Base 2 period, for one week following the end of the practise, the participants were asked to rate their subjective stress levels each day.

The methods of practising Jikan-ho and the breathing technique used in this experiment are as follows.

Figure 1 Process of Experiment 1

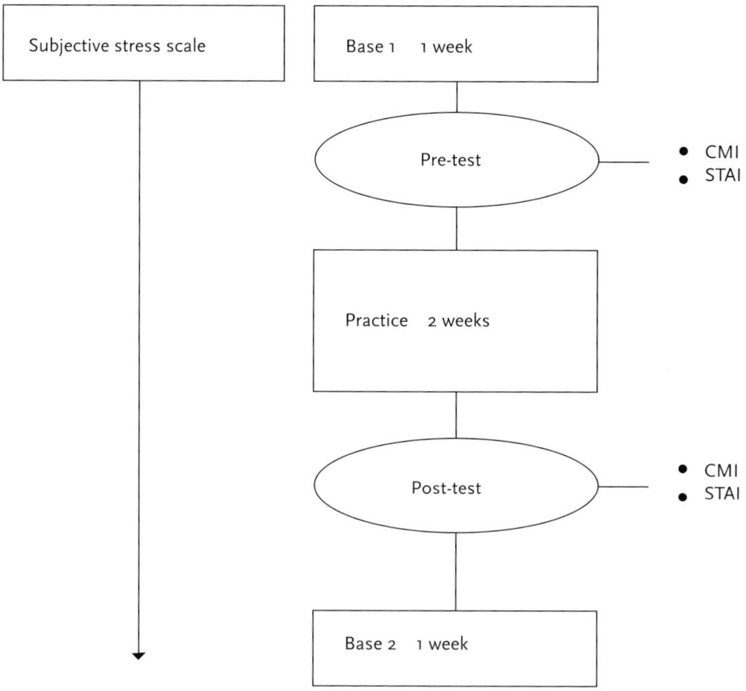

Method of practising Jikan-ho

Participants were instructed on how to practice the Jikan-ho technique for about 90 minutes. After receiving instructions the participants practised the technique twice. On each occasion the participants were asked individually to give their impressions and to discuss any unsuccessful or difficult points, on which they were given advice by the experimenters.

As for their daily practise of the technique, the participants were instructed that when faced with a stressful situation they should use Jikan-ho immediately and directly, in other words, they should just look at the situation from the perspective of the "self" who observed without evaluation and interpretation. Further, they were instructed that in their ordinary daily living they should just look at what they were doing at each moment from the perspective of the "self" who did not make any judgment or who just watched the circumstance unfurl in front of him/her (i.e. the self who was watching an unpleasant circumstance in the course of training). They were also told to practice the Jikan-ho technique at least once each day even in a stress-free situation.

Method of practising breathing technique

Participants were instructed on how to practice the breathing technique for about 90 minutes. The breathing technique's specific training procedures were as follows.

1 Put your hands on your stomach with the right hand below the left hand.

2 Stretch your back as if you are pushing up the ceiling with the top of your head. Stretching your back is important, do not lean against a back support. You will stretch your back straight but let other parts of your body relax.

3 Keep your eyes open or closed, and when you keep your eyes open, please try to look down 45 degrees slantwise (half open eyes). If the scenery in front of you bothers you, you can close your eyes and if the darkness in closing your eyes makes you feel uneasy, you can use half open eyes.

4 Exhale and inhale while putting some of your strength around the navel of your abdomen. Count "on-e" when exhaling and then inhale. When you exhale again, you will count "tw-o." Go on like this until you count up to ten. When you finish counting ten, start all over again from one. If you find that you have counted beyond ten, go back to one and start again.

5 As you get used to point 4 (above) increase the length of your exhaling and shorten the length of your inhaling. Exhale as slowly, smoothly and thoroughly as possible.

What is important is that you concentrate on your counting without thinking of anything else. You may not be able to concentrate on counting when your mind gets cluttered with all kinds of thoughts. When something like this happens, just leave it alone and continue to count without forcibly trying to brush away your thoughts.

After being given the above explanations the participants were instructed to practise the technique and were individually asked to give their impressions and describe any unsuccessful or difficult points, on which they were given advice.

By way of applying the breathing technique in their daily living, participants were instructed to use the technique in their daily lives as well as in stressful situations. They were instructed to use the breathing technique at least once each day even in stress-free situations.

Results and Discussion

Figure 2 shows the results of CMI. For the purpose of comparing the effectiveness of the two techniques, an analysis of covariance was computed, with the type of technique as the fixed factor, mean CMI scores in the post-test as the dependent variable and the CMI scores in the pre-test as the covariate. The analysis showed that Jikan-ho was significantly more effective than Breathing on the reduction of CMI score ($F(1,44)=4.73$, $p=0.04$).

The mean scores of pre-test and post-test were then tested with the corresponding t-test in each technique. Only in the Jikan-ho group, the total score based on 6 subscales at post-test was significantly lower than that of pre-test (G+I+N+P+Q+R; $t(42)=2.00$, $p<05$, one-tailed test.). No significant difference was found in STAI.

Figure 3 shows resultant subjective stress levels. The mean scores of the base 1 period and the practice period were tested with the corresponding t-test in each technique. In both techniques, the practice period showed significantly lower stress levels than the base 1 period (Jikan-ho group: $t(42)=3.51$, $p<01$, two-tailed test. Breathing technique group: $t(42)=2.87$, $p<01$, two-tailed test). No significant difference in subjective stress levels was found between the two techniques.

The results if this study suggest that the Jikan-ho technique, although not differing from breathing technique in subjective stress, did bring about significantly larger positive effects on the Cornell Medical Index-Health Questionnaire. This suggests that Jikan-ho was able to bring about a wider range of psychological changes than breathing, despite the fact that individuals were being asked to bring to mind unpleasant events at least once per day. How might such wider generalization come about? One possibility is that the deliberate retrieval and 'holding in non-judgmental awareness' of unpleasant memories brings about a change in underlying cognitive processes, thus improving a person's resilience to physical and psychological stressors. In order to investigate this possibility, we undertook a further study, comparing Jikan-ho and breathing techniques, evaluating their relative impact upon biases in episodic memory retrieval.

Figure 2 Results of CMI (total of 6 sub-scales)

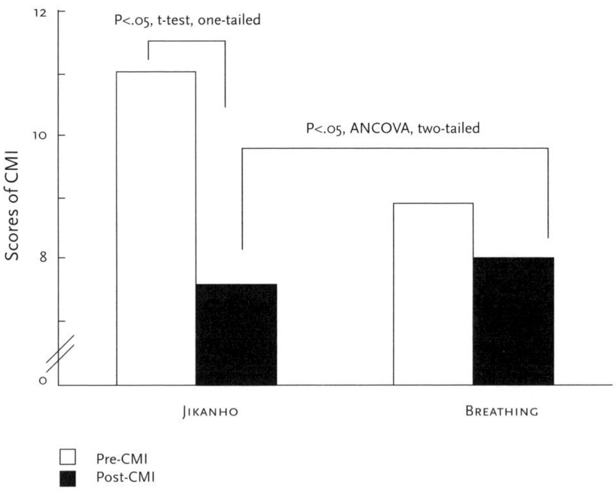

Figure 3 Results of subjective stress scale

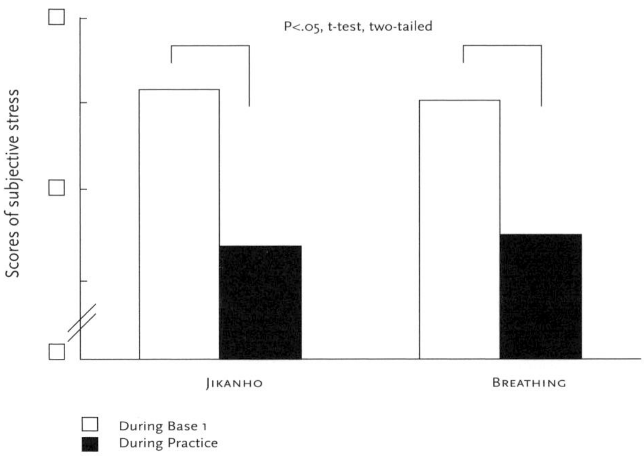

Experiment 2: the effects of Jikan-ho on biases in accessibility of episodic memories

Method

The participants were 62 undergraduate students and they were divided into three groups, a Jikan-ho group, a breathing technique group and a control group. The process of the Experiment 2 is shown in Figure 4. The former two groups were given explanations of the respective techniques (Jikan-ho, breathing) prior to the experiment. At the outset of the experiment, the participants were asked to recall certain unpleasant incidents they experienced in the past and to retain the images for five minutes for the purpose of inducing unpleasant moods. Then, the first selective recognition test was conducted as a pre-test. The test consisted of two different sheets, "a stimulus-words sheet" and "a check-list sheet for recognition." In the former sheet, 20 words, 10 positive and 10 negative, were randomly listed. In the latter sheet, these same 20 words and another 10 interferer words (5 positive and 5 negative) were located randomly.

At first the participants were exposed to the stimulus-words sheet for 15 seconds. Then, with the sheet turned over, they were asked to count aloud backwards from 200 to 1 for one minute to prevent rehearsal. After that, they were asked to stare silently at the check-list sheet for 15 seconds and to recognize a maximum of 15 words, entering figures from 1 through 15, in the order of their certainty of recognition, in the brackets beside each of the words.

After this pre-test, the Jikan-ho group and the breathing technique group were asked to practise their respective techniques for 5 minutes. The control group was asked to recall unpleasant incidents for 5 minutes. Following this, the second selective recognition test was conducted as a post-test.

In selective recognition tests, two versions of the sheets were prepared. In the pre-test, version A was used for half of the subjects in each group, and version B was used for the rest. In the post-test every subject completed a different version of the sheet from that used in the pre-test.

Figure 4 Process of experiment 2

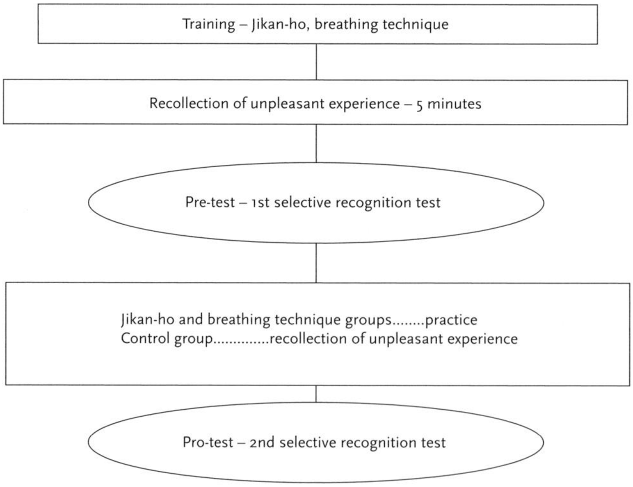

Results and discussion

For the purpose of comparing the three groups, an analysis of covariance was computed, with the type of group as a fixed factor, the number of positive words in the post-test as a dependent variable and the number of positive words in the pre-test as a covariate. The analysis shows that the main effect of the groups was significant (F(2,58)=3.65.p<.05). The multiple comparison based on Bonferroni's test showed the number of recognized positive words in the post-test of the Jikan-ho group was significantly greater than that in the control group (Mse=2.41,p<05). No significant difference was observed between the breathing technique group and the control group, and between the Jikan-ho group and the breathing technique group.

The numbers of recognized positive words in the pre-test and in the post-test were tested with a corresponding t-test. Figure 5 shows the result. In the Jikan-ho group, the number of positive words in the post-test was significantly greater than that in the pre-test (t(20)=3.51, p<.01, two-tailed test). In the breathing technique group, the difference between the pre-test and the post-test showed a significant tendency towards increased recognition of positive words (t(20)=1.78, p<.10, two-tailed test). As for the control group, there was no difference (t(19)=0.95, n.s., two-tailed test).

These results suggest a slight though nonsignifcant superiority for the Jikan-ho technique over breathing. However, the breathing technique did not perform significantly better than the control condition, whereas Jikan-ho did result in significantly more positive words being recalled than controls

Figure 5 Results of the selective recognition test

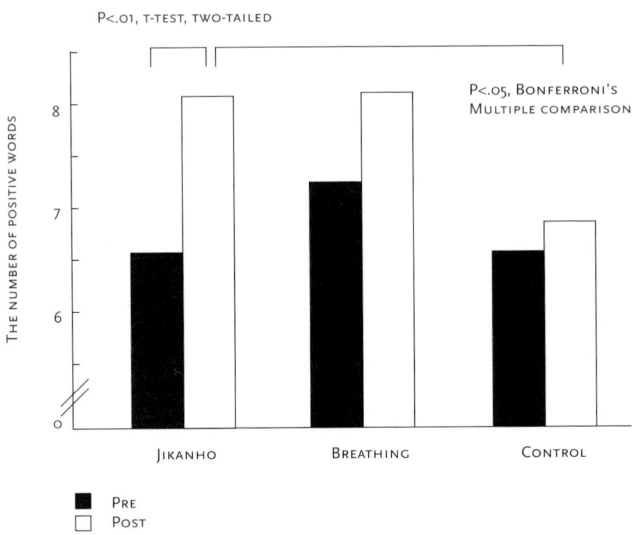

4. General discussion

The results of Experiment 1 suggest that Jikan-ho has the effect of reducing daily stress through daily practice of the technique. These results support those of an earlier study by the present authors (Koshikawa *et al.*, 2000). The results of Experiment 2 suggest that Jikan-ho has the potential to break an intensifying cycle between negative moods and cognition. According to Bower's associative network model of emotion (1981), one of the basic theories in cognitive psychopathology, an activated emotion will be transmitted through an associative memory network and will help to activate the memories connected to the emotion. In the pre-test of Experiment 2, recollection of unpleasant incidents induces negative moods in the participants, and the moods lead them to choose a greater number of negative words. In the post-test, the use of the Jikan-ho technique changes the negative moods and leads the subjects to choose a greater number of positive words. These results suggest the possibility that Jikan-ho helps one extricate oneself from the intensifying cycle between negative moods and cognition shown by Teasdale's model.

When compared with the breathing technique, Jikan-ho was found more effective in both Experiment 1 and Experiment 2. It may be assumed the relatively higher effectiveness of Jikan-ho comes from its being a cognitive technique which deals more directly with negative experiences than a physical technique like the breathing technique.

The results of the present experiments certainly point to the effectiveness of Jikan-ho in reducing stress and weakening the negative moods and increasing accessibility to positive words. These results suggest that Jikan-ho can break the vicious cycle of negative moods and cognitions and might help in the prevention of depression or anxiety disorders in their initial stages. It is consistent with a number of recent studies suggesting that mindfulness-based approaches can prevent relapse in depression (Teasdale, Segal, Williams *et al.*, 2000) and that part of this effect is accompanied by changes in underlying memory retrieval processes (Williams, Segal, Teasdale and Soulsby, 2000).

Acknowledgements

I would like to express my thanks to Dr. Catherine Crane of University of Oxford for proof-reading my text.

References

Bower, G..H. (1981), Mood and memory. *American Psychologist* **36:** 129-148.

Brodman, K., Erdman, A. J., Jr., and Wolff, H.G.. (1955), *Cornell Medical Index–Health Questionnaire Manual* (Revised, 1955), The New York Hospital and the Developments of Medicine (Neurology) and Psychiatry, Cornell University Medical College. (Japanese version, Kanehisa, T., and Fukamachi, K. 1976 CMI. Sankyo-bo: Kyoto.)

Clark, D.M. (1986), A cognitive approach to panic. *Behaviour Research and Therapy,* **24:** 461-470.

Koshikawa,F. (2000), A technique of self-awareness in the East. In W. Weidong, Y, Sasaki and Y. Haruki (Eds.), *Bodywork and Psychotherapy in the East.* Delft: Eburon, pp.195-203.

Koshikawa, F., Kubozono,Y., Ishii,Y., and Haruki,Y. (2000), Effectiveness of The Jikan-ho (a Japanese self-awareness technique) on Stress Reduction. *International Journal of Psychology, Abstracts of the XXVII International Congress of Psychology,* p.78.

Nimiya, T. (1958), *Ningen shinka no mirai* [Future in human development]. Tokyo: Hakko-sha.

Sakairi, Y. (1999), *Meisou-ho no fuan teigen kouka ni kansuru rinsyo sinrigaku-teki kenkyu.* [Clinical Psychological Study on the effects of Anxiety Reduction by Meditation. Doctoral Dissertation (Tsukuba University),

Segal, Z.V., Williams, J.M.G., Ridgeway, V., Lau, M., & Soulsby, J. (2000), Reducing risk of recurrence of major depression using Mindfulness-based Cognitive Therapy. *Journal of Consulting and Clinical Psychology,* **68:** 615-23

Spielberger, C.D., Gorsuch, R.T., and Lushene, R.E. (1970), *Manual for the state-trait anxiety inventory.* Consulting Psychologists Press. (Japanese version, Mizuguchi, K., Shimonaka, J., and Nakazato, K. (1970), Japanese Version STAI. Kyoto: Sankyo-bo.

Teasdale, J. (1985), Psychological treatments for depression: how do they work? *Behaviour Research and Therapy,* **23:** 157-165

Williams, J.M.G., Teasdale, J.D., Segal, Z.V. & Soulsby, J. (2000), Mindfulness-Based Cognitive Therapy reduces overgeneral autobiographical memory in formerly depressed patients. *Journal of Abnormal Psychology* **109:** 150-155.

Yamaguchi, R. (1991), *Jiko kakumei no genri to hoho* [Principles and methods on self-revolution]. Tokyo: Tama-shuppan.

Mindfulness meditation: a treatment of binge eating disorder

Jean L. Kristeller
Dept. of Psychology, Indiana State University
C. Brendan Hallett

Introduction

Mindfulness meditation is increasingly being used as a psychotherapeutic technique for conditions as diverse as anxiety disorders, addictions, chronic pain, depression, and as an adjunct to psychotherapy (Kabat-Zinn, Massion, Kristeller *et al.*, 1992; Marlatt & Kristeller, 1999; Rubin, 1996; Beauchamp-Turner & Levinson, 1992; Teasdale *et al.*, 2002). Meditation appears to have the potential to facilitate general self-regulation, and may enhance insight and the integration of perceptual, cognitive, and behavioral aspects of human functioning.

Disorders involving behaviors that are normally under complex self-regulatory control, such as eating behavior, may be particularly well suited for treatment utilizing mindfulness meditation. Both compulsive eating and excessive dieting reflect a lack of balanced response to normal hunger and satiation cues, as response to these are replaced by conditioned patterns triggered by emotional response and non-nutritive stimuli. Individuals with binge eating disorder appear to suffer from the disregulation of multiple areas that may be responsive to meditative practice. These areas include elevated anxiety and dysphoria, distorted and reactive thinking patterns, and severely disturbed awareness of normal physiological cues related to food intake. There have been some anecdotal reports of meditation's efficacy for treating eating disorders (Epstein, 1995) and meditation has been alluded to in self-help literature on dieting (e.g., Ray, 1981). However, meditation has not been systematically studied as an intervention for an eating disorder.

Correspondence should be addressed to Jean L. Kristeller, Ph.D., Dept. of Psychology, Indiana State University, Terre Haute, IN, 47809. Email: PYKRIS@ISUGW.INDSTATE.EDU.

BINGE EATING DISORDER

The diagnosis of binge eating disorder (BED) was first formalized in 1991 (Spitzer *et al.*, 1991) to distinguish this population from those with bulimia nervosa or non-binging obesity, and is classified as a proposed disorder in the DSM-IV (American Psychiatric Association, 1994). A binge episode is defined as eating an amount of food in a discrete period of time that is definitely larger than most people would eat, while experiencing lack of control over eating during the episode. Studies (Marcus, Smith, Santelli, & Kaye,1992; Rossiter, Agras, Telch, & Bruce,1992) indicate that obese binge eaters typically report binging 3-5 days per week. Other criteria include marked distress and guilt regarding binge eating, secretive eating, and the lack of the compensatory behaviors (e.g., purging, fasting, or laxative misuse) that characterize bulimia nervosa. Numerous studies have found that BED is a common disorder, particularly among those in treatment for obesity. Spitzer *et al.* (1993) found a prevalence rate of about 30% for obese persons in weight control programs, but BED is less common among the general population, with a prevalence rate of 3-5% in community samples. It is almost twice as common in women and equally common in Caucasians and non-whites (Spitzer *et al.*, 1992).

A number of studies have found greater levels of psychopathology and general distress among binge eaters relative to non-binge eaters with comparable weight. Greater levels of dysphoria appear to be the most common psychological factor associated with binge eating (de Zwaan *et al.*, 1994; Prather & Williamson, 1988; Wadden, Foster, Letizia, and Wilk, 1993), along with lower self-esteem (de Zwaan *et al.*,1994; Lowe & Caputo, 1991). Gormally *et al.* (1982) found that, while obese non-binge eaters did not report rigid dieting standards or problems controlling urges to eat, obese binge eaters had a more perfectionist attitude toward dieting and reported constantly struggling to control their urges to eat. Wilson *et al.* (1993) found that obese binge eaters reported significantly less control over eating, more fear of weight gain, more dissatisfaction with weight, and more food and weight preoccupation than non-bingers of similar weight.

Numerous theories and models have been put forth regarding the etiology and maintenance of BED (Fairburn & Wilson, 1993). BED can be viewed as a prototypical disregulation syndrome, exhibiting disturbances of affect regulation, cognitive and behavioral disregulation, and physiological disregulation, for which an intervention such as meditation, with a goal of increasing general psychological and physiological self-regulation, is particularly well-suited.

A disregulation model synthesizes key aspects of several other models of food intake regulation, including the restraint model (Polivy & Herman, 1993), the escape model (Heatherton & Baumeister, 1991), the abstinence violation effect (A.V.E.) model (Marlatt & Gordon, 1985), the affect regulation model (Polivy, Herman & Mc Farlane, 1994), and loss of interoceptive awareness model (Kuehnel & Wadden, 1994), into a comprehensive explanation of a typical binge eating cycle. Many, although not all, binge eaters engage in chronic dieting. The efforts made in over-controlling the amount of food that is eaten may engender a sense of physiological and psychological deprivation, making them more susceptible to triggers to binge, such as ingesting a forbidden food, feelings of anger or depression, or self-deprecating cognitions. As binge eaters' negative view of self increases, they may seek an escape from this aversive self-awareness through eating (the escape model). Having begun to eat a food that was considered off-limits, such persons judge that they have "blown it", feel even worse about themselves, and binge (the A.V.E. model). This may be compounded by their lack of physiological awareness, leading them to disregard feelings of satiety (Heatherington & Rolls, 1989; Blundell & Hill, 1993). Initially, the binge episode may bring a sense of physiological sedation and psychological relief. This is short-lived, however, and is likely to be followed by physical discomfort and guilt, leading to continued negative self-appraisal and a renewed dedication to dietary restraint. This binge cycle will vary by person, and some may not experience all of these components. Meditation may attenuate or interrupt various aspects of this cycle.

In recent years, interventions that have shown success in treating bulimia and obesity have been studied for the treatment of BED (Agras *et al.*, 1994; 1995). These interventions include cognitive behavioral therapy, weight loss treatment, and interpersonal therapy. Nevertheless, a high proportion of these individuals with BED continue to binge following these treatments and there is a tendency for post-treatment relapse. A possible limitation in these treatments is the lack of focus on increasing awareness and acceptance of bodily cues that maintain binging behavior. These include awareness of the sensations of hunger and satiety, as well as the flavors and textures of foods that are eaten in a mindful manner.

Meditation as a therapeutic intervention

Research on the effects of meditation has examined its impact on a range of disorders, including anxiety, depression, alcohol dependency and psychophysiological stress disorders (Marlatt & Kristeller, 1999). Meditation's potential for making one more aware of bodily and cognitive processes offers strong possibilities for the treatment of BED. It can help bingers become attentive to their level of physical satiety, an awareness that is largely lost by those with BED (Hetherington & Rolls, 1989; Hadigan *et al.*, 1992). Further, it offers bingers the capacity to become more aware of physical, emotional, social, and other cues that trigger them to binge eat. Greater awareness of these important areas will help subjects break out of their habitual pattern of binge eating.

Methods

Our approach to using mindfulness meditation for treating binge eating or compulsive eating is loosely modeled on the standard 10 week Mindfulness Based Stress Reduction program (MBSR) as developed by Jon Kabat-Zinn (1990) but is different in a number of respects. The key elements of the MBSR program are delivered in a large (30 people) group format, including general mindfulness meditation practiced (using a tape) for 40 minutes/day; body scan meditation also delivered by audiotape; weekly yoga; and group discussion, with introduction of some limited elements of cognitive therapy. The only aspect of the MBSR program explicitly addressing eating regulation is the "raisin meditation" used in the first session, in which participants eat one or more raisins very slowly and mindfully. This exercise is often reported as being very powerful for participants, and is used to link more general meditative experience to experience of everyday activities.

While a major component of our intervention is the use of mindfulness meditation, again facilitated by use of an audiotape, the remaining elements of the approach are specifically focused on issues related to food, eating, and some of pathological patterns often observed in individuals with binge eating disorder. Our initial study used a seven session intervention; our current treatment uses nine sessions, with two follow-up contacts. Three forms of meditation are used: general mindfulness meditation, eating meditations, and mini-meditations. The primary focus of general mindfulness meditation is to develop focused attention, and simply, awareness of the object of that attention. This practice teaches individuals to observe the contents of the mind and sensations of the body without judgment and to learn detached awareness (Kabat-Zinn, 1990). Eating meditations are oriented more specifically toward the behaviors, beliefs, and emotions associated with food intake. In addition to the raisin meditation, the treatment utilizes foods more typical of those consumed during binging: high salt and fat foods (cheese and crackers) and sweet foods (cake and cookies). These meditations are somewhat like guided imagery exercises, but include the mindfulness element in which participants are brought back to a place of detachment. For mini-meditations, instructions are to take a few moments to stop and become aware of thoughts and feelings, at times of stress, prior to meals, when binge urges occurred, etc.

Approximately 15-20 minutes are allotted at the start of each group to allow participants to discuss progress and difficulties experienced during the previous week. With the exception of this period, sessions are structured around meditation and other mindfulness practices. Each session focuses on a specific theme related to overcoming binge eating, such as becoming aware of binge triggers, hunger and satiety awareness, self-forgiveness, and relapse prevention, with related guided meditations and exercises in mindful eating, using food provided either by the leader or by participants. Homework assignments include daily meditation and mindful-eating exercises. All the intervention components are clearly specified in a treatment manual, developed over a number of years of clinical work with a range of individuals with eating disorders, including bulimia, compulsive eating and binge eating disorder, and in a range of settings, including a student counseling service, general mental health clinic and a medical center.

In our first study (Kristeller & Hallett, 1999; see paper for more details), 21 women (ages 25 to 62, average age of 46) were recruited from the community. None of the participants had previous experience with meditation. All women were overweight, with an average weight of 239 lbs (Body Mass Index = 40.33). All women met criteria for BED, and were evaluated on a number of measures assessing general functioning, depression, anxiety, and experiences around food and eating, including the Binge Eating Scale (BES; Gormally *et al.*, 1982). We also collected ratings of mindfulness, frequency of binging, and awareness of hunger and satiety cures.

Our first study employed a single-group extended baseline design. This design had proven successful in our exploratory study of a meditation intervention for treating anxiety disorders (Kabat-Zinn *et al.*, 1992) and enabled us to establish the size of effects. After an individual orientation session, participants were evaluated weekly during a waiting period of approximately three weeks to establish a stable baseline, followed by seven sessions of group treatment, and a three week follow-up. In general, participants were compliant in attending each session and doing the homework (meditation and mindful eating) that was asked of them.

RESULTS: CHANGE IN FREQUENCY AND INTENSITY OF BINGING

Table 1 Variables mean scores on pre- and post-treatment

	3 Weeks Pre-Treatment	Treatment – Week 1	Treatment – Week 4	Treatment – Week 6	3 Weeks Post-Treatment
Number of Binges/Week	5.0	3.9	1.9	0.9	1.6
Binge Eating Scale (BES)	32.3	31.1	24.5	15.1	15.1
Depression (BDI)	17.8	17.2	14.4	8.0	10.2
Anxiety (BAI)	16.3	15.2	14.6	10.9	10.5

As can be seen in Table 1, participants showed a marked decrease in the number of binges reported per week; binges dropped from 4.02 averaged across the pretests to 1.57 averaged over the posttests ($t(1,17) = 6.37$, $p<.001$). This decrease is also clinically significant in that it reduces the binging below the frequency needed to meet DSM BED criteria. Of the 18 participants, nine reduced their frequency to less than one binge per week; five reported one to two binges per week; only four were still binging more than twice per week. The magnitude of binging also decreased substantially. Prior to treatment,

70% of binges were identified as "very large" whereas this had dropped to 24% at the three week follow-up. Scores on the Binge Eating Scale, which assesses problems and preoccupation with binging more qualitatively, fell from a mean of 31.69 at pretreatment, a level judged to be "severe", to 15.1 at post treatment, a level just higher than having "little or no problem" with binge eating (t (1,17) = 9.86, p<.001) (Gormally *et al.*, 1982). Mood also improved substantially. Depression (Beck Depression Inventory: Beck, Ward, Mendelson, Mock, & Erbaugh, 1961) decreased significantly from a baseline of 17.47 to 9.11 following treatment (t(1, 17) = 4.48, p<.001), as did anxiety (Beck Anxiety Inventory:Beck, 1988) (t(1, 17) = 3.10, p<.001). There was no significant change in weight over the course of treatment or at the follow-up.

Table 2 Mean scores on weekly measures

	Pre-Treatment			Treatment						Post-Treatment		
Week	1	2	3	1	2	3	4	5	6	1	2	3
Eating Control[a]	2.1	3.2	2.7	2.7	4.4	4.0	4.8	4.3	5.2	4.9	4.8	4.8
Mindfulness[a]	3.0	4.2	4.2	3.7	4.7	4.8	4.9	4.7	5.7	5.1	5.7	5.6
Hunger Awareness[a]	1.7	3.4	3.6	3.6	4.6	4.6	5.1	5.1	5.2	5.0	5.4	5.1
Satiety Awareness[a]	2.9	3.6	3.9	4.1	4.8	5.0	5.1	5.1	5.4	5.4	5.7	5.3

a Value is on a 7-point Likert Scale.

Feelings of control over eating rose significantly from 2.65 (out of seven) to 4.91 following treatment (t(1, 17) = 9.51, p<.001), gradually increasing from the final session to the final post-measurement. Awareness of hunger and satiety cues also improved significantly, as did ratings of mindfulness during eating following treatment (t(1, 17) = 8.31, p<.001).

Over the course of the 6 week treatment program, participants reported meditating on average a total of 15.82 hours (S.D.=3.15), with general mindfulness meditation accounting for 9.0 hours (S.D.=2.24), eating meditation accounting for 5.02 hours (S.D.=2.22), and mini-meditation (which takes only a few moments at a time) for 1.81 hours (S.D.=1.41). Use of the eating meditation was highly related to decreases in BES scores (r=.66, p<.01), while use of mini-meditations predicted an improvement in depression (r=.59, p<.025). Surprisingly there were no relationships found between amount of meditation and change in mindfulness.

An increase in mindfulness was also highly predictive of a decrease in number of reported binges (r =.76, p<.001). Change in mindfulness was also correlated with an increase in sense of eating control (r=.58, p<.025). Improvement in awareness of satiety cues was also significantly correlated with a reduction in number of binges reported (r=.53, p<.025), but change in awareness of hunger cues was not (r=.19, p =.46), suggesting that a re-regulation of normal satiety experience is particularly important for treating binge eating disorder. While not surprising given that binging inherently involves failure to stop eating and thus disruption of satiety cues, this relationship has not previously been reported.

The results in this study compare favorably with treatments drawing on more traditional methods. Agras and his colleagues (1995) used cognitive-behavioral therapy to treat 50 women with BED, who had comparable levels of obesity, binge frequency and BES scores to our participants. After 12 weeks of treatment, decreases observed on the BES and the BDI were similar or slightly smaller than we observed in our study, although improvement in binging was somewhat greater.

DISCUSSION: UNDERSTANDING THE RESULTS

These results provide support for the disregulation model of binge eating, including some of the sub-theories on which it is based, such as the escape theory (Heatherton & Baumeister, 1991). Mindfulness teaches an alternative to escape or avoidance. For participants, the nature of how they paid attention to internal and external signals changed during the course of therapy. This change is evident in an apparently paradoxical shift in the relationship between mindfulness and binge eating. Prior to treatment higher ratings of mindfulness were associated with greater levels of binging (r =.30), whereas after treatment, higher levels of mindfulness was associated with less binging. The pretreatment findings appear to be consistent with the escape hypothesis, which posits that an aversive self-awareness leads persons to binge. Prior to treatment it was aversive for participants to be aware of their eating behaviors. Binging was used in order to lower this aversive self-awareness, since more adaptive coping mechanisms were not available. Once treatment began, participants began to observe the contents of their minds without reacting, whether the thoughts and emotions that came up were pleasant or unpleasant. It appears that once participants learned this form of mindfulness, self-awareness became a positive tool that they were able to use in order reduce their binging. In addition, they learned important skills, such as how to use awareness of their body's cues—specifically hunger and satiety cues—to increase their ability to self-regulate. Thus, it appears that this treatment taught participants to be aware of themselves, but in such a way that was not aversive and that provided them with a sense of comfort and control.

There is also support for the affect regulation model of binging. Mindfulness meditation provided a means to experience negative emotions, such as depression and anxiety, without reacting to them. Also of note, certain of the exercises appeared particularly powerful at producing resolution of emotional issues; for example, the forgiveness meditation resulted in about half of the participants reporting that they had substantially resolved feelings of anger toward parents or husbands, feelings that they identified as common binge triggers. Of course, it is also possible that it was the increased feelings of control and reduced behavioral dysfunction that led to improvement in mood, rather than the converse.

Most of the participants had a history of frequent attempts to gain control of their weight by using deliberate food restriction. The mindfulness intervention taught them to do the opposite of this, a concept that was initially very difficult for the participants to accept. Nevertheless, to varying degrees, they learned to regulate their food intake by being more mindful, discriminating and trusting of their bodies' cues of hunger and satiety in order to decide when to eat and when to stop eating, rather than alternating binge cycles with restrictive 'dieting' practices. Many of them noted that it was the first time that they could remember experiencing how their body felt. Previously, they had tended to fluctuate between experiencing self-denial and experiencing discomfort from over-eating. Participants found it quite surprising and paradoxical that the act of giving up a degree of conscious control over their eating led to increased control. The meditative, mindful approach also appeared to help reduce catastrophic thinking characteristic of the Abstinence Violation Approach and replace it with an increased attitude of accepting "what is".

A somewhat surprising result was that of the three types of meditation practiced, general mindfulness meditation, mindfulness meditation focusing on eating, and mini-meditations, only time spent using eating-related meditation was related to decreases in the BES. This form of meditation may have been more highly correlated to change on the BES due to the specific focus on eating behaviors and emotions related to eating. A possible explanation may be that mindfulness, not meditation, was emphasized to the participants as the primary tool for reducing binging. It was learning to eat and live mindfully, attending to cognitive, affective, and bodily cues without reacting automatically, that was expected to reduce binging, a finding that was supported by the data. Meditation was only one of the tools we introduced for practicing this form of mindfulness. It appears that spending a greater amount of time meditating did not necessarily guarantee that one had achieved greater mindfulness in relation to food intake.

In general, participation rates were high during the treatment program. During a pilot group run for this study, less effort had been made to orient individuals, either in regard to the rationale for using meditation or that the focus would be on increasing experiences of mindful control, rather than on weight loss. That first group had a very high attrition rate, suggesting the importance of careful orientation to a program using such novel interventions. In the orientation we subsequently provided, we explored possible misconceptions about meditation, such as concerns that we would be proselytizing a non-Christian religion (to date, all participants have been Christians from a region of the U.S. that is somewhat conservative in religious beliefs). We also made it clear that the focus of the group would be on gaining control of binging, rather than on weight loss per se. While some of the participants lost substantial weight over the next few months, at the end of treatment there were no significant changes in weight among participants. Interestingly, although they did not initially lose weight, participants without exception reported that they were not disappointed by this. This may have been because, often for the first time, they felt a greater sense of control and self-acceptance. Another factor appears to be that, while they did not lose weight, they also did not gain weight. Participants had a great fear that they would gain weight if they did not force themselves to restrict food. They found that allowing the body to self-regulate (eating when hungry and stopping when full) was a good deal more satisfying than the diet-binge cycle that they were used to, and they reported being pleasantly surprised by not gaining weight.

In summary, this pilot study of the effectiveness of meditation-based interventions in treating binge eating disorder is encouraging. Treatment outcomes were statistically and clinically significant and comparable to those found in other approaches to this disorder. A randomized trial comparing this treatment to both a psycho-educational control and a waiting-list control is now in progress with a larger number of participants and a 4-month follow-up. Further investigation should assess ways in which these meditation-based techniques can be embedded into a more comprehensive treatment program.

REFERENCES

Agras, W.S., Telch, C.F., Arnow, B., Eldredge, K., Detzer, M.J., Henderson, J., & Marnell, M. (1995), Does interpersonal therapy help patients with binge eating disorder who fail to respond to cognitive-behavioral therapy? *Journal of Consulting and Clinical Psychology*, **63** (3): 356-360.

Agras, W.S., Telch, C.F., Arnow, B., Eldredge, K., Wilfley, D.E., Raeburn, S.D., Henderson, J., & Marnell, M. (1994), Weight loss, cognitive-behavioral, and desipramine treatments in binge eating disorder: An additive design. *Behavior Therapy*, **25**: 225-238.

American Psychiatric Association. (1994, 4th ed.), Washington, DC: Author. *Diagnostic and Statistical Manual of Mental Disorders, 4th Edition.* Washington, DC; Author.

Beauchamp-Turner, D.L., & Levinson, D.M. (1992), Effects of meditation on stress, health, and affect. *Medical Psychotherapy*, **5**: 123-131.

Beck, A.S., Ward, C.H., Mendelson, M., Mock, J., & Erbaugh, J. (1961), An inventory for measuring depression. *Archives of General Psychiatry*, **4**:53-63.

Beck, A.T., Epstein, N., Brown, G., & Steer, R. (1988), An inventory for measuring clinical anxiety: Psychometric properties. *Journal of Consulting and Clinical Psychology*, **56(6)**: 893-897.

Blundell, J.E., & Hill, A. J. (1993), Binge eating: Psychobiological mechanisms. In C.G. Fairburn, & G.T. Wilson (Eds.), *Binge Eating: Nature, Assessment, and Treatment* (pp. 206-224). New York: Guildford Press.

de Zwaan, M., Mitchell, J.E., Seim, H.C., Specker, S.M., Pyle, R.L., Raymond, N.C., & Crosby, R.B. (1994), Eating related and general psychopathology in obese females with binge eating disorder. *International Journal of Eating*

Disorders, **15(1)**: 43-52.

Eldridge, K.L., & Agras, W.S. (1994), Instability of restraint among clinical binge eaters: A methodological note. *International Journal of Eating Disorders*, **15**: 235-287.

Epstein, M. (1995), *Thoughts Without a Thinker.* New York: Harper Collins.

Fairburn, C.G., & Wilson, G.T. (Eds.) (1996), *Binge eating: Nature, Assessment, and Treatment.* New York: Guilford Press.

Gormally, J., Black, S., Daston, S., & Rardin, D. (1982), The assessment of binge eating Severity in obese persons. *Addictive Behaviors*, **7**: 45-55.

Hadigan, C.M., Walsh, B.T., Devlin, M.J., LaChaussee, J.L., & Kissileff, H.R. (1992), Behavioral assessment of satiety in bulimia nervosa. *Appetite*, **18**: 233-241.

Heatherton, T.F., & Baumeister, R.F. (1991), Binge eating as escape from self-awareness. *Psychological Bulletin*, **110(1)**: 86-108.

Heatherington, M. & Rolls, B.J. (1989), Sensory-specific satiety in anorexia and bulimia nervosa. In L.H. Schneider, S.J. Cooper, and K. A. Halmi (Eds.), *The Annals of the NewYork Academy of Sciences: The Psychobiology of Human Eating Disorders* **75**: 387-398. New York: New York Academy of Sciences.

Kabat-Zinn, J. (1990), *Full catastrophe living: Using the wisdom of your body and mind to face stress, pain, and illness.* New York: Dell.

Kabat-Zinn, J., Massion, A.O., Kristeller, J., Peterson, L.G., Fletcher, K. E., Pbert, L., Lenderking, W.R., & Santorelli, S.F. (1992), Effectiveness of a meditation-based stress reduction program in the treatment of anxiety disorders. *American Journal of Psychiatry*, **149(7)**: 936-943.

Kristeller, J.L., & Hallett, C.B. (1999), An exploratory study of a meditation-based intervention for binge eating disorder. *Journal of Health Psychology*, **4(3)**: 357-363.

Kuehnel, R.H., & Wadden, T.A. (1994), Binge eating disorder, weight cycling, and psychopathology. *International Journal of Eating Disorders*, **15(4)**: 321-329.

Lowe, M.R., & Caputo, G.C. (1991), Binge eating in obesity: Toward the specification of predictors. *International Journal of Eating Disorders*, **10**: 49-55.

Marcus, M.D., Smith, D., Santelli, R., & Kaye, W. (1992), Characterization of eating disordered behavior in obese binge eaters. *International Journal of Eating Disorders*, **12**: 249-256.

Marlatt, G.A., & Gordon, J.R. (Eds.), (1985), *Relapse Prevention: Maintenance Strategies in the Treatment of Addictive Behavior.* New York: Guilford Press.

Marlatt, G. A., & Kristeller, J.L. (1999), Mindfulness and meditation. In W. R. Miller (Ed.), *Integrating Spirituality In Treatment: Resources for Practitioners* (pp. 67-84). Washington DC: American Psychological Association.

Polivy, J., & Herman, C.P. (1993), Etiology of binge eating: Psychological mechanisms. In C.G. Fairburn, & G.T. Wilson (Eds.), *Binge Eating: Nature, Assessment, and Treatment* (pp. 173-205), New York: Guilford Press.

Polivy, J., Herman, C.P., & McFarlane, T. (1994), Effects of anxiety on eating: Does palatability moderate distress-induced overeating in dieters. *Journal of Abnormal Psychology*, **103**: 505-510.

Prather, R.C., & Williamson, D.A. (1988), Psychopathology associated with bulimia, binge eating, and obesity *International Journal of Eating Disorders*, **7**: 177-184.

Ray, S. (1981), *The Only Diet There Is.* Berkeley, CA: Celestial Arts.

Rossiter, E.M., Agras, W.S., Telch, C.F., & Bruce, B. (1992), The eating patterns of non-purging bulimic subjects. *International Journal of Eating Disorders*, **10**:556-566.

Rubin, J.B. (1996), *Psychotherapy and Buddhism: Toward an Integration.* New

York: Plenum Press.
Spitzer, R.L., Devlin, M.J., Walsh, B.T., Hasin, D., Wing, R., Marcus, M.D., Stunkard, A., Wadden, T., Yanovski, S., Agras, S., Mitchell, J., & Nonas, C. (1991), Binge eating disorder: To be or not to be in DSM-IV. *International Journal of Eating Disorders,* **10(6)**: 627-629.
Spitzer, R.L., Devlin, M.J., Walsh, B.T., & Hasin, D. (1992), Binge eating disorder: A multisite field trial of the diagnostic criteria. *International Journal of Eating Disorders,* **11(3)**: 191-203.
Spitzer, R.L., Yanovski, S., Wadden, T., Wing, R., Marcus, M.D., Stunkard, A., Devlin, M., Michell, J., Hasin, D., & Horne, R.L. (1993), Binge eating disorder: Its further validation in a multisite study. *International Journal of Eating Disorders,* **11(3)**: 191-203.
Teasdale, J.D., Moore, R.G., Hayhurst, H., Pope, M., Williams, S., & Segal, Z.V. (2002), Metacognitive awareness and prevention of relapse in depression: Empirical evidence. *Journal of Consulting and Clinical Psychology,* **70**: 275-287.
Wadden, T.A., Foster, G.D., Letizia, K.A., & Wilk, J.E. (1993), Metabolic, anthropometric, and psychological characteristics of obese binge eaters. *International Journal of Eating Disorders,* **14(1)**: 17-25.
Wilson, G.T., Nonas, C.A., & Rosenblum, G.D. (1993), Assessment of binge-eating in obese patients. *International Journal of Eating Disorders,* **13**: 25-34.

Health is a totality

Otto Reichard

Health is a totality, balance

Whether in cure, care or commitment

Its quintessence is quality with radiance

Not just the facts but the values are meant

Consider not just what to do but how to be

Cause and consequence are entangled for all to see

System, Self and Situation are interwoven dimensions of the same system

Only Selective Integration can point to its very stem

Meditation on total health

Otto Reichard

In the beginning there was the Void

First the body took shape

Second came Consciousness, which we cannot avoid

Then came Society that changed the Ape

And so descended on us "Culture"

To change our Constitution, Conflicts and Contexts like a Vulture

But to make us hail, healing needs a total push

Even on this side of the Hindu Kush

We have to listen to all the winds of change

From whisper to wisdom, to keep our grasp within range

The past is only a prelude

The future only an anticipation

And the present only an illusion

But in Meditation they find their fusion

Words and wisdom, being and boundaries

Michael J. Mahoney[1]
University of North Texas

In the realm of wisdom, a wise being is silent. By venturing these words, I disqualify myself.

Words of wisdom may be a contradiction, but we have come to live in worlds of words.

My words here are about boundaries, words, and the mysteries of being as we are.

Imagine four acts in a play that becomes us.

Act one: the boundary

In the beginning, there were no cells.

Only soup. Primordial soup.

Then primitive coalition.

Co-operation. Moving together.

Movement together connects and separates.

Tensions develop.

A membrane forms.

Form takes form.

The cell is born.

1. Adapted from Mahoney (in preparation).

Systematic activity creates an edge.

Shared activity folds in on itself.

An inside is created. An outside is distinguished.

The boundary binds what is inside it.

The boundary separates.

In separating, the boundary connects.

What is inside is now more connected with itself.

Living boundaries are partially closed and partially open.

They must protect the integrity of what lies within them.

They must connect with what lies beyond them.

Selective exchange.

Trade at the borders.

Exchange across boundaries.

Ingest, digest, excrete.

Open to and seek what is needed.

Close from and avoid what harms.

Connect with what serves life.

Sym is with. *Bios* is life. Symbiosis.

Activity organizes itself.

Systematic activity becomes structure.

Structure is systematic process.

Act one never ends.

It just creates an inside and an outside.

That's what boundaries do.

Act two: the center

Boundaries stabilize.

They are a holding.

Within their protection, more structure can develop.

With a cell membrane, complexity accelerates.

Differences develop within.

The labors of life are divided.

Division of labor.

Specialization of function.

Differences that make a difference become specialties.

Coordination becomes a challenge.

Co-ordination.

Orderly togetherness.

Act two begins with the appearance of a center.

Call it a nucleus.

Prokaryote becomes eukaryote.

A center is activity that orders.

Co-ordination is the special function of a nucleus.

Part of the inside gets its self together.

The inside of the inside folds into its own patterns.

The center is in-formed and in-forming.

Membrane informs nucleus, nucleus informs membrane.

Activity everywhere, now more coordinated.

Boundaries and center, both of them active.

Acts one and two continue.

Act three: sex

Centered activity has more balance.

Balance helps.

But a single center has limits.

Limits do more than limit.

Limits challenge.

Tensions everywhere.

Essential tensions.

Creative tensions.

A center so tense it cannot hold.

It splits.

The cell splits.

One becomes two.

Same old center. Same old boundaries.

Now in two places.

Now in four.

Now in eight.

Grow tense and split.

Again and again and again.

It works.

But it does not learn.

And it does not die.

Just endless repetition.

Nothing new under the sun.

Until there is sex.

Act three opens with sex.

Exchange of nuclear material.

Part of the core of one being embraces part of the core of another.

Crossing boundaries.

Touching centers.

Sometimes the exchange makes a spark.

Parts of one nucleus embrace parts of another.

The embrace begets a bond.

The bond is a bound into novel territory.

A unique new center forms.

New and yet familiar.

Familiar. From familia.
A family line of novel nuclear material.

Material.

Matter matters.

Matter is from *mater.* Madre. Mother.

Is matter the mother of what matters?

Pattern in process.

Pattern is from *pater.* Padre. Father.

Is pattern the father of what mothers?

The seeds of change are everywhere.

Change and choice.

Change and choice and protection.

The souly trinity of evolution: variation, selection, retention.

Vary from the family. Be different.

Differences create choices.

From differences, select.

Choose to approach or avoid.

Choose to accept, choose to defy.

No choice but to choose.

When a difference makes a promising difference, protect it.

Preserve it.

Protect, project, and propagate that which gives promise.
Sex in the mystery.

Sex in the magic.

Sex offers promises.

Birds do it. Bees do it. Even sages on their knees do it.

Let's do it. Let's fall in love.

Acts one, two, and three continue.

Act four: the symbol

Sex adds diversity to life.

It also adds death.

Only sexy beings die.

Not so easy come, not so easy go.

Bliss in the kiss.

Death in the yeath.

There is an act after sex.

It is largely symbolic.

Of those who survive, a tiny few become aware.

Aware of death, aware of life.

Are they conscious?

Pretend that consciousness is capacity to bind space and time.

Capacity to remember.

Capacity to plan.
How?

How to connect then and now.

How to connect here and there.

Act four begins with the symbol.

Sym is with. *Bol* means to thrust or put.

Symbol. To connect. To put together.

Creatures who live together may learn to put together.

Only social creatures are symbolic.

They exchange more than their nuclear fluids.

Symbolic beings share experiences.

In their sharing, they can grow.

Relationship gives meaning.

Relate. *Relatus*. To carry back. To connect.

Creatures of the symbol live in and from relations.

Communication is communion.

Communion with companions.

Companion. *Com* is with, *pane* is bread. One with whom food is shared.

Some companions bring confusion.

Ask any couple.

Confusion is too much fusion.

We do need our boundaries.

We need connections, too.
Symbols are ligaments to the bones of being.

Religion.

From *religare*. *Re* is back to, *ligamentum* is ligaments.

Symbol-forged connections can bring joy.

They can also bring pain.

Pain is memorable.

The more one re-members pain, the more one fears and dreads.

Past pain becomes future pain.

Pain teaches "No !"

Survival depends on this lesson.

For symbol-breathing creatures, pleasure is more difficult.

It is an occasional luxury of survival.

Celebrate occasions.

Joy is a moral obligation. It requires practice.

Symbols can foster consciousness.

Symbols can also fester mindlessness.

Look at psychology.

Just look. Don't buy.

Some creatures of the symbol get drunk on their words.

Forgive arrogance.

Homo sapiens sapiens – the hominid that knows that it knows.
Relax the grip of that illusion.

Epilogue

After the symbol comes a half curtain.

The four acts continue.

As symbols loom larger, the presence of the present recedes.

Each moment bears scars from the past.

Life can become only longing.

Past and future can dominate.

The eternal present – the *always now* – is elusive.

Hear whisperings here.

Lao-Tzu, Siddharta, Socrates.

Monastics in silence.

What if suffering is the presence of pain not present?

Pain remembered. Pain expected.

What if pain is inevitable, but suffering is less so?

Is there a lesson?

Lessen.

Lessen.

In lessen lessons, there is less talk.

More presence.

Wisdom likes to be quiet.
Quiet and Embracing.

Embracing the boundaries from which all began.
Inside / outside.

Beside.

All sides. No sides.

Boundaries as <u>temporary</u> structures for being.

Temporary.

Temporary.

Just passing through.

Centers in boundaries.

Bonding in leaps and bounds of being.

Here comes a bounce.

Hop is the heart of hope.

Boundaries, binderies, books.

Authorities are only authors.

Words are only symbols.

Wisdom appreciates.

Some words **are** precious.

Appreciate. *ap preciare.* To approach the precious.

But words can also get in the way.

Look at psychology.

Look ! Look !

Then have a heart.

Bless a heart.

When connecting, heart to heart, the words slide away.

Truly connect and words slide away.

Words   slide   away.

Forgive this interruption.

References

Abram, D. (1996), *The spell of the sensuous.* New York: Pantheon.

Ackerman, D. (1990), *A natural history of the senses.* New York: Random House.

Anderson, W.T. (1997), *The future of the self: Inventing the postmodern person.* New York: Tarcher and Putnam.

Austin, J.H. (1998), *Zen and the brain.* Cambridge, MA: MIT Press.

Baars, B.J. (1997), *In the theater of consciousness.* Oxford, UK: Oxford University Press.

Bateson, G. (1972), *Steps to an ecology of mind.* New York: Ballantine.

Bateson, G. (1979), *Mind and nature: A necessary unity.* New York: Bantam.

Bateson, P., & Martin, P. (2000), *Design for a life.* New York: Touchstone.

Berman, M. (1981), *The reenchantment of the world.* New York: Bantam.

Berman, M. (1989), *Coming to our senses: Body and spirit in the hidden history of the west.* New York: Bantam.

Brown, W.S. (Ed.)(2000), *Understanding wisdom: Sources, science, & society.* Radnor, PA: Templeton Foundation.

Capra, F. (1996), *The web of life.* New York: Anchor.

Chödrön, P. (1997), *When things fall apart: Heart advice for difficult times.* Boston: Shambhala.

Combs, A. (1996), *The radiance of being: Complexity, chaos, and the evolution of consciousness.* St. Paul, MN: Paragon House.

Fogel, A. (1993), *Developing through relationships: Origins of communication, self, and culture.* Chicago: University of Chicago Press.

Garvey, J. (Ed.)(1985), *Modern spirituality: An anthology.* Springfield, IL: Templegate.

Graci, G.M., O'Rourke, N., & Mahoney, M. J. (2003), Personal meanings of spirituality. *Constructivism in the Human Sciences,* 8, 37-47.

Hanna, T. (1970), *Bodies in revolt: A primer in somatic thinking.* New York: Holt, Rinehart & Winston.

Harding, D.E. (1961), *On having no head: Zen and the rediscovery of the obvious.* London: Penguin.

Hargens, S. (2001), Intersubjective musings: A response to Christian de Quincey's 'The promise of Integralism.' *Journal of Consciousness Studies,* 8 (12), 35-78.

Harre, R. (1991), *Physical being: A theory for corporeal psychology.* Oxford: Blackwell.

Hartman, E. (1991), *Boundaries in the mind: A new psychology of personality.* New York: Basic Books.

Hunt, H.T. (1995), *On the nature of consciousness: Cognitive, phenomenological, and transpersonal perspectives.* New Haven, CT: Yale University Press.

Huxley, A. (1944), *The perennial philosophy.* New York: Harper & Row.

Johnson, D.H. (1994), *Body, spirit, and democracy.* Berkeley, CA: North Atlantic Books.

Johnson, M. (1987), *The body in the mind: The bodily basis of meaning, imagination, and reason.* Chicago: University of Chicago Press.

Kabat-Zinn, J. (1990), *Full catastrophe living.* New York: Dell.

Kabat-Zinn, J. (1994), *Wherever you go there you are: Mindfulness meditation in everyday life.* New York: Hyperion.

Karen, R. (1998), *Becoming attached.* Oxford: Oxford University Press.

Kauffman, S.A. (1993), *The origins of order: Self-organization and selection in evolution.* Oxford: Oxford University Press.

Kauffman, S.A. (1995), *At home in the universe.* Oxford: Oxford University Press.

Kegan, R.(1982), *The evolving self.* Cambridge, MA: Harvard University Press.

Kegan, R. (1994), *In over our heads: The mental demands of modern life.* Cambridge, MA: Harvard University Press.

Kornfield, J. (1993), *A path with heart: A guide through the perils and promises of spiritual life.* New York: Bantam Books.

Kornfield, J. (2000), *After the ecstasy, the laundry*. New York: Bantam.

Mahoney, M.J. (1991), *Human change processes*. New York: Basic Books.

Mahoney, M.J. (2003a), *Constructive psychotherapy: Practices, processes, and personal revolutions*. New York: Guilford.

Mahoney, M.J. (2003b), *Scientist as subject: The psychological imperative*. Clinton Corners, NY: Percheron Press.

Mahoney, M.J. (in preparation), *Good head: Grateful confessions and sensual science*.

Margulis, L. (1998), *Symbiotic planet: A new look at evolution*. New York: Basic Books.

Margulis, L., & Sagan, D. (1995), *What is life?* New York: Simon & Schuster.

Miller, W.R. (Ed.)(1999), *Integrating spirituality into treatment: Resources for practitioners*. Washington, DC: American Psychological Association.

Nepo, M. (2000), *The book of awakening*. Berkeley, CA: Canari Press.

Partridge, E. (1983), *Origins: A short etymological dictionary of modern English*. New York: Greenwich House.

Ram Dass (1970), *The only dance there is*. Garden City, NY: Anchor Press.

Russell, P. (1992), *Waking up in time: Finding inner peace in times of accelerating change*. Novato, CA: Origin Press.

Sorabji, R. (2000), *Emotion and peace of mind: From Stoic agitation to Christian temptation*. Oxford, UK: Oxford University Press.

Steindl-Rast, Br.D. (1983), *A listening heart: The spirituality of sacred sensuousness*. New York: Crossroad.

Stolorow, R.D., & Atwood, G.E. (1992), *Contexts of being: The intersubjective foundations of psychological life*. Hillsdale, NJ: Analytic Press.

Vaughan, F. (1979), *Awakening intuition*. New York: Anchor Press.

Vaughan, F. (1986), *The inward arc*. Boston: Shambhala.

Walsh, R.N. (1999), *Essential spirituality*. New York: Wiley.

Watts, A. (1963), *The two hands of God: The myths of polarity*. New York: Macmillan.

Watts, A. (1966), *The book: On the taboo against knowing who you are*. New York: Random House.

Wheeler, G. (2000), *Beyond individualism: Toward a new understanding of self, relationship, & experience*. Hillsdale, NJ: Analytic Press.

Wilber, K. (1999), *Collected works* (4 vols.), Boston: Shambhala.

Zimmerman, J., & McCandless, J. (1998), *Flesh and spirit: The mystery of intimate relationship*. Ojai, CA: Bramble Books.